D1261357

French Industrial Policy

French Industrial Policy

William James Adams *and* Christian Stoffaës

Editors

The Brookings Institution
Washington, D.C.

Library of Congress Cataloging-in-Publication data:

French industrial policy.

Includes bibliographies and index.
1. Industry and state—France. 2. Industry and
state—United States. I. Adams, William James,
1947–   . II. Stoffaës, Christian, 1947–
HD3616.F82F74   1986   338.944   85-48203
ISBN 0-8157-0098-9
ISBN 0-8157-0097-0 (pbk.)

987654321

THE BROOKINGS INSTITUTION is an independent organization devoted to nonpartisan research, education, and publication in economics, government, foreign policy, and the social sciences generally. Its principal purposes are to aid in the development of sound public policies and to promote public understanding of issues of national importance.

The Institution was founded on December 8, 1927, to merge the activities of the Institute for Government Research, founded in 1916, the Institute of Economics, founded in 1922, and the Robert Brookings Graduate School of Economics and Government, founded in 1924.

The Board of Trustees is responsible for the general administration of the Institution, while the immediate direction of the policies, program, and staff is vested in the President, assisted by an advisory committee of the officers and staff. The by-laws of the Institution state: "It is the function of the Trustees to make possible the conduct of scientific research, and publication, under the most favorable conditions, and to safeguard the independence of the research staff in the pursuit of their studies and in the publication of the results of such studies. It is not a part of their function to determine, control, or influence the conduct of particular investigations or the conclusions reached."

The President bears final responsibility for the decision to publish a manuscript as a Brookings book. In reaching his judgment on the competence, accuracy, and objectivity of each study, the President is advised by the director of the appropriate research program and weighs the views of a panel of expert outside readers who report to him in confidence on the quality of the work. Publication of a work signifies that it is deemed a competent treatment worthy of public consideration but does not imply endorsement of conclusions or recommendations.

The Institution maintains its position of neutrality on issues of public policy in order to safeguard the intellectual freedom of the staff. Hence interpretations or conclusions in Brookings publications should be understood to be solely those of the authors and should not be attributed to the Institution, to its trustees, officers, or other staff members, or to the organizations that support its research.

Foreword

SINCE THE EARLY 1980s, industrial policy, the term applied to government
intervention in the marketplace to promote or protect certain industries, has
been an important topic of debate in the United States. And given U.S. trade
imbalances, the competitive weakness of the steel and automobile industries,
and the special problems of such sunrise industries as microchip processing and
the manufacture of new-generation computers, industrial policy is likely to
remain a subject of public discussion. To inform that debate, the Brookings
Institution asked William James Adams, an affiliate of our Foreign Policy
Studies program, to organize a symposium to look at industrial policy in France,
where government has aggressively promoted or defended certain industries
for centuries. The specific goal of the symposium, held in September 1984 in
Washington, D.C., was to introduce interested Americans to the workings of
French industrial policy and to French politicians, civil servants, and corporate
executives who have decisively influenced that policy over the past twenty-five
years. The discussion was designed to permit Americans to develop a clearer
conception of how French industrial policy works in practice and the ways in
which the French experience might be relevant for the United States.

The papers and comments in this volume are the result of that conference.
They reflect the experience of leading participants in policymaking and of those
who carried out directives; they are not intended to be the analytic assessments
of scholars. Thus the papers should be considered not as attempts to resolve
explicit issues drawn from a well-defined academic literature, but rather as
essays from which readers with little knowledge of French policy can develop a
list of questions that should be asked about industrial policy. References to
sources have been kept to a minimum, and each author bears responsibility for
the evidence he cites.

The editors of this book are William James Adams, associate professor of
economics at the University of Michigan, and Christian Stoffaës, professor of
economics at the Institut d'Etudes Politiques in Paris and deputy director of the
Direction des Industries Electroniques et de l'Informatique of the French Minis-

try of Industry. Adams translated and edited all the final papers, comments, and discussions—a considerable undertaking given the gap in institutional knowledge between the French authors and American readers. Stoffaës, in addition to contributing two chapters, selected many of the French participants. Financial assistance in carrying out the symposium and producing this book was provided by the German Marshall Fund of the United States, the French-American Foundation, and the French government.

The editors wish to extend their gratitude to John D. Steinbruner, director of Foreign Policy Studies at Brookings, whose conception of the relationship between scholarly and policy activities they admire profoundly. They also wish to thank the three anonymous reviewers who provided unusually detailed and thoughtful suggestions for the manuscript. At Brookings, Nancy Brauer and Julia Sternberg prepared the conference; Virginia Riddell provided administrative assistance; James E. McKee verified the factual content of the manuscript; and James R. Schneider edited and prepared it for publication. At the University of Michigan, Thea Lee and Xavier Maret translated preliminary versions of several papers for circulation during the conference. At the German Marshall Fund of the United States, Judith Symonds and Peter Weitz provided especially helpful counsel to the editors.

The views expressed here are those of the authors and should not be ascribed to the individuals and organizations whose assistance is acknowledged above; to the trustees, officers, or staff members of the Brookings Institution; or to the other institutions with which the authors are affiliated.

Bruce K. MacLaury
President

June 1986
Washington, D.C.

Contents

Bernard Vernier-Palliez
Preface   1

William James Adams
Introduction   3

PART I. THE HISTORICAL RECORD IN FRANCE   11

Henri Aujac
An Introduction to French Industrial Policy   13

Christian Stoffaës
Industrial Policy in the High-Technology Industries   36

Raymond Lévy
Industrial Policy and the Steel Industry   63

François Perrin-Pelletier
Industrial Policy and the Automobile Industry   74

Michel Freyche
Export Promotion as Industrial Policy   82

Robert Boyer
Industrial Policy in Macroeconomic Perspective   88

Bela Balassa
Selective versus General Economic Policy in Postwar France   97

Henri Aujac, John Zysman, François Didier, George C. Eads
Comments   103

PART II. DIRECTIONS FOR REFORM   113

Martin Malvy
Modernization: The Industrial Policy of Laurent Fabius   115

Henri Guillaume
Implications of the New Indicative Planning   119

Philippe Herzog
Public Enterprises Should Promote Social Efficiency   127

François Lagrange
Industrial Policy Should Be Conducted at the
Supranational Level   133

Paul Mentré
The French Economy Should Be Deregulated   143

Christian Goux
Parliament Should Play a Larger Role in Industrial Policy   156

François de Combret
What Can the United States Learn from the French Experience?   161

Roger B. Porter
Industrial Policy and the Role of Government in the Economy   166

Donald Riegle
American Industrial Policy: Building on the Chrysler Experience   175

Robert S. Strauss
Comments   181

General Discussion   183

Bruce K. MacLaury
Concluding Comments   196

Christian Stoffaës
Postscript   198

Authors' Biographies   211

Conference Participants   215

Index   222

Tables

1-1. Industrial Subsidies, by Type, 1970–79   22
1-2. R&D Activity, by Industry, 1979   26
1-3. Export Subsidies, 1974–79   28
1-4. Importance of Public Enterprise, by Industry, before
       and after 1982   30
1-5. Expenditures on Industrial Policy, by Type of Program, 1974   33
1-6. Concentration of Industrial Subsidies among Recipient
       Companies, 1976   34
2-1. Relative Strengths and Weaknesses of French High-Technology
       Industries in World Competition   45
2-2. Structure of the Energy Sector   48
2-3. Structure of the Aerospace Sector   52
2-4. French Foreign and Domestic Arms Sales, by Company
       and Government Agency, 1981   54
2-5. Structure of the Electronics Sector   58
2-6. R&D Strategies in Selected OECD Countries,
       1965, 1980, 1985   60
3-1. Investment per Ton of Steel Produced, by Country, 1965–75   66
3-2. Debt as a Percentage of Sales in the Steel Industries of
       Selected Countries, 1970–76   66
3-3. Production and Employment in Steel: France in Relation to
       Other European Countries, Selected Years, 1960–77   68
3-4. World Consumption of Steel, by Geographic Area, 1950,
       1970, 1980   69
6-1. Determinants of Exports as a Percentage of Imports, 1950–80   96
11-1. Incidence of International Trade on the French Economy, 1963,
       1973, 1983   134
11-2. Incidence of International Trade on the Large Industrial
       Economies, 1983   134
12-1. Average Annual Percentage Increase in Civilian Employment,
       by Country, Selected Periods, 1968–82   150
12-2. Average Annual Percentage Increase in Real Gross Fixed
       Capital Formation (Machinery and Equipment), by Country,
       Selected Periods, 1960–80   151
12-3. Average Annual Increase in Total Factor Productivity,
       by Country, 1971–73 and 1974–82   151
12-4. Average Annual Percentage Increase in Real Value Added
       in Industry, by Country, Selected Periods, 1960–83   151

Figures

12-1. Evolution of Industrial Employment, Selected
       Countries, 1960–81   152
12-2. Importance of Internal Finance to French Corporations,
       1959–82   153
12-3. Factor Productivity in France, 1959–81   154
12-4. Relationship between Investment and Employment in France,
       1959–73 and 1974–81   155

Bernard Vernier-Palliez

Preface

INDUSTRIAL POLICY enjoys nearly unanimous support in France. Statesmen as diverse as Jean Monnet and Charles de Gaulle have proposed it eagerly. Even potentially controversial programs, such as those for nuclear power and weapons, have been pursued by French governments of all stripes and colors.

Not all Americans will understand the French consensus on industrial policy, and their confusion is perfectly normal. The American environment is almost devoid of economic constraints. The natural resources of the country—in agriculture, in energy, and in industrial raw materials—help to make it the economic leader of the world. As the leader, the United States is able to impose its national currency as the reserve currency of the world. No wonder it can run a deficit of $120 billion in its trade balance and $80 billion on current account without raising many eyebrows. The lack of external constraints saps the apparent necessity for industrial policy.

The natural position of France is much less enviable. In order to pay for our imports, we must export; and to export, we must be competitive. Faced with the skyrocketing price of oil in the 1970s, we had no choice but to develop nuclear power—and to do so very quickly. Maybe the United States will find itself in the same position a century from now; but a century is a very long time. Today there is no pressing problem. The United States can pay its bills by printing dollars. France does not enjoy that luxury. The hardness of the constraints it faces provides its motivation to engage in industrial policy.

I do not wish to suggest that the United States has no industrial policy. Like Molière's famous character, Monsieur Jourdain, who talked in prose without knowing it, the United States does practice industrial policy. It does so when it bails out an automobile corporation or a bank; it does so when it creates and promotes a National Aeronautics and Space Administration; and it does so when the Department of Defense spends $200 million to $250 million a year to develop automated factories.

What I know best, however, is France. On some occasions, France has practiced industrial policy very successfully. Other times, it has practiced it rather clumsily. In my view the secret of good industrial policy is the same as the secret of good cooking: the lighter the better.

1

William James Adams

Introduction

FROM THE PRESIDENCY of Franklin D. Roosevelt to that of Jimmy Carter, American norms for the organization of business activity underwent remarkably little change. In most industries, it was argued, government should promote competition. It should do so by enforcing the antitrust laws at home and by advocating liberalization of trade and investment abroad. In those few industries where competition was thought to be undesirable, government was urged to rely on independent commissions to regulate entry and profitability. Although people disagreed about the exact boundary between competition and regulation, neither the intensity nor the profundity of their debate ever sufficed to create a top-priority issue for public action. As late as 1972 any veteran of the New Deal would have felt comfortable in discussions of government's role in the world of business.

During the past decade, however, the United States has experienced structural and macroeconomic imbalance. As a result, many Americans have begun to question traditional governmental approaches to business. Some, sensitive to the problems of bureaucracy and the perversities of regulation, argue that government intervenes too much in the market mechanism. They urge a comprehensive effort to deregulate the economy. Others, confronted by structural unemployment, decaying industrial regions, and rapid technological change, have become disenchanted with reflex reliance on market forces. They advocate new forms of intervention based on the promotion or protection of specific industries. Although fuzzy in definition, and sometimes in content, "industrial policy" is the name now given to such intervention.

In its current phase of fermentation, the debate on government intervention in business has induced the United States to experiment amply with deregulation. In transportation, for example, it has eliminated the Civil Aeronautics Board and curbed the Interstate Commerce Commission. It might even return the old Penn Central railroad to private hands. In finance and telecommunications, deregulation is proceeding less decisively. Nevertheless, it promises to transform its industrial objects dramatically.

3

The United States has also dabbled in industrial policy. In some cases, such as military procurement or restraints on imports, its efforts could be interpreted as inadvertent. In other cases, however, such as the rescues of the Lockheed and Chrysler corporations and the Continental-Illinois bank, it has acted very consciously indeed. Nevertheless, in comparison with most rich countries the United States has explored deregulation a good deal more than it has experimented with industrial policy. The debate on whether to promote or protect selected industries is being waged with imported evidence—much of it from France and Japan.

In the hands of advocates and opponents alike, foreign industrial policies often become caricatures. Whether viewed as panaceas or cancers, their roles are rarely underestimated. Not only are the policies themselves described in stylized form, but so are the policy cultures in which they originate. Thus the Germans are said to believe in market mechanisms, from which it is concluded that their economy is governed by market forces, while the French and Japanese are said to believe in public policy, from which it is concluded that their economies are ruled by government initiatives.

As we rethink public policy toward business, Americans can undoubtedly learn a great deal from the study of other rich countries. In so doing, however, we must avoid the mentality of the congressional junket. We must recognize the complexity of foreign experience as well as the variety of ways it can be interpreted.

In this book the reader will find a diversity of perspectives on French industrial policy. Some essays argue strongly for industrial policy; others attempt to debunk it. Taken together with the accompanying commentaries and discussions, they constitute a lively and balanced introduction to the French experience. In fact for all their skirmishing, the authors do seem to agree on several points of interest to American readers.

What is industrial policy? Few of the French authors attempt to define the boundary between industrial policy and government policy in general. As a result it is tempting to conclude either that the authors are confusing industrial policy with other policies or that industrial policy is too amorphous a subject to bear analytical discussion. Such conclusions are, however, unwarranted. Explicitly or implicitly the authors of these essays take industrial policy to be any policy an important goal of which is to shape the industrial composition of national output. To some the alteration in question is an increase in the share of GNP accounted for by industry (that is, by manufacturing and mining industries as a group). To others the alteration in question is an increase in the production of some particular industries (for example, those in which technological change is proceeding rapidly) relative to the production of others.

When the authors discuss exports, research and development, government procurement, and indicative planning under the heading of industrial policy, they reveal their belief that the stated aims of policy can mislead. Not only should the effect of a policy not be inferred from its intent, but its intent should not be inferred from a press release. That a policy is not proclaimed by the government as "industrial" implies nothing about its intended impact on the industrial composition of output. Americans who insist on limiting the concept of industrial policy to the realm of the intentional and then infer what is intentional from a policy's label may be constricting naively the true domain of industrial policy. It is entirely possible that what is announced as industrial policy may constitute a minor part of its substance.

A good example of this problem involves the locus of governmental responsibility for industrial policy. Many observers focus on the so-called spending ministries—industry, telecommunications, and defense. Like MITI, the Japanese Ministry of International Trade and Industry, these are the departments that launch and discuss in public what Henri Aujac calls "grands projets"— blueprints of development for specific sectors of the economy. Although the authors of the following chapters do recognize the considerable and expanding powers of such ministries, they also appear convinced that the leading governmental actor is the Treasury Department of the Ministry of Finance. Recognizing Treasury's role permits the realization that authority for industrial policy is concentrated in a few hands. Such concentration facilitates (but does not guarantee) targeting governmental assistance on a few beneficiaries. Because Treasury can channel its favors through many conduits, recognition of its role in industrial policy obliges the observer to examine many more policy levers than are manipulated by the spending ministries.

What justifies industrial policy? In the United States, economists tend to recognize a single justification for industrial policy: the failure of a market system to generate socially optimal levels of information. Such failure may entail the underrepresentation in national output of industries that rely on recent knowledge. As a result it may inspire conscious promotion of such industries.

Although the authors of these essays would endorse such logic, some advance additional arguments on behalf of industrial policy. Robert Boyer, for example, stresses the relationship between industrial and macroeconomic policies. In his view, open economies do not always possess the macroeconomic tools required to achieve both full employment and external balance. Industrial policy can permit a country to alter its import and export behavior to allow the expansion of aggregate demand to the full-employment level. A second rationale for industrial policy, one that lies well below the surface discussions of many chapters, is based on the concept of second best. According to this view, market power, more than any "natural" comparative advantage, determines the international division of labor. To the extent that France cannot eliminate the market power of foreign multinational corporations, it must create market power at home. In so doing, it will ensure the country's ability to produce goods in which it suffers no natural comparative disadvantage but from which it would otherwise be excluded through imperfections in global markets. This position dovetails with a third justification of industrial policy. Many of the authors view national security (the American term) or national independence (its Gallic counterpart) as an important argument for industrial policy. To the extent that a country fails to enjoy a comparative advantage in the production of goods necessary to ensure national preservation, they argue, it is appropriate for government to promote the development of industries that will achieve that goal.

How has French industrial policy performed? Undoubtedly, it is interesting and important to study the origins and content of industrial policies. Ultimately, however, it is the performance of industrial policies—the extent to which they generate desired or desirable effects—that matters most. Unfortunately, the debate on industrial policy tends to bypass the problem of evaluation. Too many observers appear to believe that the content of a policy reveals its effect.

The authors of these chapters offer no blueprint for measuring impact. Most seem to gloss over the methodological underpinnings of their assessments. Their reluctance to make sweeping judgments on French policy may bear testament to the difficulty of isolating cause and effect.

Nevertheless, the chapters that follow are hardly devoid of significance with respect to issues of appraisal. For example, many of the authors emphasize the long-term character of industrial policy and imply that premature evaluation might dupe the observer into believing that a successful project has failed or that a dubious project has succeeded. If correct, this line of argument suggests that industrial policies cannot be evaluated easily through intertemporal analysis of an industry: too much time must elapse between implementation and evaluation.

The chapters devoted to particular industries reveal the basic problem of evaluation. Required is some method of determining how an industry would behave and perform in the absence of a given set of policies, not all of which are aimed at the industry itself. Such a determination requires an understanding of the relationships among market structure, market conduct, and market performance. In other words it requires knowledge of industry as well as of policy. We are fortunate to have here the opinions of people who possess concrete understanding of oligopolies and agencies alike.

The verdict of these experts appears unanimous in one respect: French industrial policy has succeeded in the aerospace and nuclear sectors. Had the government not promoted the production of military aircraft, nuclear weapons, and nuclear power, France would never have enjoyed the allegedly enviable position it now occupies in these activities. Whether success is measured strictly in terms of national independence or also in terms of "natural" comparative advantage is not always apparent. I suspect that some, but only some, authors believe that both criteria of performance have been satisfied.

Where is French industrial policy headed? The authors of these chapters appear to disagree stridently on how to reform industrial policy. To the extent that each proposal represents the views of a different political current, it might seem that the future of French policy depends greatly on who will exercise political power. Although certainly correct at the level of detail, such a conclusion ignores a striking and common theme in these proposals: French industrial policy should be decentralized. To some the decentralization in question entails diffusion of power within government—from the executive to the legislative branch and from national to regional authorities. To others it entails diffusion of power to the private sector—either to management or to labor. Because decentralization of government power usually results in greater consultation with the private sector, the two paths of diffusion really converge. Thus to the extent that these proposals can be taken at face value, the *dirigiste* element in French industrial policy is likely to wane regardless of who wins the presidential election of 1988.

What can the United States learn from the French experience? Just as the authors of these essays are reluctant to judge French policy, so they are reluctant to prescribe a program for the United States. To most, France is France and the United States is the United States: the two institutional soils differ too profoundly to transplant success from one to the other.

Be that as it may, and ignoring the maxim that comparisons need not entail imitations to be useful, several points of relevance still come to mind. First, the French experience clearly demonstrates that as a government becomes the major customer, major supplier, and major financier of a business enterprise, the autonomy of that enterprise evaporates. Ultimately, the French government nationalized the very companies—profitable as well as unprofitable—that received the lion's share of its support. Such an ending might well give pause to those unions and companies in the United States that seek substantial favors from government.

Second, as François de Combret emphasizes, by American standards the size of the French economy is modest. It is heavily exposed to foreign competition, and it generates a relatively small government budget. As a result, any industrial policy that attempts to contravene world market forces would deplete French means very quickly. In contrast, most sectors of the American economy remain insulated, however naturally, from foreign competition. Given the size of its economy and the role of its currency, the American government can spend substantial sums before bumping into a budgetary constraint. Therefore, an American industrial policy might attempt to fight the flow of the market for a long time. In other words the danger exists that an American industrial policy would be heavily protectionist. However much the French might relish a protectionist stance of their own, their economic position in the world dictates a market-conforming strategy.

Finally, many of the French authors assert that the United States already engages in industrial policy and that for political reasons it merely avoids the name. To those Americans who advocate an industrial policy, this point of view may appear heartening, because it may suggest that as long as the United States practices industrial policy in fact, it might as well do so consciously and systematically. Those skeptical of industrial policy may prefer another interpretation of the French view. If the French really see little difference between what is done in France and what is done in the United States—and if current American policies are truly incoherent and ineffectual—then maybe the impact of French policy on French industry has been exaggerated. Maybe industrial policy has had little to do with the vitality of the French economy since World War II. If so, the case for French-style policy in the United States would be weak even if such policy could be transplanted successfully.

But that is a matter for the reader to decide. The chapters that follow should provide ample concrete experience with which to build a reflective opinion on the merits of industrial policy. Thanks to the willingness of Bruce MacLaury to undertake this venture, as well as his skill in chairing the symposium, the reader need not be confined to speculation as to how industrial policy works in practice.

Suggestions for Further Reading

The literature on French industrial policy is huge, and even that part written in English cannot be considered petite. Rather than daunt the reader with a complete catalog of stimulating work on the French economy, I list below a few books capable of introducing the subject. I deliberately include studies written at various times during the postwar period.

Carré, Jean-Jacques, Paul Dubois, and Edmond Malinvaud. *French Economic Growth*. Translated by John P. Hatfield. Stanford, Calif.: Stanford University Press, 1975.

Cohen, Stephen S. *Modern Capitalist Planning: The French Model*. Berkeley: University of California Press, 1977 (first published in 1969 by Harvard University Press).

Jacquemin, Aléxis, ed. *European Industry: Public Policy and Corporate Strategy*. London: Oxford University Press, 1984.

Kuisel, Richard F. *Capitalism and the State in Modern France: Renovation and Economic Management in the Twentieth Century*. London: Cambridge University Press, 1981.

McArthur, John H., and Bruce R. Scott. *Industrial Planning in France*. Boston: Harvard University Graduate School of Business Administration, Division of Research, 1969.

Organisation for Economic Cooperation and Development. *The Industrial Policy of France*. Paris: OECD, 1974.

Padioleau, Jean G. *Quand la France s'Enferre: La Politique Sidérurgique de la France Depuis 1945*. Paris: Presses Universitaires de France, 1981.

Scott, Bruce R., and Audrey T. Sproat. *National Industrial Planning: France and the EEC*. Boston: Harvard University Graduate School of Business Administration, Division of Research, 1983.

Sheahan, John B. "Experience with Public Enterprise in France and Italy," in William G. Shepherd, ed., *Public Enterprise: Economic Analysis of Theory and Practice*. Lexington, Mass.: D.C. Heath, 1976.

Sheahan, John. *Promotion and Control of Industry in Postwar France*. Cambridge: Harvard University Press, 1963.

Stoffaës, Christian. *La Grande Menace Industrielle*. Paris: Calmann-Lévy, 1978.

Stoleru, Lionel. *L'Impératif Industriel*. Paris: Editions du Seuil, 1969.

Vernon, Raymond, ed. *Big Business and the State: Changing Relations in Western Europe*. Cambridge: Harvard University Press, 1974.

Zysman, John. *Governments, Markets, and Growth: Financial Systems and the Politics of Industrial Change*. Ithaca, N.Y.: Cornell University Press, 1983.

Zysman, John. *Political Strategies for Industrial Order: State, Market, and Industry in France*. Berkeley: University of California Press, 1977.

Part I

The Historical Record in France

Henri Aujac

An Introduction to French Industrial
Policy

INDUSTRIAL POLICY may be defined as an attempt by government to shape the evolution of industrial structure. During the century that ended with the depression of the 1930s, the French government largely accepted the "natural" evolution of domestic economic structure. By 1945, however, the government was alarmed not only by the physical damage resulting from World War II but also by the underdevelopment of French mining and manufacturing. Large regions of the country, such as Brittany and the area southwest of the Loire, appeared devoid of industrial activity. Other regions relied on small companies wedded to outdated technologies.[1] Markets remained local or at most national in scope. An archaic system of distribution in effect reserved French markets for French producers.

To most governments of the postwar period, it has seemed obvious that reducing inflation, curbing trade deficits, and ensuring full employment would all require an industrial policy. As a result, throughout this period, industrial policy has been considered a particularly efficacious component of general economic policy. But although French industrial policies have always been, or have always been *supposed* to have been, general in perspective, they have sought different goals and used different tools in different periods. This chapter describes some of these differences, paying special attention to the changes that have occurred since President François Mitterrand has come to power.

Philosophies

1946–63: Reconstruction and Modernization

Discussions of optimal industrial structure benefit greatly from the existence of national income accounts and input-output tables; in 1946, however, neither

---

1. Automobiles and aircraft were the exceptions. Both developed during World War I in response to massive government subsidies, and both maintained their dynamism after the war.

existed.[2] As a result, industrial policy was conducted largely within the framework of indicative planning. The government's top priority was to end the economic chaos that followed liberation. Given the shortage of funds available for reconstruction, it decided to focus immediate efforts on a small number of industries—steel, cement, farm tractors, fertilizers, transport services, energy, and automobiles.[3] Activity in these industries would accelerate the growth of demand for other products and prevent bottlenecks in supplying them.

To promote industrialization generally, planners relied heavily on a strategy of changing the attitudes of industrialists. Managers and trade union officials were sent in droves on six-week visits to the United States. In addition, at least in theory, the Commissariat Général du Plan left the bulk of indicative planning to commissions composed primarily of leading economic actors from outside government.[4]

The plans of this period are the only ones to have succeeded undeniably. With amazing speed, French GNP exceeded its prewar level. More important, economic agents began to base their calculations on the assumption that the economy would grow and modernize.

1963–69: The Technology Gap

By 1963 France had shed its colonies, and the heavy burden of expenditure on wars in Indochina and Algeria had disappeared. In the view of Charles de Gaulle, France now possessed the discretionary resources to develop into a modern military power. That meant acceleration of the program to develop an independent nuclear force. But such a force required computers—computers that the United States refused to supply. As a result de Gaulle recognized the linkage between national military strength and national expertise in production. The government attempted to develop a domestically controlled electronics industry, and in so doing it changed the nature of industrial policy. Under Jean Monnet and his successors, industrial policy had consisted essentially of building

2. The weakness of an input-output table is its failure to recognize the company, as opposed to the industry, as the unit of decisionmaking.

3. The first two were needed to rebuild and modernize other industries; the second two were needed to develop agriculture; the last would be used to earn the foreign exchange needed to pay for imports necessary to the reconstruction process.

4. It must be noted, however, that in this period, French companies exhibited sparse cash flows. Only the government possessed the funds that could permit them to invest at desired rates. Under the circumstances, it would hardly be surprising to learn that they readily followed the "administrative guidance" of the government.

a consensus. Much of the initiative for specific strategies was left to nongovernmental participants on the planning commissions. In other words, industrial policy was decentralized. Under de Gaulle, however, choices among projects were made by government. Decentralization had given way to government authority and bureaucracy.

Between 1963 and 1969 the government spent several billion francs on developing *industries de pointe*—high-technology industries such as nuclear weapons, aerospace, and conventional military equipment. The results were mixed. The French weapons industry, for instance, became highly competitive in world markets; the French computer industry remains backward by American standards.[5]

1969–74: Grand Industrial Policy

Although the Treaty of Rome was signed in 1957, French companies were not exposed fully to foreign competition until the late 1960s. At that time the economy was seen to consist of an exposed and a sheltered sector. Manufacturing and mining lay in the first, while agriculture, construction, commerce, and the services lay in the second. Faced with acute competition, the exposed sector began to decline. Between 1962 and 1970, for example, the share of industrial employment in total employment fell from 45 percent to 41 percent. Unemployment began to rise.

President Georges Pompidou proposed to mitigate these problems by promoting the emergence of one or two large enterprises in each major industry. These so-called national champions would protect the legion of small and medium-sized producers that supplied and bought from them. In addition to working through the national champions, government could develop agencies designed to deal with regional problems—agencies such as the Délégation à l'Aménagement du Territoire et de l'Action Régionale (DATAR). The agencies could aid those enterprises facing bankruptcy that accounted for large parts of total employment in regional labor markets.

The creation of national champions usually occurred within the framework of *plans sectoriels*, government blueprints for the structure of particular industries. During the 1970s such plans were developed for the steel, textiles, footwear, and leather goods industries. The plans included provisions designed to promote the creation of national champions through mergers. Between 1970 and

---

5. On the effort to develop a national computer industry during these years, see Jacques Jublin and Jean-Michel Quatrepoint, *French Ordinateurs: de l'Affaire Bull à l'Assassinat du Plan Calcul* (Paris: Editions Alain Moreau, 1976).

1974 major mergers did occur. They involved consolidation of already-large companies and left the fringe of small and medium-sized firms intact. Thus Saint-Gobain merged with Pont-à-Mousson, Pechiney with Ugine Kuhlmann, de Wendel with Marine-Firminy, and Banque de l'Indochine with Banque de Suez. Whether these mergers permitted French enterprise to compete effectively in world markets is another matter. Some companies—for instance, the Compagnie Générale d'Electricité—displayed both dynamism and profits. Others such as the steel companies never performed particularly well. In general, the *plans sectoriels* cannot be considered successful.

As for the regional policies, some parts of the country—Paris and the Rhône-Alpes—developed well; other areas—Dunkerque in the north and Fos in the south—developed poorly. The efforts of DATAR to preserve employment in regions with declining employment met with mixed results.

1974–78: The Promise of Market Mechanisms

Between 1974 and 1978 the French economy experienced many shocks: the explosion of petroleum prices, the disintegration of the international monetary system, competition from low-wage countries, and the post-1968 reexamination of the desirability of modern growth. To combat these problems, President Valéry Giscard d'Estaing initially relied heavily on market mechanisms and macroeconomic policy. True, the government did formulate rescue plans for particular industries—footwear, leather goods, watches and clocks, and machine tools, for instance—but the grand industrial policies of President Pompidou definitely receded in importance.

1978–81: Grand Industrial Policy Once More

By 1978 the first oil shock had hit France with all its force. To most observers, including those in government, the customary diet of competition and Keynes no longer seemed adequate to deal with France's economic problems. With great ceremony, industrial policy was returned to a state of grace. Both the ends and the means of Giscard d'Estaing's policies resembled those of Pompidou, but in one respect the market-based approach of 1974–78 remained in force. The national champions were no longer to dominate all parts of all markets. Rather, they were supposed to develop expertise in particular niches of markets, expertise that would permit them to become truly competitive in those segments of world markets. This strategy was labeled the *politique des créneaux*.

Giscard d'Estaing's industrial policy did not prevent inflation; nor did it prevent a gradual rise in unemployment. It did, however, reduce France's trade deficit and led to important economies in the use of energy.

Since 1981: A Socialist Revolution?

In some respects it is difficult to determine the essence of President François Mitterrand's industrial policy. After all, he has come to power relatively recently. Moreover, his political allies disagree violently in matters of economic policy. Some favor the continued pursuit of policies initiated by government and controlled by the bureaucracy. Others favor decentralization—both in the sense of transferring power to regional governments and in the sense of involving extra-governmental constituencies in the policy process. In other words, under President Mitterrand, one simultaneously hears advocates of the Monnet approach and advocates of the de Gaulle approach: gone are the days when French economic policy sounded rational and coherent. True, in the early days most of the debate on industrial policy occurred in the Commissariat Général du Plan. Then, under President Pompidou the focal point shifted to the Ministry of Industry.[6] Today, several agencies of government seek to control industrial policy, including the Ministry of Research and Industry, the Ministry of International Trade, and the Ministry of Planning.[7] As ever, the Ministry of Finance has the final say on industrial policy, but the diversity of opinion reaching ears outside the government has increased dramatically.

Among those who wish the government to pursue an activist industrial policy, strong pressure has developed to abandon the *politique des créneaux*. According to Louis Gallois, the top civil servant at the Ministry of Industry, "the experience of the leading industrial countries reveals a simple truth: the ability of an economy to compete depends on the capacity of its industrial sector to satisfy the large bulk of domestic needs, on the existence of a tightly knit and diversified industrial fabric, and on an ample stock of large as well as small firms. It is time to realize that 'there are no doomed industries, only outmoded technologies.' "[8]

To replace the strategy of niches, the Socialists proposed a *politique de*

6. In both periods the Ministry of Finance had the last word on industrial policy, but it was not in the habit of debating.

7. Since this chapter was written the Ministries of Industry and of International Trade have been consolidated.

8. Ministère de la Recherche et de l'Industrie, *Une Politique Industrielle pour la France: Actes des Journées de Travail des 15 et 16 Novembre 1982* (Paris: La Documentation Française, 1982), p. 387.

filières, a strategy based on providing aid to entire vertical streams of production. According to this view, no niche is viable on its own. Each depends on the vitality of upstream and downstream industries. As a result government should intervene at every needy stage of every vertical stream of production. This permits *la reconquête du marché intérieur*, the renewal of the ability of French companies to compete effectively in French markets.

Preoccupation with vertical streams lends itself to industry-specific plans. Thus the sectoral plans launched in earlier years—the machine tools plan of 1976 and the steel plan of 1966, for instance—were renewed. Individual companies were asked to merge, increase spending on research and development, increase production and employment, increase ratios of exports to production, or modify product lines. In return the government agreed to help finance the companies' investments, increase public training of skilled labor, increase government purchases of their products, and stimulate such purchases by parties in the private sector.

Because it is too soon to judge these efforts, two observations must substitute for an appraisal. First, even in its bureaucratic incarnation, the philosophy of the current government includes a preference for increased dialogue: although final decisions remain with the government, discussion with and reflection by economic agents outside government has been encouraged. Moreover, the government has increased its recourse to formal contracts when dealing with industry and labor. Such contracts underscore an interest in the views of others.

The second observation concerns the likelihood that these policies will bear fruit. More than ever before, important decisions regarding French industry are being made by the European Communities (EC) in Brussels. For example, Brussels sets tariff levels with respect to goods imported from outside the EC. It also sets national production quotas within the community in such important industries as steel. Finally, it decides the legality of national subsidies to particular industries. For example, in 1982 the French government had to submit its plan for the French steel industry to the European Commission. The plan proposed Fr 26 billion in subsidies during 1982–83. The commission authorized only a fraction of that amount and made approval of that fraction contingent on further reduction of French capacity to produce "long" products such as I-beams and rails.

The constraints imposed by Brussels have become so confining that the French Ministry of Industry has occasionally rebelled. In March 1982 the French government offered to reduce employer contributions to the social security system by 10 to 12 percent (some Fr 2.5 to Fr 3 billion in a good year) for those textile companies that innovated or invested or both. Brussels refused to allow these tax expenditures, arguing that they were not accompanied by sufficient obligations on the part of the manufacturers to reduce the industry's capacity. In reply the French Ministry of Research and Industry said "the plan is well suited to its objectives and should be continued."[9] While awaiting the ultimate outcome, the French government has put off the day when it is obliged to reduce its influence on the French textile industry.

Even when Paris is not ordered to defer to Brussels in matters of industrial policy, France cooperates voluntarily with other countries.[10] Such cooperation has occurred frequently in the aerospace industry: Concorde, Airbus, Ariane, and Eurodif are all joint policy ventures that would otherwise have been too expensive for any single government to undertake. Although beneficial in many respects, however, international cooperation makes it difficult for France to control its own industrial policy.

There is, then, a continuity in philosophy between the strain of Socialist thought described above and the philosophies of de Gaulle and Pompidou. Another current viewpoint, one that stresses decentralization, has not been expressed with vigor in a very long time indeed.

France is divided into twenty-two regions. Before the Socialists came to power in 1981, regional governments exercised virtually no power in matters pertaining to industry. Most decisions were made by the *préfet*, an administrative official appointed by the national government. The regional council deliberated, but it could neither legislate nor execute economic policy. The same was true of each region's *comité économique et social*. For all intents and purposes, the préfet controlled the region's budget.

On March 2, 1982, the Socialists passed a law that delegated major responsibilities for economic policy to the regions. By the implementing decrees of September 1982, these responsibilities were quickly expanded. The regions can now intervene on behalf of companies in difficulty. They can also decide in which industries to subsidize the creation of new employment.[11]

Nevertheless, the regions are effectively required to limit their interventions to small and medium-sized companies. Otherwise, it is felt, decisions made at the national level might be subverted, and industrial policy might lose all coherence. For example, if the Aciéries de Decazeville wishes to invest in a new technique of production and the investment is sufficiently large that adopting the new technique would alter the chances of steel companies in other regions to develop similar capacity, the decision will be made by the national not the regional government.

In addition to the decentralization of industrial policy per se, the Socialists

9. *Les Echos*, January 31, 1983.
10. See the chapter by François Lagrange in this volume.
11. For details, see the DATAR newsletter, no. 71 (November 1982).

have also decentralized indicative planning. By the law of July 29, 1982, regional plans will be established side by side with the national plan. In addition the national plan will be submitted to the regional councils for comment. The first experience with these procedures has been far from ideal. The regions lack the qualified personnel needed to engage in economic policy. Reliance on the national government for an important share of their resources has meant that the regional councils have often had to formulate their industrial policies without knowing how much money they would have to support their choices. Because of the lack of time they had to consider the Ninth Plan, they exerted little influence on its content.

In the long term the biggest obstacles to decentralization will be the reluctance of the national bureaucracies to relinquish their control of industrial policy[12] and the power of the large industrial companies created during past rounds of industrial policy. The companies produce in many regions; frequently they sell in global markets. In many cases, they account for over half a region's industrial investment. Until now these companies have contracted with the national, but not the regional, governments regarding future behavior. Contracts have not specified the regional composition of the companies' activities.

Which is the real industrial policy of the Socialists—the grand industrial policy in the Pompidou style or the effort to decentralize economic decisionmaking that might be traced to Jean Monnet? More important, to what extent do these approaches conflict?

Again, it is too soon to answer such questions. My own view, however, is that the two types of policy complement rather than conflict with each other. Decentralization will occur tomorrow only if the centralized decisions succeed today. In other words, industrial policies of the de Gaulle–Pompidou style are being used to create a healthy industrial sector. Meanwhile, regional institutions are being developed and planning is being democratized to the point that decentralization will have a chance to succeed. Today, maybe only ten officials in each region are competent to engage in economic policy. But when Jean Monnet began, he had no more than that at the national level.

Tools

Since World War II there has been a broad continuity in the goals of industrial policy: relief from external constraints, achievement of high employment, pro-

12. In this regard, it is interesting to note that the national ministries are suddenly establishing regional branch offices. The Ministry of Industry, for example, now has a Délégation aux Affaires Régionales.

motion of new technology, and preservation of national independence. A similar continuity has characterized means. With one major exception—public enterprise—the techniques of industrial policy have remained the same, weathering the creation and destruction of agencies and the hiring, redeployment, and coordination of bureaucrats. These techniques can be divided into two categories: those that are traditionally considered under the heading of industrial policy and those that have major influences on industrial structure even if they are sometimes classified in other compartments of economic policy.

Instruments of Industrial Policy Narrowly Defined

Narrowly defined, the instruments of industrial policy include subsidies, public procurement, and research policy.

Subsidies. Conventionally, subsidies are described as horizontal or vertical. Horizontal subsidies are available to any company that meets a given set of criteria; vertical subsidies are open only to companies within a certain industry. Frequently, vertical subsidies are further limited to certain companies within the industry. The Finance Commission of the Seventh Plan described this system as

> complex and multifaceted. It owes its form to the placement of successive layers of government action on a preexisting stock of government policy. Each layer constitutes a response to a new set of priorities. Once in place, each policy acquires a life of its own. Over time, policies become increasingly permanent and decreasingly selective. In one form or another, firms are led to seek subsidies from the state. Sometimes they obtain multiple subsidies for the same purpose. The danger of such a system is that selectivity will be drowned in a shower of interventions; the system as a whole will be very costly, but the efficacy of each policy will be very slight.[13]

The durability of small subsidies is especially troubling: they hardly affect industrial outcomes, yet they complicate the policy system enormously. For example, in 1977 wholesale consumers of electricity in Brittany collectively received Fr 1 million in subsidies. The sum is trivial, but the program must be administered nonetheless.

In general, companies prefer horizontal subsidies. Such subsidies do not depend on subsequent performance, and they avoid the appearance of being arbitrary. The impact of horizontal subsidies on industrial outcomes is relatively difficult to measure, however; hence the preference within government for vertical subsidies.

Amounts spent by government on subsidies are difficult to measure with precision. A variety of sources, including different ones at different times, must

13. Report of the Commission on Finance of the Seventh Plan.

Table 1-1. *Industrial Subsidies, by Type, 1970–79*
Millions of current francs unless otherwise specified

Subsidies	1970	1971	1972	1973	1974	1975	1976	1977	1978	1979
Sector-specific subsidies	2,446	3,357	3,676	3,495	4,444	5,270	5,982	5,502	4,666	6,915
Aerospace	1,131	1,668	1,865	1,507	1,992	2,294	2,170	1,774	1,893	1,257
Shipbuilding	309	465	610	626	784	1,124	1,071	964	1,042	1,563
Electronics and information processing	0	283	223	215	329	701	1,228	741	444	335
Steel	494	534	370	530	760	570	1,260	1,637	515	3,246
Agriculture and food	142	142	110	121	153	186	178	174	192	204
Capital grants	370	265	498	496	426	395	75	212	580	310
Subsidies not tied to specific sectors	1,245	1,473	1,565	2,255	2,937	3,224	5,038	5,627	5,068	8,021
Regional subsidies	424	346	299	453	435	256	213	447	452	1,364
R&D subsidies	116	128	150	154	179	417	507	421	567	530
Industrial policy subsidies[a]	0	0	72	107	109	148	141	106	124	203
Interest subsidies[b]	129	189	170	240	283	401	525	637	717	907
Insurance of exporters against cost inflation	164	459	550	585	650	1,155	2,100	1,661	1,035	1,660
Loans to exporters	402	302	293	654	1,217	775	1,471	2,310	2,064	3,255
Miscellaneous	10	49	31	62	64	72	81	45	109	102
All subsidies listed above	3,691	4,830	5,241	5,750	7,381	8,494	11,020	11,129	9,734	14,936
Subsidies as a percentage of value added	1.9	2.1	2.0	1.9	2.2	2.2	2.5	2.3	1.8	2.4
Subsidies as a percentage of gross fixed capital formation	10.0	12.2	12.2	12.3	13.9	16.1	17.3	16.4	13.5	19.1

Source: Henri Aujac and Jacqueline de Rouville, *La Politique Industrielle en France Depuis 1945 et Surtout Depuis 1969* (Neuilly-sur-Seine: Bureau d'Informations et de Prévisions Economiques, 1983), p. 53.
a. Crédits de politique industrielle.
b. Bonifications.

be consulted, and comparability is thus difficult to achieve. It is important to realize, however, that industry receives only one-third of all subsidies destined for business enterprises. A larger share is spent on commerce and the services, the balance going to energy, agriculture, and food. The lion's share of subsidies goes to public enterprises. Even before the recent round of nationalizations, public enterprises received at least 80 percent of transfers to industry.

In May 1981 the new Socialist government established a commission to study the use of subsidies in France. Table 1-1 shows the commission's measurement of subsidies for the years 1970–79 and illustrates several features of the French system: the concentration of subsidies in a few activities, the attention devoted to restructuring mature industries (shipbuilding and steel, for instance), the attention devoted to promoting new industries such as aerospace, electronics, and information processing, and the substantial increase in export promotion.

The subsidies under discussion are dispensed by a wide variety of departments in a wide variety of ministries. Most of the funds employed as government subsidies appear either in the budget of the Fonds de Développement Economique et Social (FDES), or under the heading of *crédits de politique industrielle*. To a large extent, however, decisions as to how these funds should be allocated are made elsewhere. Many, for example, are made by interministerial committees, which are designed to achieve rapid and coherent deployment of the government's resources. The major government participants include:

—The Fonds de Développement Economique et Social. Between 1962 and 1974 the budget of the FDES declined considerably in real terms, but since then it has played a major role in dramatic cases of industrial reorganization. During 1974–75, for example, it devoted Fr 1.45 billion to the acquisitions of Berliet by Renault and Citroën by Peugeot. It also spent Fr 1.4 billion on the development of Fos. Since then it has devoted substantial sums to the steel industry.

—The Comité Interministériel pour l'Aménagement des Structures Industrielles (CIASI). Created in 1974 and renamed in 1982 as the Comité Interministériel pour les Restructurations Industrielles (CIRI), this committee is supposed to help independent companies of small and medium size that find themselves in temporary difficulty (in principle, large companies and their subsidiaries are excluded). Between 1974 and 1981 CIASI spent Fr 1.5 billion in the form of standard loans from the FDES, Fr 474 million in loans entitling the government to benefit from subsequent profits, and Fr 815 million in subsidies drawn from the *crédits de politique industrielle*. During this period the committee reviewed 1,100 cases involving 380,000 jobs. It awarded funds in 700 cases— an average of Fr 10,000 per job. On average, every franc committed by CIASI permitted a company to raise an additional eight francs from other sources. Some 40 percent of the jobs saved were in mechanical equipment and textiles. Fully one-third of the situations qualifying for support resulted in failure within five years, however. The work of the CIASI has been handicapped in two respects. Because the funds are awarded on a revolving basis, the committee cannot distribute them according to a coherent plan. In addition there are large disparities among cases in terms of government funds per job saved, which suggests that political factors have influenced the committee's decisions. The committee has, however, been able to act speedily.

—The Comité Interministériel d'Orientation pour le Développement des Industries Stratégiques (CODIS). Just as CIASI deals with mature industries, so CODIS deals with industries of the future. Since its creation in 1979 it has promoted the manufacture of office equipment, household electronics, flexible work stations, biotechnology, marine equipment, energy saving devices, and certain textiles. CODIS asks its beneficiaries to sign a contract with the state (a *contrat de développement*) that specifies the obligations of each party. In 1980–81 CODIS spent Fr 2.3 billion, drawn largely from the funds of the FDES, from the *crédits de politique industrielle*, and from the plan to computerize French society. Critics have suggested two defects in the work of CODIS. First, unlike CIASI, it concentrates most of its aid on very large companies. Second, because CODIS finances most of the investments undertaken by its beneficiaries, it exercises substantial influence over their behavior. In some cases, such as that of CII-Honeywell Bull, the influence has led to confusion over who does and who should manage the recipient company.

—The Comité Interministériel pour le Développement des Investissements et le Soutien de l'Emploi. Founded in 1979, CIDISE finances medium-sized companies that are growing very rapidly. Between 1979 and 1981 it helped finance 600 investment projects, deploying Fr 1 billion in FDES funds in the form of participatory loans. These loans accounted for 16.35 percent of the total funds mobilized by the recipient companies for these projects. Close to one-third of the money loaned went to companies in agriculture, food, and textiles.

—The Fonds Spécial d'Adaptation Industrielle. Created in 1978, FSAI is supposed to encourage investment in regions with high unemployment. During 1980 the fund loaned Fr 592 million, which resulted in Fr 2.3 billion in invest-ment. The automobile industry accounts for 70 percent of the loans outstand-ing; steel and shipbuilding also receive substantial aid.

—The Institut de Développement Industriel (IDI). Created in 1970, the institute is supposed to finance dynamic medium-sized companies that lack equity funds. In fact, however, it has also helped companies in declining industries.

—The Agence Nationale de Valorisation de la Recherche (ANVAR). The agency helps small and medium-sized industrial companies to invent and innovate. The agency has been very successful, and its role in French industrial policy is growing.

—The sociétés de développement régional (SDR). These organizations are supposed to aid medium-sized enterprises that cannot obtain bank credit on market terms. In addition to lending money themselves, they guarantee loans extended by banks to relevant companies.

—The comités départementaux d'examen des problèmes de financement des entreprises (CODEFI). In principle these organizations reflect an intention to decentralize industrial policy. In fact, however, they have averaged fewer than one loan per committee per year. The loans are designed to complement short-term credit extended by traditional banks.

Public Procurement. In addition to cash subsidies, the government promotes industry through its purchases of goods and services. The national and local governments, together with public enterprises, purchased 7 percent of GNP in 1979. Almost 60 percent of the Fr 167 billion of public purchases were attributable to Electricité de France (Fr 42 billion), the Ministry of Defense (Fr 36 billion), and the postal-telephonic system (Fr 20 billion). The chief beneficiaries of government procurement have been construction, mechanical equipment, electrical equipment, and aerospace companies. The government has used its purchasing power to favor French-owned companies at the expense of others. Most purchases involve big stakes: almost half of all public orders are worth over Fr 10 million. From the perspective of suppliers, the orders of Electricité de France are especially prized both because they typically guarantee purchases over the medium term and because suppliers are rarely obliged to depend only on EDF for business. In contrast, neither the French Railways nor the Paris transit authority has succeeded in planning its purchases for a series of years.

Research Policy. During the 1960s the government concentrated its research budget on military needs, including aerospace development, nuclear weapons, and computers. More recently, it has attempted to use its funds to support economic modernization. Three channels of funding exist: broad research programs established at the time the budget of the Ministry of Research is set, interministerial committee budgets, and the R&D contracts, or *marchés d'études,* offered by particular ministries. Frequently, funding takes the form of loans or advances. Rarely, however, is the government reimbursed. Between

Table 1-2. R & D Activity, by Industry, 1979
Percent

Industry	R&D expenditure divided by value added	Share of total industrial R&D expenditure
Agriculture	0.1	0.6
Food, beverages, and tobacco	0.3	1.4
Energy	1.8	6.6
Building materials and ceramics	0.6	0.5
Metallic mining and basic metals	1.6	2.2
Foundries and fabricated metals	0.5	1.1
Mechanical equipment	1.7	3.2
Electrical equipment	4.4	3.7
Electronic equipment	19.6	20.7
Information-processing equipment	14.5	4.6
Chemicals	4.9	9.0
Pharmaceuticals	22.5	5.9
Rubber and plastics	3.8	3.5
Textiles	0.6	0.6
Aerospace	39.1	18.1
Automobiles	5.2	12.0
Shipbuilding and miscellaneous transport equipment	1.5	0.4
Instruments	3.6	1.2
Glass	3.4	0.8
Miscellaneous manufacturing	0.2	1.0
Construction	0.1	0.7
Transport services	0.1	0.4
Other services	. . .	1.8
All industries	2.4	100.0

Source: Aujac and de Rouville, Politique Industrielle, p. 66.

1965 and 1967, the Délégation Générale à la Recherche Scientifique et Technique admitted to having spent more than Fr 1 billion on R&D, only 5 percent of which was reimbursed. Table 1-2 summarizes the research effort of French industries in 1979.

Instruments of Industrial Policy Broadly Defined

The broadly defined instruments of industrial policy include export subsidies, monetary policy, tax expenditures, and competition policies.

Export Subsidies.   These subsidies are described fully by Michel Freyche elsewhere in this book. Table 1-3 shows the extent of export subsidies between 1974 and 1979. The table does not show that export subsidies have gone almost exclusively to a small number of giant companies. As a result, the program has not increased the number of companies that sells abroad. Nor does table 1-3 reveal the special privileges accorded to exporters of capital equipment (special opportunities to rediscount at the Bank of France and special opportunities for foreign governments to borrow from French financial institutions). These privileges distort the structure of French exports toward lumpy orders by foreign governments and away from ordinary international trade.

Monetary Policy.   In most respects, French monetary policy is macroeconomic: the rediscounting and quantitative control of bank lending undertaken by the Bank of France tend to apply equally to all nonfinancial borrowers. So do the various measures designed to increase national saving and to develop the securities market. Industry benefits only insofar as such policies make all credit cheap.

In some respects, however, monetary policy is selective. Construction tends to be favored more than industry, and investments in certain regions are favored more than those in others. In response to government pressure, banks have lent money to companies they consider to be unworthy of credit (some large steel manufacturers have obtained loans in this way).

The government has urged public enterprises to borrow abroad so as to leave national saving to the use of private enterprise. Given the decline of the franc, this policy has jeopardized future investment in industries dominated by public corporations.

Tax Expenditures.   Typically, tax expenditures are available to all companies on an equal basis. Thus depreciation rules, investment tax credits, and inducements offered to households to hold corporate stock[14] inherently are nondiscriminatory. Use of tax expenditures usually takes the form of selective reductions in employer contributions to the social security system. Such reductions tend to apply to specific industries or companies.

Competition Policy.   Until about 1965 the government helped to preserve an industrial structure made up of small and medium-sized companies through a variety of tax advantages available only to such enterprises. After 1965 the government began to promote mergers of already large companies, an activity that appears incompatible with French antitrust laws. Legally, French compe-

14. Under the Monory Law of 1978.

Table 1-3. *Export Subsidies, 1974–79*
Billions of current francs

Program	1974	1975	1976	1977	1978	1979
Loans to exporters	1.36	1.11	1.59	2.75	2.79	3.58
Insurance of loans to exporters and their foreign customers	0.05	−0.01	−0.31	−0.57	0.59	1.67
Insurance of market prospecting activities of exporters	0.03	0.04	0.04	0.04	0.05	0.05
Insurance of exporters against cost inflation	0.65	1.15	2.10	1.69	1.04	1.66
Total	2.10	2.29	3.41	3.91	4.47	6.98

Source: Aujac and de Rouville, *Politique Industrielle*, p. 68. Figures are rounded.

tition policy is based on an ordinance of June 30, 1945, and laws of July 1, 1977, and July 19, 1977. These documents give the government very broad powers to control collusion, abuses of dominant positions, and mergers. In fact, however, French antitrust law has been a dead letter because the Commission de la Concurrence has no power to decide cases. Antitrust decisions are made by such members of the cabinet as the minister of economic affairs. An indication of the views of such politicians was given during preparation of the bill that became law on July 19, 1977, when the prime minister stated that the law would not be used "to call into question the policy of industrial concentration that has been pursued for many years by successive French governments." Between its creation in 1977 and November 30, 1981, the Commission de la Concurrence considered only 150 cases involving collusion or the abuse of a dominant position. During the same period, only 4 mergers were considered worthy of its attention, and all were ultimately allowed, subject to conditions established by the relevant ministers. Clearly, competition policy is not an important element of French industrial policy.

Recent Developments

With one exception the Socialists have employed the tools of industrial policy bequeathed to them by their predecessors. The exception is public enterprise. In February 1982 five of France's largest industrial enterprises—Compagnie Générale d'Electricité, Pechiney Ugine Kuhlmann, Rhône Poulenc, Saint-Gobain–Pont-à-Mousson, and Thomson-Brandt—were nationalized. The government also took control of both major steel companies (Usinor and Sacilor) as well as the Compagnie Générale de Constructions Téléphoniques (CGCT)—

the French subsidiary of ITT—and CII–Honeywell Bull, Dassault, and Matra. Finally, the government took over virtually all of the banking sector that had escaped the nationalizations at the end of World War II. From holdings made up mostly of public utilities,[15] the public sector came to account for 30 percent of value added and 50 percent of research and development in the industrial sector. Table 1-4 shows for each industry the share of value added attributable to the public sector as defined both before and after the 1982 round of government acquisitions.

To many, industrial policy provided the rationale for expanding the public sector. According to the office of the prime minister, public enterprise would constitute the principal lever of a grand industrial policy. For one thing, since the 1960s these companies had been the chief beneficiaries of French subsidies: it was time for the government to exercise direct control so that public monies would not be spent for purely private purposes. In fact, by reducing the chance that business would subvert government objectives, nationalization would increase the ability of government to resort to subsidies. On another plane, the enlargement of the public sector was thought to facilitate industrial policy because it permitted the government to intervene directly in the distribution of lines of business among companies. Several observers believed that large French companies had come to consist of incoherent hodgepodges of subsidiaries. By nationalizing the lot of them, government could concentrate a certain activity in a single company. In other words it could continue its promotion of national champions. As a result, nitrogenous fertilizers have been concentrated in the Compagnie Française de l'Azote (COFAZ), halogens have become the responsibility of Elf-Aquitaine, organic chemicals and plastics of CDF-Chimie, and specialty chemicals of Rhône Poulenc (petrochemical refining is to be shared by Elf-Aquitaine and CDF-Chimie). Thus Pechiney Ugine Kuhlmann has been stripped of virtually all its chemical operations, while Rhône Poulenc has lost its fertilizer manufacturing activities.

Unlike the nationalizations of the industrial sector, those of the financial sector were motivated less by industrial policy than by general economic policy.[16] The impact of these nationalizations will depend heavily on the ability of government to control its banks. If history is a guide, the government will not

---

15. For instance, companies in electricity, natural gas, coal, railways, and urban mass transit. The principal public enterprises other than public utilities were Renault, Société Nationale Industrielle Aérospatiale, and Ato-Chimie.

16. Proposals not adopted by the Socialists would have influenced industry more directly. For example, the Socialist platform envisaged a national investment bank and also considered creating a series of industrial banks, each designed to cater to a single industry.

Table 1-4. *Importance of Public Enterprise, by Industry, before and after 1982*

Industry	Share of value added in 1979 attributable to the public sector as defined	
	Before 1982	After 1982
Coal	99.3	99.3
Petroleum and natural gas	39.7	39.7
Electricity	97.8	98.2
Distribution of gas	96.6	96.6
Distribution of water and steam	. . .	3.7
Ferrous ores	0	68.3
Crude steel	. . .	66.4
Semifabricated steel	0	16.8
Nonferrous metallic ores	0	. . .
Basic nonferrous metals	16.3	60.7
Miscellaneous nonmetallic minerals	. . .	52.6
Building materials and ceramics	. . .	5.8
Glass	0	34.7
Basic chemicals	11.6	47.8
Specialty chemicals	5.1	9.2
Pharmaceuticals	6.6	24.3
Foundries	. . .	26.3
Fabricated metals	. . .	6.7
Farm machinery	1.0	. . .
Machine tools	2.8	3.3
Industrial equipment	1.7	18.3
Handling equipment	0.4	1.6
Office equipment	0	8.7
Electrical equipment	0	18.7
Electronic equipment	. . .	45.7
Household durables	0	8.7
Automobiles and transport equipment	. . .	31.4
Shipbuilding	0	0.0
Aerospace	53.8	84.3
Instruments	7.6	9.6
Synthetic and artificial fibers	0	. . .
Textiles	0	1.2
Leather	0	0
Footwear	0	0
Apparel	0	0
Wood	0	2.4

Table 1-4 *(continued)*

| Industry | Share of value added in 1979 attributable to the public sector as defined | |
	Before 1982	After 1982
Furniture	0	1.3
Paper and board	. . .	7.6
Printing and publishing	0	0.3
Rubber	. . .	3.3
Plastics	2.2	10.4
Miscellaneous manufactures	0	. . .
Total: industry including energy	17.3	29.9
Total: industry excluding energy	8.0	22.5

Source: Aujac and de Rouville, *Politique Industrielle*, p. 125.

always get its way. For years, the Crédit Lyonnais, the third largest bank in France, failed to comply with the government's system of quantitative credit controls—even though it was owned by government.[17] Apparently the government now exercises greater control over its banks. The Ministry of Economic Affairs has named a new president for each bank, and every week the presidents are summoned to a meeting at the ministry. The investment bankers in particular complain that they are being forced to lend to companies unworthy of credit, however deserving they might appear to the politicians or their electors.

The experience with the banks might also appear to signal the inability of government to control its industrial properties, but such is not the case. First, the Council of Ministers, upon nomination of the sponsoring minister, names the head of each public enterprise.[18] On occasion, people are chosen less for their competence than for their willingness to embrace the views of the sponsoring minister. Second, sponsoring ministries exercise financial and industrial oversight. Each company must present its proposed investment program, projected cash flow, and proposed financial structure. It negotiates with its sponsoring ministry until the sponsor approves the overall plan and agrees to do its part. As for industrial oversight, the sponsoring ministry decides the range of activi-

17. To be sure, the bank was punished for its behavior. It had to deposit at the Bank of France double the amount by which it had exceeded its allowed rate of lending. Because these deposits earned no interest, the profits of the bank declined precipitously.

18. Typically, the sponsoring minister is the minister of industry (for industrial companies) or the minister of economic affairs (for financial firms).

ties in which each company should engage and hence implicitly the degree to which each will face competition from domestic rivals. From the perspective of the sponsor, both the feasibility and the desirability of controlling the behavior of public enterprises are assumed. It is difficult to see how managerial autonomy can be preserved in such a system.[19]

Who Benefits from Industrial Policy?

Most studies of industrial policy occur ex ante rather than ex post. As a result, they emphasize what the government would like to happen as opposed to what happens in fact. Under the circumstances it is easy to exaggerate the success of industrial policy.

The lack of ex post studies is hardly surprising. Because industrial policy is merely a convenient name for a heterogeneous collection of tools and strategies, any attempt to measure the impact of the collection as a whole is fraught with difficulties. As table 1-5 shows, it is difficult to measure even the amount of government subsidies: policies differ in subsidy content and cannot be added together directly. Nevertheless, it is important to ask some questions regarding impact. The one to which I shall respond is, who really benefits from French industrial policy?

Industrial policy has served to expand dramatically the power of the state and its bureaucracy over French society. Government has become one of industry's best customers. In some markets its position approaches monopsony. Beyond purchases of their products, the government offers massive subsidies to certain industrial corporations. Since the 1982 round of nationalizations the state has also constituted the country's leading industrial enterprise. Through its longstanding monopoly of television broadcasting, in particular, it has been able to manipulate public opinion.

The government has used its power over private enterprise to reinforce the big against the small. In 1979 Hervé Hannoun, a high-ranking official in the Ministry of Finance, was asked to study the impact of government subsidies. His report, which the government refused to publish,[20] clearly demonstrated that a very few industries receive the bulk of government support, a finding that is

19. By the end of 1982 each public enterprise was to submit a plan to its sponsor containing production and investment objectives, macroeconomic hypotheses, and financial needs. By February 1983, after bilateral discussions, these enterprise plans were to become *contrats de plan*, with terms of three years. The contracts were designed to guarantee the autonomy of management. We shall see if they succeed.

20. The essential contents of the report are described by Gilbert Mathieu, *Le Monde*, September 27, 1979.

Table 1-5. *Expenditures on Industrial Policy, by Type of Program, 1974*
Millions of francs

Program	Amount of expenditure
Subsidies	16,200
Capital grants (net of shareholder income)	1,300
Tax expenditures	3,500
Loans of the FDES (capital grant to FDES for the year)	3,450
Loans of the Crédit National	4,700
Loans of the sociétés de développement régional	1,200
Cash advances for R&D and for aerospace	1,350
Underpricing of public utilities	22,000
Subsidies associated with undertaxation of corporations	15,500

Source: Anicet Le Pors, *Les Béquilles du Capital: Les Transferts Etat-Industrie Critère de Nationalisation* (Paris: Editions du Seuil, 1977), p. 44.

confirmed in the results of Anicet Le Pors.[21] Moreover, government support is highly concentrated in five large enterprises: Compagnie Générale d'Electricité (including Alsthom), Thomson-Brandt, CII–Honeywell Bull, Dassault, and Empain Schneider. These five received nearly 50 percent of all government support of industry, as measured by R&D subsidies, export subsidies, regional development subsidies, and sectoral subsidies. The concentration of support is confirmed in data gathered by the Committee on Industrial Finance associated with the Eighth Plan (see table 1-6). These data show that three public enterprises received nearly one-third of all subsidies and nine companies (some public, others private) received over half.

Some observers believe that figures of this sort exaggerate the degree to which subsidies benefit only giant companies. They argue that the big recipients should be viewed as conduits of government support to smaller companies. In 1982, however, the Bureau d'Informations et de Prévisions Economiques conducted a survey of small and medium-sized firms. It asked whether government support of big business ultimately trickled down to their level. They replied that apart from funds distributed by ANVAR, most government subsidies flowed only as far as the subsidiaries of the large recipients. Small, independent companies lacked the knowledge of government programs and the clout with bureaucrats to obtain their share of aid. Moreover, such companies are especially dependent on the speed with which they can obtain help: to receive aid far

21. *Les Béquilles du Capital: Les Transferts État-Industrie Critère de Nationalisation* (Paris: Editions du Seuil, 1977).

Table 1-6. Concentration of Industrial Subsidies among Recipient Companies, 1976

	Share of this type of subsidy in all listed subsidies	Nine largest beneficiaries				All other beneficiaries	All beneficiaries
Type of subsidy		3 large public enterprises	1 large mixed enterprise[a]	5 large private enterprises	Total		
Industries of the future	39	45	18	17	80	20	100
Mature industries	22	59	0	11	70	30	100
Industrial reorganization	11	0	0	1	1	99	100
Regional subsidies	6	0	0	4	4	96	100
Export subsidies	22	2	0	41	43	57	100
All of the above	100	31	7	18	56	44	100

Source: Aujac and de Rouville, *Politique Industrielle,* p. 86.
a. A minority of the voting stock of this company is controlled by government.

in the future is barely preferred to not receiving aid at all. To a member of the competitive fringe, trickle down is no alternative to direct and immediate support.

Households, too, have probably been hurt by industrial policy. Admittedly, the spread of telephones and televisions has contributed warmth and opportunity to the isolated household, but the value of Concorde to the average citizen is far from obvious, nor is the type of television programming that serves primarily to distribute the advertisements of business enterprises and the filtered news reporting of the state. Without a doubt the chief beneficiaries of French industrial policy during the past fifteen years have been the state, its bureaucracy, and a few large industrial corporations.

Christian Stoffaës

Industrial Policy in the High-Technology Industries

THE PERSISTENCE of economic crisis during the past ten years has forced the governments of industrialized nations to search for powerful economic policies. Techniques ranging from Keynesian reflation to radical monetarism have been used to fight stagflation. So far none can be considered an unqualified success. Keynesianism has achieved only moderate increases in growth and employment; even so, it has stimulated inflation and deficits in international trade. Monetarism seems to have reduced inflation, but it has also spawned stagnation and unemployment. Given these failures of macroeconomic policy, many observers conclude that the current economic crisis is one of industrial adjustment, that existing industrial structures must be adapted to the new realities of global competition, rapid technological change, and new consumer tastes. Without adaptation, existing economic structures will doom Keynesianism to the production of inflation and doom monetarism to the proliferation of bankruptcy.

If this analysis is correct, then a number of questions arise. Is it possible to develop new industries and diffuse new technologies as long as stagnation, excess capacity, and meager profits discourage risk taking and financially productive investment? Should the governments of free-market countries adopt a more interventionist attitude to foster the development of new technologies and the growth of new and promising industries? Or should they stay instead with their traditional economic policies of laissez-faire at the microeconomic level and "neutral" regulation at the macroeconomic level?

The governments of the developed market economies have responded very differently to these questions. During the past ten years the degree of public intervention in industrial structures has increased in all countries. But certain European governments (the United Kingdom, Sweden, Italy, and France) have been especially quick to rescue the lame ducks in such depressed industries as steel, chemicals, textiles, and shipbuilding. These interventions have usually been conducted under strong political and social pressures to sustain full employment, especially in depressed areas. Rescue has taken the form of nationalization, loans, subsidies, the organization of government-sponsored cartels, and protection from foreign competition. Such policies have been criticized as inefficiently defensive; they are said to aid the obsolescence of industrial structure as a whole by preventing the reallocation of resources.

Despite the shortcomings of rescue operations, most of Europe as well as the United States has been reluctant to engage in positive industrial policies. Unlike its defensive counterpart, positive industrial intervention would involve a government in selecting new industries with promising futures (so-called sunrise industries), picking specific companies to develop them, and backing the winners in various ways to permit them to develop the desired activities.

In no small measure the reluctance of many governments to pursue positive industrial policies has been nourished by troubling questions. Is it legitimate for a democratic government to pick winners arbitrarily? Would not choices of that sort entail protectionism and unfair competition? Would they not profoundly distort both domestic and international competition? How could politicians and bureaucrats improve on the investment decisions of professional bankers and entrepreneurs?

Despite questions of this sort, some countries—especially those with a long tradition of government intervention in the economy—have engaged successfully in positive industrial policy. Among these, Japan has received the most attention, largely because Japanese industry has been very successful: it has not only challenged American and European companies in traditional industries such as automobiles or consumer electronics, but it also threatens to challenge them in sunrise industries and advanced technologies such as robots, computers, and integrated circuits.

Among European countries, France is unique in having pursued positive industrial policies for a long time. Because of these policies, while some companies in traditional industries were suffering greatly from economic crisis, other companies were able to achieve great technological and commercial success in such important sunrise industries as electronics, telecommunications, aerospace, sophisticated weapons, and nuclear engineering. In many of these advanced industries, France has increased its exports to world markets; it has even challenged the heretofore unchallenged leadership of American companies. As a result the French case, no less than its Japanese counterpart, is worthy of study.

The Institutional Framework

Economists have never been successful in drawing up a compelling rationale for industrial policy. Industrial policy is by definition a highly pragmatic matter. Its content and effects depend on the state of technology, the historical moment, and, above all, the political, sociological, and cultural features of the country under examination. Industrial policy cannot be modeled easily: it defies representation in the economists' equations. Each country has its own way of handling industry. Some countries have weak central governments, while others have strong ones. Some countries have been exposed to world markets for a long time and enjoy a dynamic and innovative entrepreneurial class; others are inward looking, with industrialists and bankers alike averse to risk.

In most Western countries, steeped in the philosophy of Adam Smith, it is fashionable to believe that the best way to make industry efficient is to have no industrial policy at all—to let the market play its games. Unfortunately, both "the market" and "government intervention" are oversimplistic intellectual concepts. They do not have the same meaning in Japan, the United States, the Federal Republic of Germany, Italy, or France. Analysis of industrial policy requires deep and interdisciplinary examination. Thus French industrial strategy can be described and understood only in the context of its historical tradition and its institutional framework. These have no counterparts in the Anglo-Saxon nations or the other countries of Western Europe.

Historical Tradition: Mercantilism

The French government has a long tradition of intervening to foster the growth and development of new industries and advanced technologies. Two main factors lie at the heart of that tradition.

France was one of the first nations in Europe to unify and centralize. A powerful civil service developed as early as the eighteenth century and used economic intervention and industrial policy to achieve such objectives as national autonomy. France can thus be considered the prototype of the mercantilistic nation. It has used control of international trade and promotion of new industries as tools to achieve national prestige and wealth.

Government initiative can also be attributed to deficiencies of the private sector. France is a Latin and Catholic nation. Dominated by aristocratic landowners, it lacked the trading and capitalistic traditions of the United Kingdom, Germany, and the Netherlands. French bankers and industrialists were unusually averse to taking risks, and what ventures they did untertake showed little dynamism. After the Protestant merchant class was expelled in the eighteenth century, the wealthy preferred investing their capital in land or government bonds rather than in industry and trade. These handicaps caused the backwardness of French industry in relation to the rest of Western Europe, especially in the nineteenth and twentieth centuries. Thus it was necessary to substitute government initiatives for deficient private ventures, especially in the context of capital-intensive or technology-intensive industries.

Colbertisme (named after Jean-Baptiste Colbert, a minister of Louis XIV) was the first global and consistent national industrial strategy. Colbert's administration attempted to develop modern industries and complex technologies on French soil. The strategy combined protection from foreign competition with such incentives as monopolies, patents, subsidies, and training programs. The industries favored most were those linked to the production of weapons. Also receiving attention were those facing stiff competition from imports—linen, clothes, glass, tapestries, furniture, and porcelain. In these industries the government founded a set of royal manufacturers, some of which—Les Gobelins, the Manufacture de Sèvres, and Saint-Gobain, for instance—still exist.

These tactics were pursued throughout the eighteenth century. New branches of the civil service were created to encourage industrial development, and elite technical schools, the grandes écoles, were formed to staff these bureaucracies. During the nineteenth century the Saint-Simonian movement promoted a close association between dynamic industrialists, dynamic bankers, and the government bureaucracy. Together, they would foster the development of the sunrise industries of the times: coal, pig iron, steel, waterways, steamships, and railroads. By following these ideas, the Second Empire enjoyed a particularly high rate of growth and productive investment between 1850 and 1870. The country reverted to Malthusianism and protectionism, however, during the Third Republic, a reversion that lasted until World War II. In 1940 France still had more than one-third of its working population in agriculture. In spite of some technological leadership, its industrial structure consisted of geographically dispersed companies that were small or medium in size and conservative in behavior. The Vichy government introduced some changes: it developed the combination of liberalism and dirigisme that is known today as the mixed economy. A new technocracy emerged in the government ministries that helped organize the economy to deal with the constraints of wartime scarcity.

Following World War II, France enjoyed a true economic miracle. Government planning and nationalized enterprises became key instruments for channeling funds to transportation, coal, hydroelectricity, steel, cement, and chemicals. Once a strong industrial base was established, the economy was able to face the competition that arose when the Common Market was formed. During the Gaullist period, as responses to the American challenge, government backed new ventures in high-technology industries. The so-called *grands projets* were designed to give France national independence in technologies associated with aircraft, space, nuclear weapons, nuclear energy, oil drilling and refining, computers, and electronics. In the 1970s the high-technology industries that had been promoted during the 1960s were able to achieve noticeable success in world markets, even challenging American leadership in military and civil aeronautics, helicopter production, and nuclear engineering. At the same time, the government undertook new projects, especially in the nuclear generation of electricity, telecommunications, and electronics, to adapt to continued technological change.

Policy Tools and Instruments: Government Technocracy

The national institutions of French industrial policy are no less distinctive than the country's historical tradition. Some, such as the grandes écoles, are very old; others, such as the government's high-technology laboratories, are relatively recent. Old or new, however, few of these institutions have counterparts in other developed countries.

The technical ministries and their professional staffs are important in formulating and implementing industrial strategy. The degree of influence exerted by a ministry depends upon the nature of its links with the industries dependent on it. For example, the links between the Ministry of Defense and the armaments industries, or between the Ministry of the Post Office and Telecommunications and the telecommunications and electronics industries, are very close. Through public procurement, the ministries are able to shape such key industrial decisions as the technical standards of the equipment purchased, the prices, the structure of the industry, and the export strategy. The Ministries of Industry and Transportation have responsibility for nationalized enterprises in manufacturing, energy, and transportation. Through this tutorship they influence the strategies of the companies in these sectors.

Public procurement, which guarantees long-term orders and adequate research and development funds, appears to have been a key element in the technological success of such industries as electronics, aerospace, electrical engineering, and railroad equipment.

The Ministry of Research and Technology sets the budgets of the government's laboratories and research centers and also ensures that public spending on R&D is not sacrificed to short-term fiscal cuts. The financial ministries—

Treasury, Budget, and Foreign Trade—also participate in many aspects of industrial policy. The financial markets are closely regulated by Treasury and the nationalized banks. Treasury also monitors the debt strategy of the major public enterprises, and it distributes long-term loans or grants to both public and private enterprise. The Budget and Foreign Trade Ministries monitor the various subsidies and export-promotion loans to industry.

The ministries are staffed by professional civil servants who devote most of their careers to a particular ministry. The number of political appointments in most ministries, especially in the technical ones, is thus very limited. The professional staffs of these ministries are educated at the grandes écoles, which are run by the ministries and not by the university system. They recruit their students through highly respected competitive examinations, and they, not the universities, attract the best students.

Among the grandes écoles, the Ecole Nationale d'Administration supplies the administrative and diplomatic corps. More significant for industrial policy are the scientific and engineering schools. The Ecole Polytechnique, founded in 1794, provides the basic technical training for the various corps of state engineers. Its students then matriculate in one of the écoles d'application and upon graduation automatically join a corps of the same name. Thus the Ecole des Mines and the Corps des Mines supply the staff of the Ministry of Industry; the Ecole and the Corps des Ponts et Chaussées play the same role for the Ministries of Public Works, Urban Development, and Transportation; the Ecole and the Corps de l'Armement serve the Ministry of Defense; and the Ecole and the Corps des Télécommunications serve the Ministry of the Post Office and of Telecommunications.

Policy Tools and Instruments: Public Enterprises and Laboratories

The key participants in industrial policy are of course the companies themselves, especially the large corporations that operate in high-technology industries. The structure of each strategic industry is shaped by the relevant government ministry. This holds for public as well as private enterprise. For a long time the ministries believed in the doctrine of national champions, in the need to concentrate subsidies and other government favors on a single company in each industry. The rationale for such concentration was the need to achieve economies of scale. During the 1970s, however, the ministries adopted a pragmatic approach: wherever possible, they have attempted to maintain competition by helping more than one company in each industry. As a result, some industries have a single national champion (Dassault in military aircraft, Aérospatiale in civilian aircraft, Framatome in nuclear engineering, CII–Honeywell Bull in computers, Alsthom in heavy electrical equipment). In others the government backs two companies (Total–Compagnie Française des Pétroles and Elf-Aquitaine in petroleum, CIT-Alcatel and Thomson-CSF in telecommunications). When the Left came to power in 1981, it reverted to the strategy of encouraging national champions.

In comparison with other Western countries, France has a large nationalized sector. The first wave of nationalizations occurred just before and after World War II as the transportation and energy industries, the main commercial banks and insurance companies, and several manufacturing companies (for example, Renault) came under government ownership. The purpose of these nationalizations was political, but the nationalized enterprises subsequently became important instruments of economic policy. First they facilitated postwar reconstruction, then they promoted investment in basic industries.

Another extension of the public sector occurred during the Gaullist period. In connection with the *grands projets*, government enterprises were created or expanded in oil (Elf-Aquitaine), aerospace (Aérospatiale), nuclear materials (Cogéma), and information processing (CII).

In 1982, following the political shift to the left, another wave of nationalizations extended the public sector to about 25 percent of manufacturing industry and about 50 percent of large-scale industry. Twelve major industrial companies as well as most private banks came under government control. Thus most of the basic industries (steel, metals, chemicals, materials) and most of the high-technology industries (aircraft, electronics, telecommunications, heavy engineering) are now dominated by nationalized enterprises.

Although managed autonomously and free in their day-to-day decisions, the nationalized companies operate in close cooperation with, and under the guidance of, the ministries. Their long-term strategies are negotiated with the state within the framework of planning contracts. These contracts are designed to induce public enterprises to invest countercyclically and to take long-term risks by providing them with public loans and capital endowments to sustain their investment and research.[1] In fact, since it came to power in 1981, the Left has argued that industrial policy must rely very heavily on public enterprises to fight the effects of industrial crisis, to modernize such traditional sectors as steel and chemicals, and to develop new risk-taking ventures in such industries as electronics, information processing, and biochemicals.

Government laboratories and research centers in applied sciences are also important instruments of industrial policy. Most were created or considerably extended during the 1960s when the governments of General de Gaulle in-

---

1. See the chapter in this volume by Henri Guillaume.

creased the amount of public spending on R&D for national independence. Significant among these laboratories are the Commissariat à l'Energie Atomique, which develops nuclear engineering and materials; the Centre National d'Etudes Spatiales, which develops space launchers and satellites; and the Centre National d'Etudes des Télécommunications, which develops advanced telecommunications equipment. There are also laboratories studying oceanology, information processing, and biology.

From their beginnings, most of the public enterprises and government research centers have been staffed by former civil servants. For some time now such people have also been recruited to manage many private enterprises. Because most of them were trained in the same *grandes écoles* and the same technical subjects, they tend to think alike. The resulting interpenetration of administrative and industrial technocracies has no equivalent in the western world, not even in Japan. More than any other factor, this interpenetration explains the close coordination and mutual trust that exist between policymakers in government and planners in large corporations.

It is often argued that industrial policy inevitably suffers from myopia, that politicians are constrained to demand results in the short term even though the benefits of many worthy projects can occur only in the long term. It is certainly true that the ability to sustain industrial strategies for a long time has been a key element of French success. It is also true that political stability, as provided by the Constitution of the Fifth Republic, helps to explain the ability of recent governments to develop a long-range industrial strategy. Nevertheless, even during the Fourth Republic, when governments displayed chronic instability, long-term industrial policy was feasible. Administrative stability substituted for political stability. The role of the bureaucracy was evident: major industrial and technological projects of the day could be associated with particular civil servants—particular engineers who occupied senior positions in their corps and enjoyed the complete confidence of the politicians. Such people as Pierre Guillaumat (who founded Elf-Aquitaine in the 1960s), André Giraud (who redirected the strategy of the Commissariat à l'Energie Atomique in the early 1970s) and Gérard Théry (who reorganized the Telecommunications Administration in the late 1970s) are best described as administrative entrepreneurs: they behaved very much like the legendary capitalists of other countries.

Sectoral Policies: Recent Achievements and Current Patterns

During the past ten years, following a quarter century of fast growth, French industry has experienced depression and structural change of an unusual magnitude. Traditional industries with obsolete technologies have encountered stagnation, harsh foreign competition, bankruptcies, and layoffs. New industries have emerged and developed their investment, employment, and exports. Some 300,000 workers are employed in electronics, 150,000 in nuclear and electrical engineering, and 100,000 in aerospace. The rapid development of these industries is, in great part, the result of ambitious government industrial policies that were pursued for several decades before they reached maturity.

The recent achievements and current patterns of industrial policy in energy, aerospace, and electronics are especially notable. In these three sectors, French industry has been able to reach an advanced technological level and an internationally competitive position. In selecting these three, I do not wish to suggest that industrial policy failed to operate elsewhere. Pharmaceuticals, advanced shipbuilding, and railroad equipment, among others, have all received government attention. Nor do I wish to suggest that France has attained excellence in all sunrise industries. French industry is not as advanced in sophisticated machinery, coal liquefaction, biochemicals, specialty chemicals, precision instruments, robots, and very-large-scale integrated (VLSI) electronic components as it is, for example, in helicopters, space launchers, high-speed trains, electronic telecommunications, missiles, nuclear reprocessing, and fast breeder reactors. Why is this so and why have these three sectors been selected for review?

A common characteristic is heavy dependence on government procurement and state intervention. In advanced technologies France appears successful in industries for which government is the main customer; it appears less successful in those producing consumer goods and general industrial equipment (see table 2-1). The reason is because the main objective of government in the more successful sectors has been national security. The quest for national independence explains the government's desire to build domestic industries producing military aircraft, nuclear power, and computers. The quest for assured supplies of strategic products motivated the national oil policy and the nuclear electricity program. Even if these industrial policies have subsequently produced applications in nonmilitary areas, their origins can almost always be traced to a desire to preserve national independence. Given France's historical predilection for mercantilism, this is hardly surprising.

The quest for national independence continues unabated. In 1982, for instance, the Ministry of Defense, Direction des Recherches Techniques de l'Armement, spent Fr 17 billion on research and development related to the military. Of that amount the electronics industry received Fr 4.25 billion (25 percent), the nuclear industry Fr 3.40 billion (20 percent), rockets Fr 3.40

Table 2-1. *Relative Strengths and Weaknesses of French High-Technology Industries in World Competition*

Industry	Relative position of France	World leaders
Technologies highly dependent on government procurement		
Aerospace	Superior	United States, United Kingdom
Energy	Superior	United States, United Kingdom
Military electronics	Superior	United States
Transportation equipment	Good	United States, West Germany
Technologies largely independent of government procurement		
Chemicals and pharmaceuticals	Average	West Germany, United States, Switzerland
Metallurgy and materials	Weak	United States, Japan, West Germany
Industrial and consumer electronics	Weak	Japan
Mechanical equipment	Weak	Germany, Japan, Switzerland
Engineering and consulting	Good	United States, United Kingdom

Source: Christian Stoffaës, *Politique Industrielle* (Paris: Les Cours de Droit, 1983), p. 398.

billion (20 percent), aerospace Fr 3.40 billion (20 percent), and miscellaneous projects Fr 2.55 billion (15 percent).[2]

Energy

The government has been active in energy for some time. Energy is, of course, essential to all kinds of manufacturing activities. But France is relatively poor in coal, gas, and oil and has always been obliged to import a significant part of its energy. Such sources as it does possess could not be left to private development because of the heavy capital requirements and high degree of risk associated with the sector.

Since the nationalizations of 1946 the energy sector has been run by state monopolies in coal (Charbonnages de France), natural gas (Gaz de France), and electricity (Electricité de France). Energy policy is coordinated by the Ministry of Industry and the Ministry of Finance, which together set the prices, direct the

2. Christian Stoffaës, *Politique Industrielle* (Paris: Les Cours de Droit, 1983), p. 406.

investment, and ratify the financial strategies of the public enterprises.

Oil and gas imports have been regulated by the state since 1928. The oil industry is run jointly by the subsidiaries of three international corporations (British Petroleum, Shell, and Exxon) and two government-controlled French companies—Total–Compagnie Française des Pétroles, established in 1923 to exploit that part of Iraq's oil reserves that went to France by treaty after World War I, and Elf-Aquitaine, created in 1966 from the merger of smaller state-owned companies exploiting reserves on French territory and in former colonies. (For the current status and organization of the energy sector, see table 2-2.)

The two main achievements of energy policy in sunrise sectors relate to the production of crude oil and nuclear power.

During the 1960s, when oil's share of the national energy market rose from 20 percent to 60 percent, the main objective of energy policy was to build up an independent French oil industry. Using oil import regulations, the government helped Total and Elf boost their share of the national oil market to 50 percent. The companies used the resources they owned in the Middle East, the Sahara, and West Africa to meet increases in demand. With their profits and with the aid of government subsidies and tax credits, they were able to expand exploration both at home and abroad, hoping to find a substitute for the Saharan oil reserves that Algeria nationalized in 1970.

Elf and Total have been (and in some cases still are) active in Iran, Iraq, the Gulf emirates, the Gulf of Guinea, Indonesia, Canada, and the North Sea. They have also developed significant domestic capacity to refine oil and produce petrochemicals. Under government monitoring, the two companies have helped create a technologically advanced industry in various oil-related services. One example is the Institut Français du Pétrole, an advanced center for basic research and a training center for all kinds of petroleum engineers. Another example is Technip, an advanced refinery and petrochemical engineering company. Successful companies have also been developed in such other sophisticated technologies as geophysical exploration, offshore drilling, and tanker construction. All these service companies are internationally competitive.

France now has the third largest national oil industry in the Western world (after the United States and the United Kingdom). This achievement is all the more remarkable because France initially possessed neither the expertise of the Anglo-Saxon nations nor important natural resources to exploit.

In nuclear engineering France started to accumulate technological expertise by creating the Commissariat à l'Energie Atomique in 1945. Initially the CEA was devoted to basic research, in which French scientists such as Antoine-Henri Becquerel and Pierre and Marie Curie were well advanced long before World War II. The CEA also did research with military applications.

These orientations were reinforced when, in the 1960s, General de Gaulle decided to develop a French nuclear force. In the same decade the CEA acquired or exploited uranium mines in France and Africa, and built a uranium enrichment plant at Pierrelatte in southeastern France for military uses. The agency also tried to develop a reactor for generating electricity using natural uranium, the graphite–carbon dioxide process (that is, the *filière graphite-gaz*). But that technology encountered problems, and in the early 1970s the government decided to acquire the pressurized-water reactor (PWR) license from Westinghouse and to build a giant low-enrichment uranium plant. That plant, Eurodif, at Tricastin, is operated cooperatively with Italian, Spanish, and other foreign partners.

In 1973 France received a strong jolt from the first oil shock. At that time, it imported 75 percent of its energy needs: oil, representing 60 percent of French energy consumption, was almost entirely imported. Within a few weeks the government decided to launch a nuclear electricity-generation program so ambitious that it had no counterpart abroad. Electricité de France (EDF) was encouraged to begin construction of six PWR plants a year, each with a capacity of 900 megawatts. At the same time, the nuclear engineering industry was reorganized.

The contractor for the nuclear boiler is Framatome, a joint venture of CEA and a private, French-owned engineering group (Schneider). Framatome is also a licensee of Westinghouse. The agreement with Westinghouse provided that the licensee would recover the right to behave independently by 1980. Electricité de France gave the electric generator contracts to Alsthom, a subsidiary of the now-nationalized CGE. Simultaneously, it was decided that the CEA should expand the enrichment activities of Eurodif to build a reprocessing plant for used nuclear fuels at La Hague and to study the construction of a commercial fast breeder reactor (Superphénix), which would reduce as much as possible the problem of inadequate uranium supply.

After a decade of rapid development, the nuclear engineering industry now employs 150,000 workers. Because most Western countries have chosen to reduce their nuclear programs, the French industry now leads the world. It has mastered all nuclear technologies and controls each step of production, from mining to enrichment to electricity generation to reprocessing to fast breeding. Safety is overseen carefully by a special agency independent of both EDF and CEA.

Table 2-2. Structure of the Energy Sector

Item	Oil and gas exploration and production	Oil and gas transportation and refining	Nuclear materials (uranium enrichment and reprocessing; fast breeders)	Nuclear boilers and nuclear engineering
Relative position of French industry	Good	Good	Superior	Superior
Public research laboratory	IFP[a]	IFP[a]	CEA[b]	
Government department in charge of industrial policy	Ministry of Industry: Direction des Hydrocarbures Public enterprises in the petroleum industry	Ministry of Industry: Direction des Hydrocarbures Public enterprises in the petroleum industry	Ministry of Industry: Direction Générale de l'Energie et des Matières Premières CEA[b]	Ministry of Industry: Direction Générale de l'Energie et des Matières Premières EDF[c]
Main industrial firms	SNEA[d] CFP[e]	SNEA[d], CFP[e], Technip, Gazocéan, Gaz de France	COGEMA[f]	EDF[c]: Direction de l'Equipement Framatome
Main projects			La Hague Eurodif Superphénix	
International cooperation			Eurodif Superphénix	Westinghouse

Table 2-2 *(continued)*

Item	Electrical equipment	Coal	Solar energy	Geothermy
Relative position of French industry	Good	Poor	Good	Good
Public research laboratory	LCIE[g] EDF[c]: Direction Etudes et Recherche	Charbonnages de France: CHERCHAR[h]		BRGM[i]
Government department in charge of industrial policy	Ministry of Industry: DIMME[j]	Ministry of Industry: Direction de Gaz, de l'Electricité, et du Charbon	AFME[k]	AFME[k]
Main industrial firms	Alsthom-Atlantique Creusot-Loire Merlin-Gérin Jeumont-Schneider	Charbonnages de France		
Main projects			Thémis	

Source: Stoffaes, *Politique Industrielle*, p. 407.

a. Institut Français du Pétrole. b. Commissariat à l'Energie Atomique. c. Electricité de France. d. Société Nationale Elf-Aquitaine. e. Compagnie Française des Pétroles. f. Compagnie Générale des Matières Nucléaires. g. Laboratoire Central des Industries Electriques. h. Centre d'Etudes et de Recherches des Charbonnages de France. i. Bureau de Recherches Géologiques et Minières j. Direction des Industries Métallurgiques, Mécaniques, et Electriques. k. Agence Française pour la Maitrise de l'Energie.

Sales of equipment for nuclear power plants amount to some Fr 25 billion a year (in 1983 francs). In 1981 the government cut back on its program to build new plants. Instead of launching six 900 megawatt plants a year, it decided to build two or three 1,300 megawatt plants a year. As domestic orders level off, the French nuclear and electrical engineering industries are trying to reorient their production toward exports. Some contracts have already been captured abroad. Despite the decline in domestic orders, nuclear generation has already totally or partially replaced oil and coal in generating electricity at EDF. Nuclear-generated electricity now represents about 50 percent of all electricity consumed in France. By 1990 it is hoped that it will represent 75 percent of all electricity produced (most of the rest would be hydroelectricity), and 30 percent of total domestic consumption of energy. By then, the share of oil will have been reduced to 33 percent, about half the 1973 share. This means that electricity will have to be able to satisfy a variety of final uses, such as industrial and domestic heating. It also means that the use of electrical equipment will increase.

Nuclear electricity generation is not the only focus of the government in the energy sector. Programs have also been launched to develop energy conservation and new energy sources, such as solar photovoltaic cells, geothermy, and biomass. These programs are overseen by the Ministry of Industry and Research and its subsidiary, the Agence Française pour la Maitrise de l'Energie.

The magnitude of the French program of energy transition is by far the most ambitious in the world. It has already developed a fast-growing new industry employing highly trained workers and engineers. It will alleviate the burden of imported oil on the French economy. And it is to be hoped that sunrise energy industries will constitute a powerful locomotive for all of French industry and French exports.

Aerospace

French engineers contributed greatly to the birth and development of aircraft technologies at the beginning of the twentieth century, and the army rapidly understood the rising importance of these new technologies for warfare. Hence the tradition of French excellence in aeronautics and of government intervention in all parts of the aerospace industry. France now holds second place in the world in this industry. It is admittedly still far behind the United States, but it is ahead of many other industrial powers, including the United Kingdom, Germany, and Japan.

After several waves of merger and consolidation, the aerospace industry is now organized into three main companies, all under government control: Société Nationale Industrielle Aérospatiale, or SNIAS (civil aircraft, helicopters, missiles, space launchers, and satellites); Dassault-Bréguet (military aircraft); and the Société Nationale d'Etude et de Construction de Moteurs d'Aviation, or SNECMA (aircraft engines). There are also several smaller companies and many subcontractors such as Matra (missiles and satellites), Turboméca (helicopter engines), and Messier-Hispano. (For the current status and organization of the aerospace industry, see table 2-3.)

The main instruments of industrial policy in aeronautics have been public procurement, subsidized research, subsidized exports, and industrial diplomacy. Most important, companies have received long-term research and production contracts from the Ministry of Defense. The central objective of aerospace policy has been national independence in military aircraft, an objective that followed from General de Gaulle's decision to leave NATO. Unlike most of Western Europe, France chose not to rely on U.S. aircraft for its defense needs and has developed its own highly successful generation of military aircraft, including the Mystère 20, Mirage III, and Mirage IV.

To reduce unit cost through economies of scale, government policy included promoting exports, a feature of policy especially visible during the 1970s. Thanks to export subsidies and government diplomacy, the French aircraft industry was able to develop sales in the Middle East (for example, in Saudi Arabia and Iraq) as well as in Latin America, Asia, and Africa. Similarly, successful generations of missiles (such as Roland and Exocet) and of helicopters (Alouette) were developed for national needs and then exported.

France is a major seller in the world market for armaments. It exports Fr 30 billion in arms each year while importing Fr 1 billion. It controls 10 percent of the world trade in arms—the U.S. share is 38 percent and that of the Soviet Union 30 percent. Some 70 percent of all domestic and foreign sales of the French aerospace industry involves armaments; the corresponding figure for the electronics industry is 65 percent, for the nuclear industry 50 percent, and for shipbuilding 50 percent. Three companies—Thomson-CSF, SNIAS, and Dassault-Bréguet—accounted for over half of French arms sales at home and abroad in 1981 (see table 2-4).[3]

Defense constitutes by far the largest market for the aeronautics industry, but the industry has used the technological strengths it built up through military procurement to develop civilian applications. In return, companies receive financial support from the Ministry of Transportation and public procurement from the national airline (Air France).

The short-range civilian carrier Caravelle, developed in the 1950s, was not

3. Ibid.

Table 2-3. Structure of the Aerospace Sector

Item	Aircraft engines	Helicopters	Space launchers and satellites	Aircraft parts and equipment
Relative position of French industry	Good	Superior	Good	Superior
Public research laboratory			CNES[a]	
Government department in charge of industrial policy	Ministry of Defense: Délégation Générale pour l'Armement	Ministry of Defense: Délégation Générale pour l'Armement	Ministry of Industry: DIELI[b] CNES[a]	Ministry of Defense: Délégation Générale pour l'Armement Ministry of Transport: Direction Générale de l'Aviation Civile
Main industrial firms	SNECMA[c]	SNIAS[d] Turboméca	SNIAS[d] Matra Société Européenne de Propulsion	SFENA-Crouzet Hispano-Suiza Intertechnique SFIM Messier Thomson-CSF
Main projects	Atar CFM-56	Alouette, Puma	Ariane, telecommunications and television satellites	
International cooperation	General Electric		Arianespace West Germany	

Table 2-3 *(continued)*

Item	Military aircraft	Missiles and rockets	Civil aircraft	Leisure and business aircraft
Relative position of French industry	Superior	Superior	Good	Good
Public research laboratory	ONERA[e]	ONERA[e]	ONERA[e]	
Government department in charge of industrial policy	Ministry of Defense: Délégation Générale pour l'Armement	Ministry of Defense: Délégation Générale pour l'Armement	Ministry of Transport: Direction Générale de l'Aviation Civile	
Main industrial firms	Dassault-Bréguet	Matra, SNIAS[d]	Dassault-Bréguet, SNIAS[d]	
Main projects	Mirage, Jaguar ACE	Exocet, Roland	Concorde (abandoned); Airbus	
International cooperation	Jaguar (West Germany), ACE	West Germany	United Kingdom and West Germany, among others	

Source: Stoffaës, *Politique Industrielle*, p. 408.

a. Centre Nationale d'Etudes Spatiales. b. Direction des Industries Electroniques et de l'Informatique. c. Société Nationale d'Etude et de Construction de Moteurs d'Aviation. d. Société Nationale Industrielle Aérospatiale. e. Office National d'Etudes et de Recherches Aérodynamiques.

Table 2-4. *French Foreign and Domestic Arms Sales, by Company and Government Agency, 1981*

Company or agency	Total sales of arms (billions of francs)	Exports of weapons as a percentage of total exports
Thomson-CSF	14	65
SNIAS	11	55
Dassault-Bréguet	10	75
Ministry of Defense: Direction Technique des Constructions Navales (DTCN)	10	7
Commissariat à l'Energie Atomique (CEA)	6.5	0
Ministry of Defense: Groupement Industriel des Armements Terrestres (GIAT)	6	40
SNECMA	3.5	50
Matra	3	70
Société Nationale des Poudres et Explosifs (SNPE)	1.2	35
Manurhin	1.1	75
Total	66.3	...

Source: Stoffaës, *Politique Industrielle*, p. 406.

as successful commercially as it could have been. Then, in cooperation with British Aerospace, the first supersonic commercial carrier was developed. As everyone knows, Concorde was a costly technological success and a commercial failure. Following the Concorde experience, SNIAS and the French government chose to develop a new medium-range civilian carrier. The commercial niche was well chosen, and Airbus has already captured a large share of the world market (about 30 percent in its size class). Its success comes at the expense of the heretofore unchallenged U.S. companies. Airbus is now giving birth to a whole generation of follow-on projects (notably the A310 and the A320), with other European companies coming to join the association. Although Airbus is truly a European venture, French industry has coordinated the project.

The engine for Airbus was developed by SNECMA, which used the technological expertise it had accumulated in developing military engines. One engine, the CFM-56, is being built in cooperation with General Electric: 1,000 units were sold in 1985, representing 25 percent of purchases worldwide of large jet engines. Civilian helicopters as well as business and leisure planes have also been developed by French aircraft companies.

France first entered the space industry just two decades ago. After many years of research effort, technological and commercial success has arrived. The

Centre National d'Etudes Spatiales (CNES), one of General de Gaulle's *grands projets*, coordinated the national space policy. CNES built a launching base at Kourou in French Guyana and developed projects for military and civilian purposes in cooperation with SNIAS and Matra. These included ballistic missiles for the French nuclear force, space launchers, and satellites for telecommunications, broadcasting, and scientific observations.

The civilian space launcher and the satellites have been developed within the framework of Arianespace, a European venture. The launcher Ariane began commercial operations in 1983; it has already captured a large share of the highly promising market for launchings of telecommunications satellites.

By any standard, French aerospace policy has been an undisputed success. The companies are profitable, technologically competitive, and able to export a large share of their production.[4] As in the case of energy, the national security objective proved central to formulating and implementing industrial policy.

Electronics

During the past four decades—from the discovery of the transistor to the development of very-large-scale integrated circuits—electronics has experienced technological revolutions that have extended enormously the uses of electronic goods. Earlier applications included radios, televisions, radar and guidance systems, scientific calculators, and office computers. Now a new wave of applications of microelectronics is spreading through the economy—personal computers, new generations of consumer goods, robots for manufacturing, and the combination of information technology and telecommunications. This revolution in electronics promises to be profound, not only because of the new goods and services it offers to consumers but also because of the increases in productivity it will permit. Mastery of the full line of electronic technologies and growth of the electronics industries must be key priorities of any industrial policy.

Since 1981 the French government has accorded such priority to electronics. Current policy involves a holistic approach: it is aimed at the entire *filière électronique*. The concept of the *filière* stresses the technological interdependence among the various industries that constitute the sector.

The *filière électronique* includes some of the strongest and some of the weakest French industries. The strong include telecommunications, computer

4. Two-thirds of output is exported, the highest ratio in the world. In 1985, foreign orders reached Fr 70 billion. Of those, aircraft accounted for Fr 27 billion, jet engines for Fr 12 billion, and missiles for Fr 11 billion.

software, and the manufacture of professional electronic equipment. Average positions against foreign competition are held in computers and electronic components. Weaknesses appear in consumer goods, office equipment, robots, and scientific instruments (see table 2-5).

The key idea of the new industrial strategy was to develop the weak industries by taking advantage of the strong ones. Emphasis was thus placed on developing the industries responsible for integrated circuits, computers, consumer goods, and robots. Under the plan filière électronique, investment in plant, equipment, and research would amount to Fr 140 billion (in 1982 francs) between 1983 and 1987. These industries were to grow at a rate of 9 percent a year, and a trade surplus of Fr 20 billion was to appear by 1987.[5]

This program is financed jointly by the Ministry of Defense, the Ministry of the Post Office and of Telecommunications, and the Ministry of Industry. The policy was to be implemented by four recently nationalized electronics companies—Thomson, CIT-Alcatel, Matra, and Bull—that had been reorganized to rationalize the specializations among them.

The industry shows strong positions in two areas in which industrial policy has been active and dynamic for many years: heavy electronic equipment for professional uses (such as defense and broadcasting) and electronic telecommunications. In both cases the trade balance is positive and French companies enjoy technological leadership, a strength that has been developed through government procurement. The main companies developing and manufacturing professional electronic equipment are Thomson-CSF (a subsidiary of Thomson), Matra, and CIT-Alcatel (a subsidiary of the Compagnie Générale d'Electricité, or CGE).

Since the early 1950s the Ministry of Defense and the national broadcasting authority have tended to purchase domestic electronic equipment. Research and development has been encouraged by contracts from the Ministry of Defense in such fields as radar, aircraft equipment, and missiles. Production has been encouraged by long-term purchasing contracts. Once technological maturity was reached, exports were stimulated through special loans and industrial diplomacy. During the 1970s, exports to the Middle East were so successful that they challenged the positions of the U.S. companies that led the market.

In the telecommunications industry, France has depended for a long time on multinational giants such as ITT and Ericsson. But in the late 1960s the research center of the Ministry of the Post Office and of Telecommunications, the Centre National d'Etudes des Télécommunications (CNET), developed expertise in electronic switching technology. Property rights in the resulting

5. These contrast with a 3 percent rate of growth and a Fr 10 billion trade deficit in 1981.

technology were then given to the French company CIT-Alcatel. In the early 1970s, when the French telecommunications industry was relatively backward, the government decided to increase massively its investment in the design and manufacture of telecommunications equipment. After securing the approval of their foreign parents, the government merged Ericsson-France and ITT-France into Thomson-CSF. The total amount of investment in telecommunications equipment has been around Fr 30 billion a year (in 1983 francs) for the past ten years. In 1983, as part of its rationalization of the public sector, the government merged Thomson-Télécommunications into CGE-CIT-Alcatel. Thanks to these public purchases and to the research subsidies associated with public procurement, the telecommunications industry has been able to develop state-of-the-art technologies and to produce on a mass scale. Active R&D programs have been developed in fiber-optic networks, computers, and domestic terminals. Simultaneously, exports have been promoted, especially in the new markets of the third world.

In two other industries of the *filière électronique*, computers and electronic components, French competitive strength remains uncertain despite substantial support from the government.

The Plan Calcul, launched in 1966 as one of General de Gaulle's *grands projets*, was designed to make France independent in the design and manufacture of scientific calculators. One reason for the development of such a plan was the acquisition of Bull, the leading French computer company, by the American General Electric. In order to reestablish a French presence in the industry, the government created an enterprise (CII) that was owned partly by the state and partly by two private enterprises (Thomson and CGE). The government supported the company with research grants and public procurement, the Ministry of Industry overseeing the execution of the plan. In 1975 CII was merged with Bull, which by then had been purchased from General Electric by Honeywell. The resulting enterprise was named CII–Honeywell Bull (CII-HB). Nationalized in 1981, CII-HB is now the largest European computer company.

In spite of public subsidies and procurement, however, CII-HB still loses money and carries a heavy debt. In 1982 the government decided to increase financial support to CII-HB and to rationalize the structure of the entire industry. SEMS and Transac, smaller companies engaged in producing minicomputers and peripheral equipment, were merged with CII-HB to form the Bull group. The strategy of the new group has been reoriented toward the new generation of computers and office equipment.[6]

6. In addition to its position in computer hardware, France enjoys a leading position in software services. In this area, French companies are medium-sized and show technological sophistication and competitive ability.

Table 2-5. *Structure of the Electronics Sector*

Item	Electronic components and integrated circuits	Military electronics (radiocommunications, guidance systems, avionics)	Telecommunications (electronic switching systems)
Relative position of French industry	Average	Superior	Good
Public research laboratory	CNET-CNS Commissariat à l'Energie Atomique-LETI	Laboratories of the Délégation Générale pour l'Armement	CNET[a]
Government department in charge of industrial policy	Ministry of Industry: DIELI[b] Ministry of the Post Office and of Telecommunications: DGT[d] Ministry of Defense: DGA[c]	Ministry of Defense: DGA[c]	Ministry of the Post Office and of Telecommunications: DGT[d]
Main industrial firms	Thomson-CSF Matra	Thomson-CSF Matra ESD	Thomson-CSF CIT-Alcatel CGCT
International cooperation	Matra-Harris Eurotechnique-NSM Thomson-Motorola		

Table 2-5 (continued)

Item	Computers and electronic office equipment	Computer software	Industrial electronics	Consumer electronics
Relative position of French industry	Average	Superior	Poor	Average
Public research laboratory	INRIA[e]			
Government departments in charge of industrial policy	Ministry of the Post Office and of Telecommunications: DGT[d] Ministry of Industry: DIEL[b]	Ministry of the Post Office and of Telecommunications: DGT[d] Ministry of Industry: DIEL[b]	Ministry of Industry: DIEL[b] DIMME[f]	Ministry of Industry: DIEL[b]
Main industrial firms	Bull-CII, Matra, Intertechnique	Cap-Sogeti, CISI, SG2, STERIA, GSI	Matra CIT-Alcatel Renault	Thomson-Brandt
International cooperation	Bull-Honeywell Bull-NEC, Bull-Ridge, Matra-Norsk Data			Thomson-JVC (Videocassette recorders) Thomson-Telefunken

Source: Stoffaës, Politique Industrielle, p. 409.
a. Centre National d'Etudes des Télécommunications. b. Direction des Industries Electroniques et de l'Informatique. c. Délégation Générale pour l'Armement. d. Direction Générale des Télécommunications. e. Institut National de Recherche en Informatique et Automatique. f. Direction des Industries Métallurgiques, Mécaniques, et Electriques.

Table 2-6. *R&D Strategies in Selected OECD Countries, 1965, 1980, 1985*

Item	United States	United Kingdom	France	Japan	Other OECD
Expenditure on R&D *as a percentage of GNP*					
1965	3.0	2.4	2.1	1.6	1.3
1980	2.3	2.0	1.8	2.0	1.9
1985	2.6	1.9	2.3	2.5	2.2
Priority accorded to various R&D goals[a]					
National defense and specific major projects	1	1	1	3→4	3
Industrial development	3	3	3	2→1	2→1
Social welfare (health, environment)	2	4	4	4→3	4
Basic research	4	2	2	1→2	1→2

Source: Stoffaës, *Politique Industrielle*, p. 403.
a. Arrows represent, evolution in the ranking of goals between 1965 and 1980.

The plan for integrated circuits was initiated in 1976. Five French companies received public research subsidies from the Ministry of Industry and public procurement from the Ministry of Defense and the Ministry of the Post Office to produce large-scale integrated circuits. The companies were encouraged to sign technology-sharing agreements with such leading U.S. companies as Harris, National Semiconductor, and Motorola. In 1982 this plan was reoriented toward the stimulation of investment in manufacturing, and the amount of public support was increased substantially, reaching Fr 2 billion a year. The electronic components industry was then restructured around two companies, Thomson and Matra.

Recently, industrial policies have been developed for two weak parts of the *filière électronique*—areas that have previously remained outside the scope of government intervention. In consumer electronics, Thomson (which still holds advantageous positions in certain markets for color television sets) has been encouraged to extend its operations in European markets. Toward that end it has acquired several smaller companies in Germany.[7] Thomson has also been encouraged to sign an agreement with the Japanese group, Matsushita-JVC, to produce videotape recorders under the VHS standard.

In 1981 an ambitious plan was launched to restructure and modernize the French machine tool industry. Emphasis is being placed on robotics. Smaller companies will be encouraged to merge and to develop numerical-command

7. Its most recent acquisition of this sort was AEG-Telefunken.

machines and automats. As inducements, the government will offer grants to support R&D, procurement from nationalized companies, and funds to develop training programs. Once again, the Ministry of Industry will oversee execution of the program, known as the *plan productique*.

Still, as John Zysman has argued, industries engaged in the development of information technologies sell to private as well as public customers.[8] As a result they tend to be volatile and decentralized. It is not clear whether French-style industrial policies can succeed as well in such industries as they have in such centralized high-technology industries as energy and weapons.

Implications of the French Experience

Can the French experience be transplanted to other countries? In particular, is it relevant to the current debate in the United States on the desirability of an active industrial policy?

At first glance it might appear that American and French institutions differ so markedly that the French experience bears no implications for the United States. After all, the American incarnation of democracy, with its fragmentation of executive, legislative, and judicial power, its unstable cadre of high-level administrative officials, and its procedure-oriented legal system could not easily accommodate the arbitrary and long-term commitments that are necessary to success in industrial policy. Consider, for example, the situation in the American nuclear power industry. As a result of hundreds of legal suits, decided at very decentralized levels, the industry has been brought to a standstill. To a French observer it is remarkable that such paralysis could come to pass without explicit decisions at the collective level. No wonder the concept of an "energy czar" or a "telecommunications czar" enjoying stable, high-level power over a long time seems completely alien to the traditions of the American administrative and political establishments. Nevertheless, the military-industrial complex, built around the Pentagon, provides a clear example of an American institution that could have been drawn from the French experience.

In terms of both culture and economic organization, France has much more in common with Western Europe and even Japan than it does with the United States. As a result, the lessons of French experience appear to apply more to Western Europe than to the United States. Nevertheless, it is important not to exaggerate either the similarities of France and Europe or the dissimilarities of

8. See his *Political Strategies for Industrial Order: State, Market and Industry in France* (Berkeley: University of California Press, 1977).

France and the United States. Regarding Europe, one must recognize that French institutions and policies often have no counterparts in the other European countries. As for the United States, one must remember that the main inspiration for French industrial policy has been military rather than economic. Given the importance of defense and space exploration in the contributions of the United States to technological change, the two countries may be less different for purposes of industrial policy than they might seem.

Raymond Lévy

Industrial Policy and the Steel Industry

THE FRENCH GOVERNMENT has always taken an active interest in its steel industry. Now that the industry is experiencing a crisis so profound that it may fail to survive in its present form, government intervention is intense. The first part of this chapter describes the means of government intervention. The rest relates government policy to the behavior and performance of the industry since World War II.

The Means

The French love regulation. They judge their public officials by the quantity of laws they produce. Rare is the minister who advocates deregulation; rarer still the minister who achieves it. As a result, government intervention in the steel industry is so pervasive that a full description would rapidly daunt the most diligent of readers. Rather than catalog the methods of government intervention, then, I shall simply describe those means that I consider to be especially important in France.

Indicative planning is the first major influence of government on the steel industry. The planners began each planning cycle by establishing a set of growth scenarios for the economy as a whole. Implicit in each scenario were growth targets for each industry. The planners then convened a series of commissions, one for each industry, to determine how the relevant industry would achieve the growth expected of it. Each commission comprised representatives of government, trade associations, companies, and unions; representatives of the Ministry of Industry chaired most commissions. The reports of the commissions outlined the steps, in the form of rules and incentives, that the government would have to take to ensure that the goals of the plan would be realized.

The commission devoted to steel has always been among the most important, for steel is especially suited to planning of this sort. In the first place, investments in this industry are both expensive and durable. In a capital market as small as that of France, special sources of funding are required. Moreover, long-lived assets require long-term forecasting. In the second place, the trade association in steel, the Chambre Syndicale de la Sidérurgie Française, happened to be very powerful. Not only did it engage in economic forecasting, the development of technical norms, and collective bargaining, but through the Groupement de l'Industrie Sidérurgique, formed in 1946, it also floated bonds on the securities market and distributed the proceeds among its members for investment. Given its strength, this trade association has been a major participant in the planning process.

The European Coal and Steel Community provides another mechanism for regulating the industry. When France signed the Treaty of Paris in 1951, it surrendered responsibility for its steel industry to an international organization. The treaty granted to a high authority (currently the Commission of the European Communities) the means necessary to shape the structure and the conduct of the industry. Specifically, the commission can control prices, mergers, and imports from countries outside the EC; it can also offer subsidies of various kinds. Of particular importance, and in contrast to the Treaty of Rome, the Treaty of Paris allows the high authority broad regulatory discretion whenever industries subject to its jurisdiction are afflicted by "manifest crisis."

Public enterprise constitutes a third important means of shaping industrial policy. In 1981 the French government decided to nationalize its steel industry. Once in public hands, all of the nationalized companies were supposed to spearhead the revitalization of the economy. The new boards of directors, each of which reserved one-third of its positions for representatives of labor, were to conclude contracts with the Ministry of Industry that would define the specific role of each company.

Although these nationalizations and the contracts that followed undoubtedly affected the industry, the government had exerted substantial influence in steel well before the elections of 1981. In 1979 the government had already determined the behavior of the companies through its acquisition of the bulk of their debt. As long as the industry needed cash from the government, ownership was not required to exercise control. Any industry that suffers from heavy debt and structural crisis is bound to be susceptible to government pressure.

Many other government policies affected the industry. Among these were general price controls, labor legislation (especially the treatment of layoffs), tax legislation (especially the treatment of mergers), and regional policy. Given the multiplicity of policies and agencies, problems of coordination and compatibility were bound to arise, and they did.

The Industry from 1945 to 1974

The history of the French steel industry since World War II can be split into three phases: reconstruction (1945 to 1958), expansion (1958 to 1974), and crisis (1974 to the present). It is the last period that affords the richest basis for the study of industrial policy.

The period of reconstruction was the golden age of French economic planning. Government eliminated obstacles to growth, and it developed an independent national economy. During these years planners attached very high priority to the development of the steel industry. They coordinated the investments of the producers,[1] controlled their prices, and financed the investments through loans from the Fonds de Développement Economique et Social (FDES), which received most of its funds from the Marshall Plan.

Apart from price control, the government's policies proved enormously successful. By 1950 French GNP had regained its prewar level. Subsequent rapid growth created a sellers' market for steel, especially for flat products. By 1958 a third strip mill had been launched, which, twenty years later, would be the principal source of strength for the French steel industry.

From 1958 to 1974 the government attempted to accelerate growth: monetary and fiscal policies were used to stimulate investment, and wages were allowed to advance rapidly. By the end of the period a variety of macroeconomic imbalances had developed.

Ordinarily, a period of rapid growth would permit sellers to diminish reliance on government. Unfortunately the steel industry continued to require support. Price controls forced producers to rely on government loans to finance investment. The need for such investment was caused not only by rapid growth of demand but also by the appearance of gaps in productivity between French and foreign companies after formation of the Common Market (see table 3-1).

Macroeconomic disequilibrium came to a head at the beginning of the 1960s. When the government found itself obliged to curb expansion, the steel industry found itself in the first of its postwar crises. The solution to this crisis was sought through a process known as *planification contractuelle*. The idea was to have the industry and the government sign a contract specifying what each party would do to end the industry's problems. In July 1966 such a contract was developed for steel. The producers agreed to modernize their plants, rationalize their production, and merge their operations. Labor agreed to a program of compen-

1. Most importantly, two strip mills of efficient scale (1.3 million tons to 2 million tons of annual capacity) were installed at Denain and at Sollac. The latter was a joint venture of several steelmakers of Lorraine.

Table 3-1. *Investment per Ton of Steel Produced, by Country, 1965–75*
U.S. dollars

Country	Investment
Italy	22.8
Japan	21.5
Netherlands	20.6
France	20.1
United States	16.3
Belgium	15.3
United Kingdom	13.2
West Germany	11.1
Luxembourg	7.2

Source: OECD statistics.

sated layoffs. Government agreed to provide interest subsidies and other forms of preferential access to savings.

The contract of 1966 could have been more successful. In Lorraine, for example, mergers occurred more at the financial than at the industrial level: ownership was consolidated, but few plants were closed and little specialization developed among previously independent companies. Then by 1969, economic growth shifted back into high gear, and the need for structural adjustment was forgotten. Both the industry and the government began to stress expansion rather than rationalization of production. In fact the government launched a new steel complex at Fos-sur-mer, exclusively for production of exports, without forcing the closing of the inefficient mills in Lorraine that the new plant was supposed to replace.

At the end of the great expansion, then, the industry looked extremely

Table 3-2. *Debt as a Percentage of Sales in the Steel Industries of Selected Countries, 1970–76*

Country	1970	1971	1972	1973	1974	1975	1976
France	55	64	84	84	67	100	104
West Germany	20	24	28	23	19	20	22
Italy	88	113	143	126	86	101	87
Belgium	37	40	35	29	20	37	38
Luxembourg	9	15	24	28	20	37	38
United Kingdom	26	40	35	31	31	45	47
United States	27	26	24	18	13	18	21
Japan	57	74	68	51	44	61	65

Sources: for 1970–1975: French Ministry of Industry; for 1976: Chambre Syndicale de la Sidérurgie Française.

healthy. In 1974 it was producing 27 million tons of steel a year, and as a percentage of revenue its income was among the highest in the world. Nevertheless, weakness lay just below the surface. The industry had incurred too much debt (see table 3-2) and it employed too many people (see table 3-3). Moreover, most investments had been undertaken to expand capacity rather than to improve productivity. The plant at Fos-sur-mer came on stream just as France was forced by world circumstances to reduce its annual output from 27 million to 21.5 million tons.

The Crisis since 1974

When the price of petroleum shot upward in 1974, the steel industry found itself faced with two crises, one cyclical, the other structural. The cyclical crisis, of course, resulted from the slowdown that occurred in the world economy after the rise in the price of oil. The structural crisis resulted from a variety of factors. Not only were traditional customers developing substitutes for steel, but those customers were themselves declining in importance relative to industries like electronics that use very little steel. Moreover, the geographical distribution of consumption was changing in a manner that put European producers at a disadvantage (see table 3-4).

In the face of excess capacity, producers had two choices: they could maintain prices, in which case they would sell nothing at all, or they could lower prices as far as the marginal cost of production, in which case they would still lose a considerable amount of money. Given the difficulty of laying off workers and even of reducing subcontracting, the gap between average and marginal cost was very large indeed. Hence the brush with bankruptcy that many companies experienced.

Because of the historical importance as well as the employment importance of the industry, no government would permit such bankruptcies actually to occur. The French government was no exception.[2] Since 1974 it has proceeded in four stages to attempt to restore the health of the industry.

The first stage lasted from the beginning of the crisis to the de facto bankruptcy of several producers in 1979. During these years the government relied on contracyclical policy as embodied in its 1975 plan for the industry. Unfortunately, government and industry alike believed that the mere existence of a plan would make the underlying structural problems disappear. As the nominal

2. In France as in other countries, the steel industry tends to be located in single-industry regions. In Lorraine and in Dunkerque steel dominates local labor markets. Workers laid off cannot find many alternative sources of employment.

Table 3-3. Production and Employment in Steel: France in Relation to other European Countries, Selected Years, 1960–77 [a]

Year	West Germany (1)	West Germany (2)	Belgium (1)	Belgium (2)	Luxembourg (1)	Luxembourg (2)	Netherlands (1)	Netherlands (2)	Italy (1)	Italy (2)
1960	50.6	64.5	240.6	253.4	423.1	736.5	890.3	1,157.2	204.2	261.3
1965	53.2	63.8	213.9	261.3	427.5	685.4	624.7	839.1	154.5	223.9
1970	52.7	63.8	188.5	244.1	435.2	643.5	472.6	652.0	137.5	190.4
1974	50.8	70.0	166.6	247.3	419.2	681.0	463.1	637.6	113.5	164.8
1975	53.3	73.1	185.8	262.1	465.6	739.5	446.4	612.3	98.6	161.9
1976	54.8	73.2	191.2	268.7	508.5	721.1	447.5	613.2	99.0	158.9
1977	56.6	71.1	196.2	287.7	510.3	835.3	448.9	612.8	94.7	147.8

Source: Chambre Syndicale de la Sidérurgie Française.

a. For each country, column (1) reports production of steel in France as a percentage of production of steel in that country. Column (2) reports employment in steel in France as a percentage of employment in steel in that country.

Table 3-4. *World Consumption of Steel, by Geographic Area, 1950, 1970, 1980*
Percent

Area	1950	1970	1980
United States	45	21	16
EEC	20	21	15
Japan	2	12	10
Eastern Bloc	19	26	29
Others	14	20	30

Source: International Iron and Steel Institute.

institutions of economic planning were experiencing a period of relative dormancy, most of the initiative lay with the trade association and the companies. They believed that structural adjustment was unnecessary. Not until March 1978 did the industry (at the initiative of its branch in Lorraine) define the conditions for restored health: competition must be attenuated, prices must be allowed to rise, and *all* plants must be allowed to improve their productivity sufficiently to survive. In other words, the industry believed that it could avoid the pain of major structural change.

The second phase began in 1978. The year before, capacity utilization had dropped to 60 percent, while the ratio of debt to sales had risen to 115 percent. The government recognized the immediacy of the need for financial and structural reform. It assumed responsibility for roughly one-half of the medium-term and long-term debt of the industry and converted some of this debt into equity. Thus government replaced the old financial holding companies (Denain–Nord Est, Chiers-Chatillon, Wendel-Sidelor) as the principal shareholder.

Encouraged by the government, the companies and the unions signed an agreement whereby workers would retire at fifty-five years of age (in some of the least efficient plants the age was fifty). The government agreed to finance the retirements and to induce people below the new retirement age to migrate to other jobs. It also promoted investments to create employment in impacted regions through the Fonds Spécial d'Adaptation Industrielle (FSAI). As a result employment in steel fell from 160,000 people in 1975 to 97,000 in 1981. In Lorraine alone employment declined from 79,000 to 39,000 people.[3] The government spent Fr 30 billion on projects of this sort.

The policies of this period concentrated heavy steelmaking in two compa-

3. The effects of this decline were mitigated by the rise of employment in other sectors. Overall, several thousand jobs were created. For example, automotive employment in Lorraine increased from 10,000 to 15,000 people during these six years.

nies: Usinor and Sacilor. Although the government impressed the importance of modernization upon those whom it named to head the two enterprises, it allowed complete autonomy of management.

The third stage of policy began with the development of a Europewide approach to the problems of the industry. After the second oil shock in 1979 the Commission of the European Communities invoked Article 58 of the Treaty of Paris and declared a manifest crisis in steel. It then used its powers to regulate the industry.

European intervention was not based on distrust of the market mechanism but rather on the belief that the industry had excess capacity and lacked efficiency. The commission reduced aggregate capacity and modernized such capacity as remained through mergers, joint ventures, product innovation, and specialization. Once these goals were achieved, the industry could be returned to market-based modes of regulation.

To reduce capital capacity, the commission established quotas on production that were to last through December 31, 1985. To ensure the availability of funds for modernization, it also established lower bounds on selling prices. The commission was prepared to allow government subsidies as long as they were of limited duration and were designed to promote its general strategy. Finally, to ensure that investments would be designed to improve, not to expand, capacity, the commission required companies to secure prior approval for all investments.

Enforcement of this European plan fell both on the European Communities and on the companies themselves. The commission levied heavy fines on those who failed to comply with its regulation of prices and production. For their part the companies banded together voluntarily to form a trade association at the European level (EUROFER). The association attempted to establish order in the European market and to monitor execution of the community's policy.

It is difficult to determine the success of the European program. On the one hand, the steel industry of Europe has never experienced as much hardship as it did in 1982 and 1983. On the other hand, productive capacity is declining, the goal of 30 million tons a year will be attained, prices are rising, and the most competitive companies are earning profits. Most important, the member states continue to say that they will comply with the commission's wish to end all subsidies by 1986.[4]

4. During the rest of the period of control, the commission must ensure that no producer and no country can manipulate the regulations to its own advantage. Equity is required to ensure successful completion of the plan. In practice, equity has required the commission to limit imports from countries outside the EC. Nevertheless it is important to recognize that these restrictions, many of which take the form of bilateral agreements, are much less disruptive of market forces than are those practiced by the United States.

The European plan for steel has impinged especially heavily on producers in France. For reasons identified above, the French companies are unusually dependent on government funds. As a result, planning at the European level has stimulated further planning by the French government. The relevant strategies are embodied in two plans for steel—one from 1982, the other from 1984.

The 1982 plan was the first to be devised by the government that assumed power in 1981. It granted to the new heads of Usinor and Sacilor, named in February 1982, a broad mandate to increase profit, stabilize employment, modernize and rationalize production, integrate downstream, and engage in R&D. The strategies designed to meet these goals were formalized in the steel plan approved by the government in September 1982. The plan called for eliminating 12,000 jobs (people displaced would be subsidized by the government), new investments of Fr 17.5 billion between 1982 and 1985, and closing certain plants (including the historically famous one at Denain). The price tag for the measures was to be Fr 10 billion a year (in 1982 francs). This may be compared with the total amount spent to aid the steel industry between 1966 and 1981: Fr 60 billion in 1982 francs.

The 1982 plan had two weaknesses, however. First, it continued to express goals in terms of volumes of output that were clearly incompatible with market demand. (For example, it set a goal of 24 million tons for 1986.) Everyone knew the goals were unrealistic, but for political and psychological reasons the government simply chose not to propose more realistic alternatives. Second, the plan failed to come to grips with the problems of Lorraine. That branch of the industry focused on long products (rails, beams, and the like), and the prospects for achieving competitive positions in those markets were bleak. On the other hand Lorraine was a depressed region, so the government did not wish to close too many plants there. By 1983, however, the financial losses of the two large public enterprises had climbed to Fr 10 billion a year (from Fr 4 billion in 1981), and budgetary constraints forced the government to revise the 1982 plan. On March 29, 1984, the government adopted its new plan. The Commission of the European Communities approved that part of the plan related to flat products, but it failed to approve the part related to long products. As in the case of its predecessors, the 1984 plan has industrial, social, and financial components.

Industrially, the plan recognized the importance of an ability to compete. If they were poorly located (as with the specialty steels produced at Fos-sur-mer), or specialized in outmoded products (the long products of Lorraine), or technologically backward, even modern plants were to be closed. Investments would be concentrated at the sites most likely to be able to compete in the future. Lorraine would reduce the capital intensity of its production once it modernized production of flat products.

Socially, the plan recognized the need to eliminate a large number of jobs. Specifically, it proposed reducing employment in steel by roughly 25,000 people, so that employment in the industry would decline from 97,000 in 1981 to 60,000 in 1987. Although early retirement would continue to be offered, the efficacy of such a policy was nearly exhausted from previous use. Thus for 10,000 workers the government would finance up to two years of retraining, during which time workers would receive incomes close to those they had earned before. By subsidizing investments in Lorraine, the government hoped that 4,000 new jobs could be created there.

Financially, the government would try to reduce further the debt of the steel companies. It would assume much of that debt itself, and it would grant the companies large amounts of new equity.[5]

It is too soon to tell whether this plan will succeed: all depends on the vigor with which it is implemented and the evolution of the situation in Europe as a whole. But I believe the plan is realistic insofar as it applies to flat and specialty products. I am less sanguine about the future of Lorraine's long products, now controlled by Sacilor. Reform is long overdue in this branch, and it may prove difficult to implement overnight.

The problems of Lorraine must be viewed in a European perspective. Other branches of the European industry are also in deep trouble. Lorraine will not be alone in requiring adjustment after the deadline in 1986. As long as the recession remains, the fragility of the industry will remain—even if the policy of the ECSC proves successful. It is unlikely that we are witnessing the last of government intervention in European steel.

Conclusion

What does the experience of the French steel industry teach regarding the efficacy of industrial policy? When the government moved to reconstruct the industry after World War II, did its reliance on quantitative goals impart some perverse incentives to the industry? Does the financial weakness of the producers in 1974 suggest that government's strategies were wrong, or simply that they had been pursued inadequately? Does the post-1974 crisis reflect the poverty of policy or a deterioration of the industry's environment?

These are difficult questions, and I shall not answer them here. Rather, I shall share my own reflections on the meaning of this history.

5. These aids will cease once the European Community's ban on state aid comes into force. It is possible, however, that French long products will require a postponement of the ban.

—Whenever an industry considered important by the public is threatened with extinction, government intervention is inevitable. Such was the case just after World War II, and such is the case today. In these situations it is essential to define correctly the goals of public policy. Instead of developing an ability to produce, France should have been developing an ability to compete. Failure to recognize the importance of cost ruined the shareholders and damaged labor. Had the number of jobs grown less rapidly during the years when output was growing so fast, France would not now be in the position of having to cope with massive layoffs in a period of high unemployment.

—Controls breed controls. The regulation of steel prices jeopardized the financial health of steel companies. In fact, even if the price of steel had been deregulated, controls on the prices of other goods would have deterred investment by their producers and would thus have curbed their demand for steel. The regulation of layoffs also weakened the ability to compete. A company can ignore the cost of mistaken investment, for it amounts to a one-shot event. If it lacks the power to fire employees, however, it must live for a long time with mistaken excesses in hiring.

—The government must learn that companies depend on fat years to balance the lean. Unless they are allowed to earn healthy profits at some points of the business cycle, they are doomed to require government support. If the government wishes to avoid excessive bailouts, it must recognize the effects on an industry of the whole array of its policy actions.

—The path of industrial policy is fraught with hazards. But such is the case for all policy paths. Danger cannot justify inaction. In addition to a clear goal and internal consistency, a successful industrial policy requires means sufficient to the task. Such means are difficult to bestow in the context of industrial democracies that reflect all too fully the complexity of their economies. Nevertheless, some believe that public enterprises constitute such means. As in the case of the steel plan of March 29, 1984, only time will tell.

François Perrin-Pelletier

Industrial Policy and the Automobile Industry

A FRENCH FRIEND of mine is the president of a large American corporation. Before he assumed his current position, he worked in the company's French subsidiary. In his experience the difference between French and American business is simple: "During my two years in the United States, I have yet to set foot inside government. In France, I was obliged to spend all of my time there." Some would argue that the incidence of government on the French economy can be attributed to the quality of the French civil service. Far be it for me, an alumnus of a school that trains top civil servants, to dispute such a claim. Nevertheless, a former president of Peugeot was probably closer to the mark when he said, "as long as companies sell to, and ask favors of, government, so long will government intervene in the economy." Given the extent to which government regulates and finances the French economy, it is difficult for French business not to ask for favors. Hence the government's control of business behavior.

In this chapter I shall discuss the role of government, actual and ideal, in the automobile industry. If familiarity with such policy has not bred contempt, it has at least immunized me against believing some of the more extravagant claims made on behalf of industrial policy.

Government and Business in the Postwar Automobile Industry

Until 1955 or so, the major goal of economic policy was reconstruction of the French economy. The Monnet plan permitted rapid achievement of this goal.[1] Thereafter the target became economic growth. Once again, government pol-

1. One should not necessarily infer cause from effect. The automobile industry was never a high priority of the planners. Even so, it too developed rapidly.

icy appeared to succeed. In comparison with other European countries, France achieved high rates of economic growth (accompanied, it is true, by high rates of inflation). During these years of rapid growth, government substantially increased its intervention in the affairs of business. With the economy booming all around them and profits unusually high, business leaders failed strenuously to contest the rise of regulation.

Only during the oil shock of the mid-1970s did the constraining nature of regulation become apparent. With the end of rapid growth the economy had to be reorganized, but the regulations then in place had reduced its flexibility. The safety net of the welfare state had become a hammock. Given the militance of trade unions on behalf of the status quo, government feared that deregulation would entail the disintegration of social consensus. As a result it left the welfare state intact.

The second oil shock merely reinforced the effects of the first. More structural adjustment was required; even less was desired. The election of 1981 should be interpreted not as a vote for socialism but as a vote for the status quo. Rather than face deregulation and resource reallocation, the French people chose the path of least resistance—preservation of de facto and de jure entitlements.

The automobile industry followed these national trends fairly closely. Until 1973 the industry seemed to perform well and was able to absorb the doses of regulation that the government applied to it. After 1973, however, problems surfaced. Japanese competition was intense—so intense that many industrial countries placed quotas on imports from Japan. To meet the Japanese challenge, French companies had to invest, but their ability to do so was limited by their financial positions. Interest payments accounted for 4 percent of revenue, and equity was difficult to raise because of persistent red ink. One of the reasons was overemployment: productivity did not justify the share of revenue spent on labor.

What accounts for the recent plight of this industry? The product itself has not lost its market: unlike steel, the automobile has not faced the development of close substitutes. Nor has there been a shift of comparative advantage in manufacturing toward newly industrializing countries. The automotive industry requires rapid technological innovation and complex organization: the industry is thus difficult to adapt to less developed economies. It is unrealistic to expect that automobiles can be designed in developed countries and produced in their less developed counterparts. Design and manufacture interact pervasively, as evidenced by the robotization of assembly lines.

To understand the predicament of the French automobile industry, therefore, one must examine in more detail the relationship between government and business in France.

The government intervenes in the automobile industry because the industry employs a large number of people. In 1979 in the European Economic Community as a whole, the automobile industry, broadly defined, employed 5 percent of the labor force (nearly 6 million people). Some 2.9 million more were engaged in selling, servicing, and fueling automobiles.[2] According to the Committee of Common Market Automobile Constructors, employment in the industry itself declined by 300,000 people between 1979 and 1982.[3] Using the European Community's estimate of two jobs in automotive services for each job in the industry itself, automotive employment must have declined by approximately 1 million people during this period, and overall unemployment increased by 4 million.[4] Clearly, any threat to the automobile industry is a threat to employment—not simply in the industry itself but also in those industries that depend on it.

The policies of the French government are directed toward four aspects of the automotive industry: sales, employment, investment, and finance.[5]

—Sales. During most of the postwar period, the French government has regulated the price of automobiles, which has decreased the revenue of producers. These controls also antagonized suppliers; after all, suppliers could not raise their prices, even when their costs rose, unless the automobile producers were allowed to raise their prices. These problems are obvious. More important is the impact of regulation on entrepreneurship. When prices are set by government, managers develop a passive outlook toward their businesses.[6]

2. These figures are estimates of the Commission of the European Communities.

3. Of the total decline, one-third was attributable to increased efficiency and two-thirds was attributable to inadequate demand.

4. Total employment declined by 2 million while the labor force increased by 2 million.

5. Another important area is regulation of the product itself—features such as safety, noise, and pollution. In this area, however, many policies are set at the European rather than national level. Such procedures ensure realization of the economies of scale. For instance, the European Economic Community is now debating the subject of noxious emissions. It has already established standards to take effect on October 1, 1986. At issue are the standards to take effect at the end of the decade. Facing political pressures and citing divergent scientific evidence, the several member states differ sharply on the subject. Some, such as France, oppose catalytic converters. They argue that in time, alternatives such as lean-burn engines will be developed. They recognize, however, that such alternatives do not currently exist. Hence they argue that standards should be tightened slowly. Other countries, such as Germany, advocate rapid adoption of stringency. Given the environmental damage they observe, they are prepared to accept converters. Although it will be difficult to reconcile these positions, such reconciliation is imperative. Inconsistent standards could result in major barriers to the free circulation of goods and people.

6. Belgium regulates the price of automobiles especially strictly. As a result, the price of automobiles is lower there than elsewhere in the EC. The Commission of the EC mistakenly

—Employment. In industrial relations the government impinges on the industry in two ways. First, it regulates wages indirectly by controlling the number of hours worked. For example, the government that came to power in 1981 reduced the length of the working week to thirty-nine hours; it also increased paid vacation time to five weeks. It did both without obliging reductions in salary. Productivity did not increase commensurately because these measures cost Peugeot some Fr 1 billion a year.

Government also attempts to control the number of people employed. Since 1975 companies have not been able to dismiss workers without approval from the Ministry of Labor. Every time Peugeot requests such authority, the ministry asks the company to reduce the number to be laid off, to delay the layoffs, and to compensate more generously those about to depart.

If only government would retire from the field of industrial relations, labor and management could resolve their differences. Nowhere is this more apparent than in the United Kingdom—a country known for animosity in labor-management relations. When Peugeot acquired Chrysler's assets in Europe, I was named president of the new subsidiary. As a result I assumed responsibility for Talbot UK, the former Chrysler UK. The first item on our agenda was to show the unions we meant business. Given the weakness of our financial position and the losses we had suffered in market share, we had to constrain wages to rise less rapidly than productivity, and we had to lay off a large number of workers. In June 1979 during the annual negotiation of wages, we offered a 5.5 percent increase. At the time the rate of inflation was 13 percent. The result was a three-month strike. Unlike Chrysler, we did not give in. We did not have the money to give in. Ultimately, the unions understood that they had to take seriously what we said. From the beginning of 1979 through 1981 our employment fell from 24,000 to 9,000 people, a decline of 60 percent.[7] Even so, no strikes were called. By 1983 Talbot UK was back in the black.[8]

Whereas the Labour government had attached conditions to the loans it had given to Chrysler—conditions such as the obligation to discuss with labor a five-year plan—the Conservative government gave us the money promised by Labour but required nothing in return.

---

attributes Belgian prices to the forces of competition. It would like the price of cars throughout the community to converge on the Belgian level. Such a measure would cost the industry $2 billion to $3 billion a year—at a time when the industry as a whole is running a deficit. It would also jeopardize the system of selective distribution.

7. Part of the decline is attributable to the sale of the Dodge truck division to Renault's truck subsidiary. But Talbot UK closed the Linwood plant, offering indemnities to those dismissed.

8. A large contract with Iran permitted increased utilization of capacity. This as well as improved labor relations played a role in the turnaround.

Naturally, those who want less intervention by government must be prepared to engage in more collective bargaining. We at Peugeot would welcome such extension of negotiations.

—Investment. The government has often prevented French companies from investing abroad in the belief that direct foreign investment would entail the export of jobs. But this belief is unfounded. Peugeot, for example, owns a plant in Nigeria. Thanks to this plant, Peugeot enjoys a 33 percent share of the market there. Because the engines and bodies of our Nigerian cars are imported from France, the Nigerian plant serves to increase employment in France.

The French government should follow the lead of the Japanese Ministry of International Trade and Industry (MITI). It should encourage not discourage direct foreign investment.

—Finance. The government controls the purchase of foreign currencies. As a result it limits the degree to which companies can obtain financing abroad. More important, however, French companies have come to rely excessively on debt, much of which is owed either to government or to banking enterprises owned by the government. In fact the government is all too willing to lend money. The halls of the ministries are cluttered with investment projects that propose to increase employment. Unfortunately, such projects are shortsighted. Unless a project can meet the market test, unless it satisfies the criterion of profitability, it will foster neither healthy expansion nor the creation of lasting jobs.[9] The truth of the matter is that equity finance must be used in periods of rapid growth and periods of acute crisis.

In the United States the high rates of interest of the early 1980s prompted management to undertake only those projects that promised a high rate of return. Even so, investment took off—a favorable omen for America's ability to compete in the future.

To this point I have discussed regulations that impinge on virtually all French companies. In principle, government does not intervene in the management of the companies it owns. Unfortunately even the best of ministers—even those who want in good faith to promote independent behavior in the enterprises they oversee—can lose sight of this principle. In my days as a civil servant at the Ministry of Transportation, any time the French national railways wanted to eliminate service on a particular line, it had to secure the approval of the

---

9. I do not wish to suggest that business itself bears no responsibility for excessive reliance on debt. Many companies wished to avoid going public so that they could retain their cloak of secrecy. They also deluded themselves into accepting the virtues of leverage. Now that the return on equity lies below the cost of borrowing, the leverage effect is working against indebted companies.

ministry. One day, the minister asked me to find out which clod had allowed the termination of service on a certain line. When I reminded him that he himself had authorized the action, he said, "Reverse the decision immediately. My wife is running for political office in that region. We cannot allow something like this to happen just now."

In general, the government has obliged the companies it owns to overproduce. Its aim has been to expand employment. To the extent that it has succeeded, the employees and customers of public enterprises have gained, but society as a whole has lost. In fact, however, government has not always been successful in its quest to control its companies. In some cases (such as Renault) competition forces even public companies to pay attention to cost. In many cases even those public officials who wish to act in the public interest can be manipulated by the enterprises they seek to regulate. This creates ambiguity in the relationship between government and business.

The Proper Role of Government

What, then, is the proper role of government within the industrial arena? I believe it should be modest. As a general rule, government should facilitate but not initiate industrial strategies. Long-term intervention should be limited to sectors in which government buys most of the output or those in which technology is changing very rapidly. Elsewhere, intervention should be short term and exceptional.

The most important thing for government to do is to end a state of affairs in which it enjoys power without responsibility while industry is left with responsibility devoid of power. It is time to recognize that companies, not governments, exert the greater influence on the course of industrial development. Without entrepreneurs there can be no industrial progress. Industrial structures can be modified, organizations can be streamlined, the tools of production can be improved; but unless top management enjoys both power and responsibility—unless it is willing to take risks—such changes will be in vain. Recall, for instance, the situation I described at Talbot UK. The desperate conditions in 1979 were caused less by the policies of a Labour government than by the fatalism of local management. If management had taken a strong stand, the health of the operation would never have become so tenuous. Consider also the current efforts of Peugeot to develop a sense of initiative and responsibility on the part of each of its employees. Peugeot's private industrial policy recognizes that strategies must be implemented at every level of the company.

Having made my case for private enterprise, let me emphasize that government does have responsibilities in the construction of a healthy economy. In France, government attracts some very able people. Young civil servants do attempt to modernize the economy; and executives of public enterprises do try to implement the principles of sound management. These sources of energy and talent should be used to the utmost.

If the government is to intervene constructively, it must bear in mind the following considerations:

—Consistency. French industrial policy has been especially effective in tele- communications and military equipment. In both cases a single ministry buys output, offers subsidies, and oversees performance. Government can thus behave coherently in its dealings with the relevant industry. What makes life difficult for an entrepreneur is the confusion of signals he receives from the several agencies of government with which he deals. The uncertainty that ensues serves to chill his enthusiasm for investment.

—Continuity. The dream of every entrepreneur is to have the government set the rules once and for all. Continuity of policy breeds business confidence, and confidence breeds innovation. In the automobile industry Peugeot and Renault are cooperating to develop an automobile that gets seventy-five miles to the gallon. The project is very costly, and so the government finances 50 percent of its budget. The success of the project will depend on the govern- ment's perseverance. Unfortunately, the budget is determined one year at a time. Under these circumstances, continuity of policy is difficult to achieve and impossible to assume.

—Time. In matters of industrial policy, it is impossible to overestimate the significance of time. Governments must recognize that the success of business enterprises, no less than that of nation-states, will depend on their abilities to react quickly and flexibly to environmental change. Companies cannot afford interminable discussions with government and labor. Only where technology is changing rapidly should indicative planning be allowed freedom of play. Else- where its forecasts are revised too frequently to be useful.

For other purposes, however, governments often place too much of a pre- mium on speed. They do not recognize that corporate strategies require time to bear fruit. For example, in 1977 Peugeot decided to standardize the compo- nents used in its automotive subsidiaries. Not until 1983, however, could it be said that a Peugeot, a Citroën, and a Talbot all used the same engine and the same transmission.

—The world outside. Governments act as if national sovereignty still existed. In the world of business, however, markets are multinational, and companies must frequently respond to events originating outside national frontiers. Yet governments impose regulations that contradict the realities of the market-place. They must recognize that they cannot expect their companies to compete effectively in world markets if they prevent them from responding to the forces prevailing in those markets.

Conclusion

In the United States, industrial policy is a fashionable topic. This is as it should be: every thoughtful person should ponder the extent to which governments are required to ensure that national economic and social goals are pursued. On the basis of the French experience, however, I believe the role of private enterprise is underplayed. Managers themselves have been taken in by the rhetoric of civil servants and all too often forget the virtues of free enterprise. I hope the current taste of Socialist rule has reminded the French business community of the dangers of overreliance on government.

In 1958 France reformed its economic institutions in major ways. The changes proved to be as successful as they were bold. In my opinion the French business community is prepared to lead another such round of reform. All it needs is the confidence of the country and the freedom to act.

Michel Freyche

Export Promotion as Industrial Policy

ALL GOVERNMENTS seek to influence the niches their countries occupy in the international division of labor. Although they differ in their methods of intervention—often on the basis of prevailing economic ideology—all concoct some mixture of legislation, public procurement, public enterprise, and public subsidy to influence the structure of their international trade.

France is no exception. It has a long tradition of economic intervention by governments of all political complexions. After World War II, for instance, intervention in international trade and development was spurred by the necessity for reconstruction and the trend toward the liberalization of world trade. In the absence of government action, France would not have been able to open its economy without provoking massive disequilibrium in the structure of its trade.

France's promotion of exports must be appraised with some subtlety. Its system of export promotion has certainly stimulated the expansion of trade in general and the development of certain industries in particular. But the system is not omnipotent: it deserves neither the credit nor the blame for making French companies as competitive as they have been in world markets. It would be incorrect to argue, as it sometimes is in the United States, that French companies are subsidized so heavily that they compete unfairly with foreign rivals.

The Export-Promotion System

The current system of export promotion, created at the end of World War II, consists of three components. The first is the network of commercial missions abroad that comprises some 250 career civil servants (graduates of the Ecole Nationale d'Administration) and another 2,000 people recruited from schools of business and engineering for temporary assignments. Although nominally under the authority of the relevant ambassador, this commercial staff reports not to the Ministry of Foreign Affairs but to the Ministry of Economic and Financial Affairs.

A second component of the system is the Compagnie Française d'Assurances du Commerce Extérieur (COFACE). Founded in 1946, COFACE, which is not owned entirely by the state, insures French exporters against a variety of risks (its activities parallel those of similar organizations in other countries). On its guarantees against commercial risk, political risk, nonconvertibility of foreign currencies, and foreign exchange risk, COFACE ran a modest surplus until the first oil shock. In these areas, then, COFACE cannot be accused of subsidization.

COFACE also insures against economic risk and prospecting unsuccessfully in foreign markets. In neither case do insurance premiums cover indemnities paid. Insurance against economic risk permits French exporters to offer firm bids on potential sales abroad. This is the type of insurance that most aggravates foreign countries. Unfortunately, critics often fail to note that indemnities cover only that fraction of cost increases that exceeds changes in cost abroad. As of September 1984, for example, only that part of cost increase that exceeded 8.5 percent a year was covered by insurance. It is difficult, therefore, to argue that the system does anything other than equalize the conditions of international competition.

Insurance against economic risk has served French exporters, especially those who produce capital equipment, in two types of situations: when unforeseen devaluations of the franc entailed sharp increases in the prices paid for imported materials and when wages exploded unexpectedly (for example, after the events of May 1968).

The third component of the French system is the Banque Française du Commerce Extérieur (BFCE). Founded in 1947, BFCE is the only subsidiary of the Bank of France. Like COFACE, it keeps the government at arm's length. Whenever the BFCE acts on behalf of government, it does so in the context of a formal contract. It is expected to earn a profit and to distribute dividends to its shareholders.

The BFCE offers long-term credit at fixed rates of interest to French exporters and to foreign purchasers of French goods. The rationale for such an institution is simply that the French banking system is not sufficiently developed to mobilize enough long-term credit at fixed rates of interest. The role of the BFCE has, in fact, gradually adapted to the evolution of the regular banking system.

Admittedly, the standard loans of the BFCE (the *crédits commerciaux classiques*) did tend to carry rates of interest slightly below those prevailing in the market, and under the pressure of the exporters, the BFCE's rates sometimes exhibited upward stickiness when market rates began to rise. In a few cases agreements between the French government and governments of importing countries also established fixed rates for periods as long as two to three years. These practices were eroded, however, by the formation of the European Economic Community; they were suppressed entirely by the OECD consensus of 1976.

The importance of these interest subsidies should not be overestimated. From the standpoint of most foreign buyers, low interest rates were not the chief rationale for purchasing French goods. Instead the chief advantage of French exporters lay in the perception of the franc as a weak currency. Many buyers believed that devaluations would lighten the burden of their debt.

In addition to its *crédits classiques*, the BFCE assembles packages of funds known as *crédits mixtes*. These are funds offered by the bank to the governments of poor nations buying French goods. The funds comprise a mixture of traditional export loans, development loans, and outright transfers.

The *crédits mixtes* generate a good deal of controversy abroad. Especially in the United States, they are discussed as if they alone bear responsibility for all disorder in international trade. But their role has also been exaggerated. In 1983, for example, France exported Fr 723 billion worth of merchandise. Of this total, only Fr 55 billion (8 percent) received some kind of export assistance. Only 10 percent of this 8 percent (0.8 percent of all French exports) involved recourse to *crédits mixtes*.

Another indication that the importance of the *crédits mixtes* has been overemphasized is that in 1983, under the terms of the 1976 consensus, the OECD identified 123 instances of questionable export finance. Of these, 7 were sufficiently important to trigger the procedure known as undermatching, and only 3 involved France (a rapid transit system in Colombia and telecommunications systems in Cyprus and Indonesia). Although the *crédits mixtes* are less important than foreigners believe, the French system taken as a whole has demonstrated its ability to exert desirable influences on both the structure of French industry and the balance of French trade.

One dimension of success has been increased purchases of French capital goods by third world governments. Between 1973 and 1983 the surplus in French trade in equipment other than automobiles rose from Fr 1.5 billion to Fr 47 billion. As a result of these contracts, France has also been able to export business and engineering services. Between 1973 and 1983 the surplus related to such services rose from Fr 3 billion to Fr 27 billion.

Expansion of their exports served to strengthen producers of capital equipment. This strength developed at a propitious moment for French industry. As the other sectors of industry (consumer goods and intermediate products) began to feel the force of competition from the newly industrializing countries, manufacturers of industrial equipment were able to pick up the slack. During the 1970s they imparted a new vigor to French industrial structure. Although much remains to be done, France now produces and exports a range of capital goods that exceeds dramatically the range that existed before the first oil shock.

Limits of Export Promotion

There are limits to the extent that exports can be promoted. Of the four most prominent, two involve constraints imposed by the outside world and the others involve constraints imposed from within France.

—Since the deregulation of the international monetary system that occurred in the early 1970s, free trade has been on the decline. Some countries now engage in barter. Others conclude bilateral agreements to reduce trade (as with the quotas imposed by the United States and France on Japanese automobiles). Many are erecting general barriers—tariff and nontariff alike—to imports, not a few of which violate the rules of the General Agreement on Tariffs and Trade and the EEC. Nevertheless, they continue to flourish. Under these circumstances, the governments of importing nations can sterilize all attempts to promote exports.

—When aggregate demand contracts abroad, it is very difficult to expand exports. Thus following the oil shocks, foreign demand for capital goods fell. During the recent period of high interest rates, it fell especially sharply in the third world. This decline in orders prompted sharp escalation in the subsidies offered by governments of exporting countries. In their attempts to maintain export volume, many have resorted to subsidies that defy the bounds of propriety.

All governments of exporting countries have thus felt the need for cooperation to limit subsidies. At first such cooperation took the form of exchanges of information among agencies engaged in export promotion. It was reinforced by measures taken by the EEC and by the OECD consensus of 1976. The objective of this consensus was to move, however gradually, to a system devoid of subsidy.

Far be it for me to criticize such cooperation. As chairman of the OECD's working party on the subject, I expended a great deal of effort on its behalf. And the consensus does represent tangible evidence of a willingness on the part of member states to compromise. Nevertheless, one should not be so naive as to ignore the limitations of these agreements. The exemptions offered with respect to certain practices and certain countries (notably Japan) make a sham of the effort at harmonizing practices. More important, harmonizing—in the form of a single rate of interest for all export finance—depends for its legitimacy on equality among countries in monetary conditions. Such conditions do not exist, however, and this is hardly surprising. Even within the EEC, capital does not traverse borders freely; in 1983, for instance, as powerful a financial center as Switzerland enacted substantial protection for its financial sector.

On the basis of my experience in export promotion, I am convinced that transparency of subsidy and convergence on a single rate of interest will not ensure free trade. Other features of export finance affect decisively the benefits of a given package. Most important among them are the fraction of the purchase that is financed, the length of the loan, and the period of grace before repayment begins.

—The importance of domestic government budgetary constraint on export promotion should not be neglected. The chief reasons that government has had to commit funds to export promotion despite the premiums paid by exporters to the relevant agencies have been the prevalence of fixed-rate loans in a period of rising rates of interest and the need to indemnify many French exporters for the failures of buyer countries to repay their loans on time.

—Within France, many criticize the promotion of exports. They argue that only a few industries and only a few companies within those industries benefit.[1] They also argue that most of the promotion involves exports to the third world, even though 70 percent of exports and most of France's bilateral deficits involve developed countries. Finally, they argue that today's exports of industrial equipment will merely exacerbate tomorrow's challenges to French producers of consumer and intermediate goods—that France is in effect subsidizing its competitors.

Whatever the efficacy of export promotion, if France is to compete effectively, it will have to modernize its agriculture, industry, and commerce. Such modernization is occurring gradually.

At the beginning of the 1970s, multinational enterprises were spreading rapidly throughout the world, but government regulations served to keep most French enterprises national in scope. In 1971 and 1972, as they began to recognize the positive effects of activity abroad on strength at home, the authorities changed their stance and began to favor direct investment. Since 1972 the government has frequently confirmed its new position. The BFCE now guarantees direct investments against political risk, and the Treasury has

---

1. Most promotion is focused on a few large producers of heavy capital equipment. Nevertheless, many companies benefit indirectly through subcontracting.

modified advantageously both its fiscal treatment of such investments and its rules regarding transactions in foreign exchange.

Although this strategy has helped reduce the geographical myopia of French companies, they still fail to match the internationalization of their foreign competitors. Lack of infrastructure abroad has hindered the ability to sell abroad. As a result, French companies have not developed the foreign revenues necessary to finance foreign infrastructure. Thus in the world arena, French enterprise has encountered a vicious cycle. Many believe that a system of joint investment in foreign countries, similar to the German system, would promote the presence of French enterprise on world markets.

Expansion of direct foreign investment will not suffice, however, to modernize France's industrial base. Toward the end of 1981, the government concluded that French enterprises could not compete abroad unless they invested more at home. To end the stagnation in investment that had begun around 1973, it attempted to fortify the equity capital of business enterprise. Several measures—development of mutual funds, expansion of the stock market, control of wage inflation—served to channel more saving toward productive investment in general. Other measures were designed to provide special help to small and medium-sized producers of nondurable goods.[2] Such domestic measures, if successful, could be expected to have a major impact on French exports.

Conclusion

In the United States many people believe that massive subsidization of exports constitutes a key ingredient of French industrial policy. But appearances can deceive: France spends no more on export promotion than do its foreign rivals. If France appears to subsidize relatively heavily, it is merely because the subsidies are transparent—other countries tend to rely on tax expenditures. Although such expenditures have not yet attained the status of controversy in the halls of international organizations, they remain a potent form of subsidy.

Whatever the history of French export promotion, the overwhelming priority of the current government is modernization. In effect, its motto is, "Show me some vigorous industries, and I will show you some vigorous exporters."

2. Producers of capital goods relied on sales to foreign and domestic governments. Their situation proved less alarming than that of companies devoted to the production of consumer and intermediate goods.

Robert Boyer

Industrial Policy in Macroeconomic Perspective

IN THE UNITED STATES most observers are skeptical of the desirability of industrial policy. To begin with, many dispute the existence of an industrial problem. They point out that in the long term, industry's share of GNP has remained stable. Any future decline, they continue, would merely confirm the felicitous arrival of postindustrial society. Among those willing to admit the existence of an industrial problem, few believe that industrial policy offers a solution. To this group, the plight of industry stems from maladroit selection of macroeconomic policies. And if monetary and fiscal policies do not suffice, they add, there is no reason to believe that industrial policy would succeed: even Japan does not offer convincing evidence that industrial policy improves industrial performance. After all, how can bureaucrats be expected to beat the choices of the marketplace?

The European experience has led European, and especially French, observers to a different perspective: industrial vitality is considered essential, and industrial policy is viewed as a potential catalyst of such vitality. The interrelationships between industrial and macroeconomic policies are especially important for industrial health. Governments should not be trying to decide between general and selective policies. Rather, they should recognize the complementarities that bind them together. Each policy performs best when deployed in concert with the other.

The Importance of Industry

Historically speaking, industry has served as an engine for growth. If the experience of seven European countries (Belgium, Denmark, France, Germany, Italy, the Netherlands, and the United Kingdom) from 1963 to 1984 is aggregated, the relationship between growth of total output and growth of industrial output is as given in equation 1 (t-ratios are in parentheses).

$$(1) \qquad \dot{Q} = 0.57\dot{Q}_{ind} + 1.2 \qquad\qquad R^2 = 0.85$$
$$\phantom{(1) \qquad \dot{Q} = } (10.4) \qquad (6.0)$$

More generally, Yves Barou and Bernard Keizer have established a correlation between good macroeconomic performance (rapid growth, slow inflation, low unemployment, external balance) and a vigorous industrial base (large share of industry in total output, large share of saving in national income, specialization of production and trade within manufacturing).[1]

Correlations of this sort are, of course, merely suggestive. They do not imply that growth of industrial output causes additional growth in total output. Nor do they rule out the possibility that autonomous modernization in the service sector stimulates the production of industrial goods. A priori, however, there is good reason to believe that industrial growth causes growth in other sectors. Engineering, insurance, finance, and commerce depend on industrial activity. Services can be complements to, as well as substitutes for, industrial products.

From the perspective of external balance, the need to maintain a vigorous industrial base is clearer still. Many European countries, including France, must import most of their raw materials and energy. Because most services are not tradable, such countries must develop an export surplus in the industrial sector to pay the bill for their natural resources.

Industrial Health and Industrial Policy

Industrial health does not necessarily require industrial policy. Some countries, it is argued, have experienced rapid industrial growth without the benefit of explicit industrial policies. Others are said to have experienced modest industrial growth despite an ambitious industrial policy. Germany is said to illustrate the first situation, France the second. Although such views are not beyond question, they do serve to remind us that industrial performance depends on factors other than industrial policy.

In my view the health of industry depends on three groups of factors: business strategies, general economic policies, and selective industrial policies. Rather than view each in isolation, one should recognize that the three interact in their effects on industrial health.

---

1. *Les Grandes Economies: Etats-Unis, Japon, Allemagne Fédérale, France, Royaume-Uni Italie*, (Paris: Editions du Seuil, 1984).

Just after World War II, for example, it was the interaction between general economic policy and business strategy that ensured the rapid growth of investment. Historians who study France's first two economic plans (1947–53 and 1954–57) usually conclude that the Commissariat Général du Plan helped to create an optimistic, expansionary climate in the business sector. This generation of bureaucrats (surely a misnomer for Jean Monnet) was leading, not watching, industrial modernization. Those who believe that modernization results from market forces alone will find little support in this period of French economic history.

Between reconstruction and 1973, general and selective policies interacted to create a beneficial cycle of growth. Among general policies the introduction of the value-added tax, the development of stabilization policy, the maintenance of cheap credit for industrial investment, recurrent devaluation of the franc, and the reduction of barriers to international trade all contributed. As for selective industrial policies, many ambitious programs appeared in such industries as aircraft, nuclear power, and computers. These programs developed technological expertise and hence an ability to compete. Given the buoyant economic conditions ensured by general economic policy, the selective programs were easy to finance. At the same time, technological progress served to increase the responsiveness of industry to macroeconomic stimulus.

In retrospect the miraculous growth led early observers to overestimate the effect of industrial and macroeconomic policies. Industrial policy in particular is very difficult to evaluate directly. Its effects occur over long periods, and verdicts cannot be rendered until well after money is spent. Thus the aerospace program looked like a failure in the era of Concorde, but the expertise that was gained permitted the development of Airbus.

Perhaps the best evidence of the importance of industrial policy is the failure of purely macroeconomic solutions to industrial problems. That expansionary policy will not suffice is evidenced by the effects of two periods of reflation—the first under Prime Minister Jacques Chirac in 1976, the second under Prime Minister Pierre Mauroy in 1981. In both cases the expectations of a beneficial cycle did not materialize, and policy had to be revised in order to curb inflation and external imbalance. In large measure the failure of expansionary policy after the Socialists came to power should be imputed to the sluggish response of industrial production to increases in effective demand.[2] Recessionary conditions

2. Institut National de la Statistique et des Etudes Economiques, *Informations Rapides*, May 20, 1983.

in the United States and elsewhere may have aggravated the failure, but they did not cause it.

According to the conventional wisdom of the 1960s, the stimulation of household income should have been transmitted to the productive sector, and idle capacity should have been returned to operation. But the opening of the French economy as well as the subtle and unnoticed loss of ability to compete internationally had changed the dynamics of the Keynesian beneficial cycle. The pattern of domestic demand failed to mesh with the structure of domestic production. During 1981 and 1982, only the sheltered sectors were stimulated by increases in aggregate demand. Simultaneously, French exports declined. Under these circumstances, macroeconomic stimulation failed to boost industrial investment beyond the rate it had attained before 1973.

Restrictive macroeconomic policy is no more successful than its expansionary counterpart. Such is the conclusion to be drawn from the austerity program of Prime Minister Raymond Barre that was in force from 1976 to 1980. Barre's strategy consisted of careful management of effective demand, freezes on prices, control of incomes, and strict monetary targets. These led to slow disinflation. Nevertheless, inflation was not curbed, nor was it possible to lower dramatically the ratio of French to foreign prices. Contrary to expectations, the shares of industrial profit and investment in GNP failed to rise. The decision to maintain an overvalued franc weakened industrial structure.

Thus the performance of macroeconomic policies depends heavily on the underlying health of the industrial sector.[3] Between 1973 and 1983, French macroeconomic policies performed poorly because French industry was in poor health. In constant prices the level of investment in 1983 was 16 percent below that of 1973. The capital stock aged and technological change slowed. Although deceleration in the rate of increase in productivity was greater in the United States than in France, the latter was nonetheless afflicted by the disease.[4] Since 1979 the index of production has been more or less stagnant. Except in 1976 and 1982, industrial employment has fallen. During the 1970s, increases in service employment balanced declines in industrial employment, but by the 1980s the crisis had become severe enough to reduce the creation of new jobs in the service sector.

3. Michel Aglietta, André Orléan, and Gilles Oudiz, "L'Industrie Française Face aux Contraintes de Change," Economie et Statistique (February 1980) pp. 35–63.

4. Gilbert Cette and Pierre Joly, "La Productivité Industrielle en Crise: Une Interprétation," Economie et Statistique (May 1984) pp. 3–24; and Robert Boyer and Pascal Petit, "Politiques Industrielles et Impact sur l'Emploi: Les Pays Européens Face à la Contrainte Extérieure," Revue d'Economie Industrielle (First Quarter 1984).

Industrial Policy in a Macroeconomic Model

The role of industrial policy in a macroeconomic setting can be formalized with the help of a simple model (variables with bars above them are exogenous with respect to domestic policymakers, at least in the short run). This model emphasizes the necessity for external balance. Effective demand (D) depends on several types of expenditure—consumption (C), investment (I), exports (X), imports (M), and government (G):

$$(2) \qquad D = C + \bar{I} + X - M + \bar{G}.$$

Consumption is a fixed fraction of domestic output (Q) after taxes (T).

$$(3) \qquad C = c(Q - \bar{T})$$

Imports depend on the elasticity of imports with respect to domestic output (m), domestic output, the elasticity of imports with respect to the price differential between domestic and foreign goods (n), domestic prices (P), and foreign prices (P_F),

$$(4) \qquad M = mQ + n(P - \bar{P}_F).$$

Exports depend on the elasticity of exports with respect to foreign production (x), foreign production (Q_F), the elasticity of exports with respect to the differential between domestic and foreign prices (y), domestic prices, and foreign prices,

$$(5) \qquad X = x\bar{Q}_F - y(P - \bar{P}_F).$$

Production occurs subject to a production function (F) with labor (N) and capital (K) as arguments:

$$(6) \qquad Q = F(N,\bar{K}).$$

Finally, maximum profitable output ($\tilde{Q}$) depends on the real wage (W/P):

$$(7) \qquad \left.\frac{\partial F}{\partial N}\right|_{Q=\tilde{Q}} = \frac{W}{P}$$

Within this framework, there are three constraints on output: effective demand, full employment, and external equilibrium. Equilibrium output and employment occur when the first of these constraints is encountered. The demand constraint is embodied in equation 2, as supplemented by equations 3 through 5; the full-employment constraint is embodied in equation 6, with $N = N_{FE}$. The last is given by

$$(8) \qquad\qquad P_m M = P_x X,$$

in which P_m is the price of imports and P_x of exports. Let us consider how the relations among these constraints affect the difficulty of achieving full employment.

The external constraint does not bind. In this case the output permitted by external balance exceeds the full-employment level. Fiscal policy can be used to ensure a level of aggregate demand that will result in full employment. If profitable output falls short of full-employment output, then incomes policy can be used to establish a real wage consistent with marginal productivity at full capacity utilization. Although full-employment equilibrium can be achieved without industrial policy, it remains possible that industrial policy can speed adoption of technological change, enhancing thereby the rate of growth.

The external constraint does bind. Suppose now that maximum output consistent with external equilibrium is less than profitable output, which in turn falls short of full-employment output. Fiscal policy alone will not be able to achieve full employment. Let us consider four possible supplements to such policy.

—Exchange Rates. In principle, governments could attempt to relax the external constraint by changing the prices of their currencies. In fact, however, governments are not always free to do so. The European Monetary System, for example, reduces the control of France over the price of the franc. Even when feasible, changes in exchange rates may not prove effective: in a perfectly indexed economy, devaluations change nominal but not real economic magnitudes. As a result they leave unemployment intact. Finally, manipulation of exchange rates can be a painful prescription indeed, given its effects on the standard of living. Other policies might work as well yet cost society less.

—Protection from imports and promotion of exports. At best, these policies work only in the absence of retaliation. More important, in a dynamic world a purely defensive strategy may reduce export as well as import elasticities. It might even reduce the maximum rate of growth compatible with external equilibrium. Even if successful, protectionism will adversely affect the standard of living.

—Incomes Policies. Incomes policies are designed to influence domestic prices, but the evidence suggests they can do so for only a year or two. Structurally, price is not the only determinant of the ability to compete in world markets. At best, then, incomes policies can mitigate the cyclical component of vulnerability in world trade.

—Industrial Policies. The theoretical case for industrial policies follows from equation 9, a representation of the maximum output consistent with external equilibrium:

$$(9) \qquad Q_{EXT} = (x/m)(P_x/P_m)\overline{Q}_F - [(y/m)(P_x/P_m) + n/m](P-\overline{P}_F).$$

Assuming that, in the medium term, export and import prices change at the same rates and that domestic and foreign prices also change at the same rates, it follows that the rate of growth of domestic output according to the external constraint will be

$$(10) \qquad \dot{Q}_{EXT} = (x/m)\dot{Q}_F.$$

To the extent that excessive specialization results in low export elasticity and high import elasticity, the output attainable according to the external constraint may be well below that required to generate full employment. In such a case, industrial structure must change before full employment is attained, and industrial policy may be one way of effecting such a modification. The desirable industrial policy is offensive in the sense that government must promote innovation and investment, especially in new industries. Politically, such promotion is no mean task. The most compelling objections to industrial policy are practical rather than theoretical.

Conclusions

Studies conducted during the preparation of the Ninth Plan paint a gloomy picture. Unless industrial structure and behavior change, French growth will fail to attain the OECD average, unemployment will climb to record levels, and investment will fail to increase sufficiently to modernize old industries and develop new ones.

The same studies suggest that changes in industrial structure will require deployment of all the adjustment mechanisms at the government's disposal. One of these is industrial policy. According to the government's econometric model, DMS, industrial policy could play a significant role in reviving investment. Interestingly, the model predicts that the effect of increased investment on external equilibrium is negative for the first five years but positive thereafter. This confirms the view that industrial policy should be considered a medium-term instrument of policy. The model also predicts that the impact of increased investment on employment is positive but modest: even if Fr 23.7 billion were invested in industry, fewer than 100,000 jobs would be created by 1990. Finally, the model predicts that directing the extra investment toward sectors competing with imports will promote employment but aggravate inflation. Industrial policy may be part of the solution to the present crisis, but it must be used in concert with economic policies of a more general nature.

Appendix: Structural Transformations of French Foreign Trade and Their Effects on Medium-Term Economic Growth

The model embodied in equations 2 through 8 suggests the importance of the relationship between movements in exports and movements in imports. Let us simplify equations 4 and 5 to 4.1 and 5.1, respectively:

(4.1) $$M = mQ$$

(5.1) $$X = x\overline{Q}_F.$$

Then the rate of change over time in the ratio of exports to imports (at current prices) can be expressed as the sum of three effects:

(11) $$(P_xX/P_mM) = (\dot{P}_x - \dot{P}_m) + (x - m)\dot{Q}_F - m(\dot{Q} - \dot{Q}_F).$$

The first effect represents variations in the terms of trade; the second represents the pull effect of foreign growth; the third represents the effect of differential national growth. Barou and Keizer have calculated estimates of each effect during the period 1950–80 for several OECD countries. For France, their results are summarized in table 6-1.

The work of Barou and Keizer provides a number of insights regarding French economic performance since World War II. First, in the long run the terms of trade had a negligible effect on maximum sustainable growth. In the shorter run the deterioration of the terms of trade after the two oil shocks did not constitute the principal explanation of the disequilibrium in trade and deceleration of growth that occurred between 1975 and 1980. Second, French

Table 6-1. *Determinants of Exports as a Percentage of Imports, 1950–80*

Effect	1950–1955	1955–1960	1960–1965	1965–1970	1970–1975	1975–1980	1950–1980
Terms of trade							
$\dot{P}_x - \dot{P}_m$	0.8	−0.2	0.8	−0.4	−1.2	−0.2	−0.1
Pull $(x-m)\dot{Q}_F$	−0.5	3.7	−1.8	1.1	3.1	−2.4	0.6
Differential growth							
$-m(\dot{Q}-\dot{Q}_F)$	0.7	−2.1	−0.8	−1.5	−1.7	0.4	−0.9
Combined $P_x X/P_m M$	1.0	1.4	−1.8	−0.8	0.2	−2.2	−0.4

Source: Yves Barou and Bernard Keizer, *Les Grandes Economies: Etats-Unis, Japon, Allemagne Fédérale, France, Royaume-Uni, Italie* (Paris: Editions du Seuil, 1984), p. 288.

economic growth, relative to economic growth in the OECD as a whole, has declined. Between 1955 and 1975 the French economy grew more rapidly than did the OECD average; between 1975 and 1980 it grew more slowly than did the OECD average. Even so, France has suffered from the slowdown in the growth of the world economy. Third, and most important in the present context, France has suffered from a decline in export elasticity (x) and a rise in import elasticity (m). Such deterioration of the income elasticities of foreign trade serves to reduce domestic growth for a given pattern of international trade. Economic policy has had to adjust to the decay of industrial competitiveness by reducing effective demand through increases in taxes. For a decade now the weakness of French industrial structure has constrained French macroeconomic policy.

Bela Balassa

Selective versus General Economic Policy in Postwar France

MANY STUDENTS of the French economy believe in the continuity of French industrial policy. They claim that Jean Monnet and Charles de Gaulle, who are subject more to veneration than criticism, in particular wished to establish an industrial policy within the framework of indicative planning. They also claim that such an industrial policy has been in force since World War II. I question the validity of this view.

Monnet's task was essentially to rebuild infrastructure and basic industries after the destruction of World War II. Such reconstruction may be regarded as an appropriate role for the state. It is only the successors of Monnet who changed this process into one of state interventions throughout the industrial sector, a process that took place under both the Second and the Third Economic Plans (1953–57 and 1958–61, respectively).

These plans aimed to ensure the coherence of supply and demand in each industry, and they did so in a manner that exhibited protectionist tendencies. In general they aimed to keep imports unchanged during the life of each plan despite the expectation of economic growth. In particular industries, *arbitrage* (bargaining) was used to determine the role of imports in market supply, with the planners serving as arbitrators. For example, when the cotton-yarn and garment industries disagreed about how much of the latter's requirements of yarn should be met through imports, the planners for cotton yarn intervened and made the decision.[1]

At the same time, the state had at its disposal a number of instruments, including quotas, import tariffs, and export subsidies, to ensure that the forecasts of the planners were realized. Thus the state relied not on the carrots and

1. Pierre de Calan quoted in *French and Other National Economic Plans for Growth*, Report from an international conference on French planning held under the auspices of the French Group of the European Committee for Economic and Social Progress at Paris on June 4 and 5, 1962 (New York: Committee for Economic Development, 1963), p. 68.

sticks of competition but on the carrots of import protection and export subsidies along with the stick of withdrawing such support from companies that did not go along with the planners.

The situation changed in 1958 as France subscribed to the liberalization code of the Organization for European Economic Cooperation (OEEC) and entered the European Economic Community (EEC). This meant that the instruments of industrial policy used earlier were no longer available to the state. As put in one official report, "No special measure is available anymore that would permit the regulation of imports; there is no mechanism that would guarantee that export objectives could be regarded with confidence. Everything depends on international competition."[2]

In the new situation, companies were subject to the uncertainty associated with competition from foreign enterprises in domestic as well as foreign markets, an uncertainty that assumed considerable importance for business decisions. In conjunction with these developments, industrialists wanted to increase their freedom of action. This desire was expressed in a resolution of the Conseil National du Patronat Français: "In matters of the management of business, the authority for making decisions cannot be divided. Above all, the illusions of a systematic dirigisme whose failure can be ascertained everywhere should be renounced."[3]

There was thus a reversal in business attitudes from an earlier acceptance of planning to its rejection. In fact the planning process changed profoundly with the abandonment of physical balances. As two American economists from the Harvard Business School observed, "the utility of planning physical coherence of inputs and outputs declined very sharply—virtually to the vanishing point."[4] With the increase in import competition at home and the decrease of subsidized sales abroad, physical coherence of supply and demand was impossible to plan.

At the same time, a shift occurred from "vertical" policies—the French term for selective promotion and control of particular industries—to "horizontal" policies—the corresponding term for incentives available to all industries. Horizontal policy measures included tax relief for those who invested or engaged in research and development, credit guarantees and insurance against fluctuations in prices and exchange rates for those who exported, and fiscal and credit measures favoring those who engaged in industrial concentration.

2. Commissariat Général du Plan et Services des Etudes Economiques et Financières, "Projet de Rapport du Groupe d'Equilibre de la Commission de l'Economie Générale, du Financement, et du Plan" (June 1961, Mimeographed), p. 57.

3. Statement of the Conseil National du Patronat Français, January 19, 1965.

4. John H. McArthur and Bruce R. Scott, Industrial Planning in France (Boston: Harvard University Graduate School of Business Administration, Research Division, 1969), p. 494.

Measures promoting mergers and buy-outs were of particular importance because the French economy had to adjust to the EEC. The results were spectacular. The value of assets of companies absorbed by other companies increased from an annual average of Fr 85 million during the 1950s to Fr 1 billion in 1965 and Fr 5 billion in 1970.[5]

Concentration was accompanied by modernization. According to an authoritative study, "the industrial structure underwent greater transformation in ten years than during the preceding half century."[6] Also, before 1958 the growth rates of manufacturing and GNP were lower in France than in Germany; but after 1958 France became the fastest-growing country in the EEC. This was the case irrespective of whether one takes the entire fifteen-year period between 1958 and 1973 or each five-year subperiod.

The dynamism of the years following 1958 contradicts the Malthusian view of the French economy. In particular, the share of gross fixed investment in GNP rose from 18 percent in 1953–58 to 24 percent in 1968–73. Most of the increase occurred in the private industrial sector. All in all, the opening of the economy to increased foreign competition, the shift to horizontal microeconomic policy, and the stabilization associated with the Pinay-Rueff reforms account for the improvement in French economic performance in relation to the earlier planned system.[7]

Apart from horizontal policies, some selective measures were also employed. Many of these measures promoted the grands projets—programs like the development of a supersonic transport or a large mainframe computer. Much has been written about the successes and failures of these projects. I share the view of John Zysman that "state support appears to have reduced the pressure on firms under its tutelage to adopt structures more suited to their technological and market problems."[8] Unsurprisingly, the French government was ultimately obliged to increase foreign, and specifically American, participation in its computer industry.

Debate over the success of the grands projets often obscures the central fact of this period: most expansion came in sectors that remained largely untouched

5. Bernard Guibert and others, "La Mutation Industrielle de la France," Les Collections de l'INSEE, Series E, Nos. 31–32, vol. 1 (November 1975), pp. 93–97.

6. Ibid., vol. 2, pp. 207–08.

7. For a detailed discussion, see Bela Balassa, "The French Economy under the Fifth Republic, 1958–1978," in William G. Andrews and Stanley Hoffmann, eds., The Impact of the Fifth Republic on France (Albany: State University of New York Press, 1981), pp. 117–38. A French translation appeared in Revue Economique, vol. 30 (November 1979), pp. 939–71.

8. Political Strategies for Industrial Order: State, Market, and Industry in France (Berkeley: University of California Press, 1977), p. 88.

by such programs. Sectors such as automobiles and machinery grew in response to horizontal rather than selective policies.

Heavy reliance on horizontal measures continued after 1973, notwithstanding the statements made by Georges Pompidou about the importance of industrial policy. Vertical measures were applied mainly in nuclear energy—a sector in which the state had to intervene to reduce reliance on imported petroleum— and in armaments.

An important change occurred in 1978 when Raymond Barre freed industrial prices that had been traditionally controlled in France. While price decontrol was only partially effective, the change was nevertheless significant psychologically even where it had no practical effect. More generally, under Barre the government gave a greater role to market forces.

In May 1981 the Socialist electoral victory led to a reversal in the process of liberalization, with new nationalizations, increased government interventions, and the reinstitution of price controls for part of industry. This does not mean, however, that the Left implemented a genuine industrial policy: it reacted to situations as they emerged, without developing a consistent policy.

In this connection, reference may be made to steel and coal. As Raymond Lévy points out elsewhere in this volume, the 1982 target for steel production was set at 24 million tons at a time when actual production was only 17 million tons. One may add that the measures that accompanied the setting of this target contributed to increases in the losses of the steel industry from Fr 3 billion to Fr 11 billion between 1980 and 1983.

These measures represented a reversal of policy. Between 1957 and 1981 employment in the steel industry had been allowed to decline from 160,000 to 97,000. Further restructuring of the industry was envisaged. Yet the Socialists attempted to increase employment. By 1984 they came to understand that their policy was untenable; target production was reduced to 18.5 million tons, and a plan for reducing employment was adopted. Nevertheless the costs of the measures taken in earlier years continue to burden the industry.

A similar series of events occurred in the case of the coal industry. While coal production was reduced from 40 million tons in 1970 to a little over 20 million tons in 1980, the Socialist government set a target of 30 million tons for 1990. As a result, employment in the mines was increased. If grants and subsidies from government are included, losses then rose from Fr 4 billion in 1980 to over Fr 7 billion in 1983. Again, a new production target was set between 11 million and 12 million tons, but reducing the labor force will be costly.

After May 1981 the Socialist government gave considerable emphasis to technologically advanced industries. In his discussion of high-technology industries earlier in this book, Christian Stoffaës writes that this emphasis continues. And yet in April 1984 the funds approved for research declined substantially. The effects of this decline were undone only partly when, a few months later, borrowed funds came to be used for research. The cuts adversely affected industrial research in particular.[9]

When he was minister of industry, Jean-Pierre Chevènement declared that "there are no condemned industries, only outdated technologies." His words have been repeated often. On its face the statement seems to endorse a horizontal policy, but at the same time, one finds that most financial assistance was devoted to specific industries—and declining ones (coal and steel) at that.

In 1982, when they nationalized several large industrial companies, the Socialists claimed to be acting to reverse a tendency toward insufficient financial resources at the disposal of business enterprise.[10] My research shows a different picture. It indicates that much of the decline in profitability occurred after May 1981, a result of factors such as price control, social legislation—including higher social security taxes, a fifth week of paid vacation, and reduction in working time from forty to thirty-nine hours a week with full compensation—and limitation of the right of the company to reduce the size of its labor force.

In this connection a comparison may be made between the periods following the two oil crises. Both crises resulted in decreased profitability. After the first crisis, however, the decline was reversed within a few years. Such a reversal did not take place after the second oil crisis. Thus the decline in profitability that occurred in 1980 continued in 1981 and 1982. At the same time, the financial positions of companies have been aggravated by interest charges on the debt they were obliged to accumulate.[11]

The situation appears even worse if, following Edmond Malinvaud, one employs a measure of profitability that is obtained by subtracting the real rate of interest from the book value of profitability. According to Malinvaud, this ratio should be 3 or 4 percent; in fact during the 1960s and 1970s it generally stayed between 4 percent and 6 percent in France. The ratio declined from 4.0

9. A more detailed discussion of policies relating to technologically advanced industries and industrial policy in general appears in Bela Balassa, "French Industrial Policy under the Socialist Government," American Economic Review, vol. 75 (May 1985), pp. 315–19.

10. See the chapter by Henri Guillaume in this volume.

11. See Bela Balassa, "La Politique Economique Socialiste: L'An III," Commentaire, vol. 7 (Spring 1984), pp. 13–22. The English version appeared in Tocqueville Review, vol. 6 (Spring–Summer 1984), pp. 183–98.

percent in 1979 to 0.4 percent in 1980; it was −1.3 percent in 1981 and −3.4 percent in 1982.[12] While improvements have occurred since, the earlier ratio has not been attained.

In conclusion, I wish to emphasize the conflicts that characterize French industrial policy today. First, there is a conflict between the state's attempt to develop all industries simultaneously and its concentration on only some of them. Second, there is conflict between choosing a national champion in each sector and having competition in the sector. Third, there is a conflict between orienting exports toward sheltered markets and toward competitive markets. Fourth, there is a conflict between modernization and what has been called national solidarity. Finally, there is a conflict between regional interests and the national interest.

In resolving these conflicts, France should rely on horizontal measures. All companies, public as well as private, should be allowed to decide their own fates. If such decisions are to be effective, companies must be provided with appropriate means. In particular, price controls should be eliminated, employers' contributions to social security reduced, and the labor market deregulated. The successes of the 1960s and 1970s bear ample witness to the virtues of horizontal policy.

12. Edmond Malinvaud, *Essais sur la Théorie du Chômage* (Paris: Calmann-Lévy, 1983), p. 218.

Henri Aujac, John Zysman, François Didier, and George C. Eads

Comments

HENRI AUJAC   In order to explain the early and expansive development of industrial policy in France, one must look to two features of the French environment. The first is nationalism, a trait in evidence from Joan of Arc to Charles de Gaulle. Nationalism explains why France insists on cultivating homegrown versions of important industries. Although the definition of "important" has varied over the centuries, it has always involved military or economic strength.

The second key feature is the French version of capitalism. The institutions of capitalism have flourished only moderately in the French setting. Private venture capital does not exist in sufficient quantities to launch big companies or new technologies. If the government wishes to ensure a French presence in sunrise industries, it must expect to finance that presence itself. Only then will employees and managers, suppliers and customers, be assured of the long-term funding necessary to develop an ability to compete in world markets.

In some cases French industrial policy has succeeded; in others it has failed. The policies of the 1950s tend to have been successful. Those since the 1960s have not. Among the policies of recent vintage, those controlling the development of nuclear power must be considered successful, while those dealing with electronics and computers have been failures. What accounts for these variations in performance?

During the 1950s France still felt the impact of World War II. The major problem was reconstruction. Technology had changed very little; the major problems were to accumulate enough savings to rebuild, and to reserve most of those savings for the rebuilding process. After the trauma associated with the war, the labor force was prepared to adapt itself to the requirements of a modern economy. The modesty of labor's aspirations facilitated saving and hence investment. In addition, France emerged from World War II with a new elite forged by war and resistance and eager to devote itself to some great cause. The combination of leadership in government and the civic responsibility of labor accounts for the success of industrial policy in the late 1940s and the 1950s.

As the war faded further into memory, however, the objectives to be pursued by government became less obvious. In the public eye, only one objective—fighting unemployment—commanded quasi-universal support. Regarding the promotion of robotics as opposed to biotechnology, or telecommunications satellites instead of neutron bombs, people do not hold firm opinions. They do not even know whom to trust—the politicians, the "experts," or "the market."

Darkening the cloud surrounding policy goals has been the cloud surrounding means. In 1979 a famous but unpublished report showed that almost 50 percent of the government's aid to industry was received by five large industrial companies and their subsidiaries. (At the time, the companies were private enterprises; not coincidentally, perhaps, they were nationalized in 1982.) Even the aid reserved for companies of small and medium size went to subsidiaries of large corporations instead of to independent enterprises. This concentration of aid, attributable to the prevalence of former civil servants at the tops of large corporations, has led many to question the equity and hence legitimacy of industrial policy.

The importance of popular consensus also appears in the context of current industrial policies. The development of nuclear power has succeeded, while the development of electronics and computers has not. The first oil shock brought home the need for nuclear power, and government pursued its objective clearly and constantly. In the case of electronics, however, the specific objectives and the commitment of funds tended to fluctuate.

The efficacy of industrial policy cannot, therefore, be predicted without an understanding of its political and sociological context. Without inspiration on the part of their authors and commitment at the grass-roots level to their implementation, government industrial initiatives are bound to fail.

JOHN ZYSMAN   The institutions that characterize French industrial policy have exhibited remarkable continuity for a very long time. Broadly speaking, the same types of policies have been applied in a wide variety of circumstances. In some cases the policies have succeeded, in others they have failed; it is important to identify the determinants of success.

French industrial policy has been successful at achieving two types of goals: sustained increases in an industry's rate of investment and increases in purchases of French goods by foreign governments—goods such as weapons, telecommunications systems, and nuclear power plants. Whether the Airbus breaks even, whether it can be competitive in world markets if the value of the dollar falls, French industrial policy must be considered to have been successful in these industries.

French industrial policy has been less successful where, as in telecommunications, the government has not been able to control the market mechanism. In the past each European government controlled its own system of telecommunications. Each was able to use its ownership to guarantee that requirements in equipment would be satisfied by domestic producers. As deregulation overtakes telecommunications, however, such control will no longer be feasible. As a result, I would expect the successes of French policy to fade away.

Unfortunately for the French, the technologies of the future are precisely the technologies that government will have difficulty controlling. Whether one looks at microelectronics, semiconductors, or computers, whether one looks at programmable automation, computer-aided design, or computer-aided manufacturing, the markets, not the governments of the world, will dominate. That explains why French policy has not met with much success in these areas.

This analysis suggests that the weaknesses of French industrial policy do not stem from vacillation. Nor do they stem primarily from a lack of budgetary commitment. Instead they are the result of a more fundamental problem: government intervention does not work well when market forces are strong and changing rapidly. Under such conditions government policy is buffeted by shifts in competitive conditions.

Here lies the major difference between Japanese and French industrial policy. From my perspective as an outsider to both systems, the Japanese seem to have been more successful at employing the forces of competition as instruments of policy. Instead of attempting to suppress the market, they endeavor to amplify and channel it.

I do not wish to belittle the accomplishments of French industrial policy. During the past thirty or thirty-five years, an economy firmly anchored to agriculture, small business, and technological backwardness was transformed into a modern economy with large-scale, competitive companies. That is a major transition—one that could not have been accomplished without the active intervention of government. The role of the government was to make sure that market forces were left free to do their work of selecting efficient, and only efficient, companies for survival.

But the transition is over, and the very patterns of policy that helped achieve the transformation now handicap France in the next round of international competition. France emerged from its structural transformation in a much weaker competitive position than did Japan. Given the similarity of French and Japanese policies, it is important to determine why those policies produced dramatically different results. In critical sectors such as electronics, Japanese companies are structurally far stronger than their French counterparts.

Instead of recognizing the importance of the market, the French government is relying on the policies of the past: it is trying to expand the role of government when it should be trying to determine how to ensure survival in competitive world markets. Witness its nationalization of five large industrial companies in 1982. Witness also its more recent decision to move the telecommunications branches of Thomson-Brandt to the Compagnie Générale d'Electricité—a move designed to create a single national champion within the electronics sector.

From a political standpoint the recent round of nationalizations may actually impede the government from acting in synchrony with market forces. Nationalization brings to the public arena issues that are best handled out of the limelight. Paradoxically, nationalization may weaken rather than strengthen the government's attempt to conduct a vigorous industrial policy.

From these observations, I draw two conclusions. First, the French experience, no less than the Japanese, suggests that governments can create enduring competitive advantages: government can intervene in markets to alter the competitive positions of various companies. These alterations can be enduring in the sense that they can continue after subsidies are removed. Nevertheless, and this is the second conclusion, government volition does not automatically translate into government success. Governments must understand the dynamics of the marketplace if they wish to influence the evolution of industries in which market forces are indomitable.

FRANÇOIS DIDIER   Most discussions of industrial policy are undertaken from an academic or a government perspective. I will discuss the subject from the standpoint of the business community.

Business sees the pragmatic as much as the ideological side of government. Thus from its perspective, the American government does engage in industrial policy, as when it bailed out Chrysler Corporation or Continental Illinois bank, and the French government sometimes fails to do so, as when it allowed a major manufacturer, Creusot-Loire, to go bankrupt. Although the French economic system is traceable to Louis XIV while that of the United States owes its origin to New England Yankees, the results are not as different as one might think.

A major problem of industrial policy is continuity. Corporations need to satisfy their shareholders at least every year and possibly every quarter. Governments need to satisfy their electorates approximately every two years. As a result it is very difficult to implement and sustain long-term policies. Under such circumstances industrial policy may work especially well in a political regime that relies heavily on a stable, powerful civil service.

The French experience bears out this expectation. French industrial policy has been successful in a number of areas: the offshore technologies of the petroleum industry provide one example. During the past twenty years the French government must have spent Fr 400 million on the development of such technologies. Today, France realizes Fr 40 billion a year in exports because of that effort. Throughout Europe the French record is held up as the model of success.

I do not wish to suggest that French industrial policies have always been successful. If Arianespace represents a happy ending, the early days of policy in the electronics sector were sad indeed.

The importance of continuity appears not only in the strategies of companies whose names are household words; it also shows up in the behavior of other French enterprises. For example, the Accor hotel group, known until recently under the name of Novotel, has developed into one of the largest chains of hotels in the world. Similarly, it was a man from Grenoble who invented a process for developing color film in less than one hour. His corporation, Kis, accounts for one-half of the devices now used in Japan to develop color film automatically.

It is fashionable to talk of winners and losers. It is important to know the sense in which such terms are applicable. Too often, students of industrial policy talk as if whole sectors of economic activity should be labeled winners or losers. Such is not the case. Even in the industries of the future, some enterprises will fail. Witness the recent experience of Osborne in computers. Crucial to success is not one's industry but one's willingness to embrace new technology. That is what the chairman of General Motors meant when he suggested that his goal was to infuse the automotive industry with new technology. In France a good example of this phenomenon is the evolution of the textile industry. Although much of its business has been lost to the third world, the industry has found niches in which, thanks to technological sophistication, it has been able to maintain a comparative advantage.

The term "industrial policy" is misleading insofar as it causes one to focus on productive efficiency or innovation. Marketing is equally important. Unfortunately marketing strategies are apt to cause misunderstandings between government and business. For example, a fierce competition is now developing among video recorder, cable television, and direct satellite television technologies. In the midst of this free-for-all the French government is increasing the number of channels it allows for television. However desirable in principle, this policy will be implemented in such a manner that not all of the new channels will sell.

In many industries the fixed costs associated with developing new products loom extremely large. In the pharmaceutical branch of my corporation, for example, some 17 percent of gross revenue is allocated to research and development. Because it is impossible to amortize such expenses on the French market alone, we are obliged to think in worldwide terms. As a result, industrial policy must take account of the importance of international markets.

One of the most important features of industrial policy must accordingly be to stabilize the values of national currencies. As one example of this phenomenon, consider energy. As of September 1984, the price of a barrel of oil was $27.50. Before the second oil shock the price was $12.00. In dollar terms the price of oil rose by a factor of 2.3. During the same period the price of a dollar in terms of French francs also increased by a factor of 2.3. Because the price of oil is set in dollars, the change in the value of the franc was tantamount to a third oil shock, the magnitude of which was just as large as that of its second cousin.

In conclusion, I have participated in industrial policy as both a civil servant and a member of a large industrial corporation. I have seen many mistakes and many achievements. My observations convince me that good industrial policy, like good cooking, is more an art than a science.

GEORGE C. EADS   I do not claim to be an expert on the French economy, but I do know something about the health of industry in the United States. I am struck by the degree of similarity between the situation in mature French industries and that in their American counterparts. The chapters by Raymond Lévy and François Perrin-Pelletier could have been written by American executives. They identify foreign competition as a major challenge. Incorrectly in my view, they question the ability of domestic producers to survive without government support. Finally, they describe the efforts of government to solve the problems of specific industries through rescue plans. Each plan seems to prove inadequate and mergers among producers are required, but faith in the ability of a new plan to solve the industry's problems is never diminished by the shortcomings of its ancestors.

Although these observations apply in some measure to the American experience, it would be wrong to suggest that the situation is identical in the two countries.

One major difference is observable in business rhetoric. In the United States, business does not accept the legitimacy of government intervention; in France it does. Whether or not this difference affects the outcomes of public policy, it does alter the set of tools available to government. Legitimacy of intervention permits France to rely on subsidies. The United States tends to resort to protection. To the extent that the United States does employ subsidies, they take the form of tax loopholes. It is hard to know whether the prevalence of such loopholes should be attributed to something deep in the American psyche or merely to the choice by Senator Russell Long of a committee that handles taxes rather than expenditures. In either case the methods of intervention clearly differ between the two countries.

A second difference lies in the implications to be drawn from foreign challenge. The French recognized well before the Americans that structural adjustment was required; executives in the American automobile and steel industries have recognized it only recently.

The final difference is the most important, and it forms the basis of most pleas in this country for industrial policy. Unlike its American counterpart the French government has negotiated broad packages of policies with the private sector. That is, the government has offered certain carrots to industry in return for the performance of certain acts. In the United States such packages do not exist, and any commitments of the private sector tend to be vague and unenforceable.

The apparent coherence of French policy has been held up as a model for the United States. In my view the appeal of the French model can be determined on the basis of three criteria: first, how quickly did government or business or both perceive the existence of a problem? Second, how smoothly does government policy move an industry toward its new equilibrium? Can the burden of transition be diffused sufficiently to eliminate most of the tensions attending the transition? Third, does government policy enhance the likelihood that the new equilibrium will be reached? In this regard, let me say that my norm for equilibrium is an internationally competitive industry.

What, then, does the experience of the two countries reveal about the performance of their systems for dealing with crisis in mature industries? On the first criterion—perception of a problem—it is difficult to distinguish the two countries. In both cases the underlying problem—loss of competitiveness—was initially denied. After it was recognized, it was imputed to the unfairness of foreign competition. Finally the remedy was seen to be expansion rather than contraction of the industry—witness the plans of the French steel industry as late as the 1970s to expand. In the United States the industry was arguing for expansion as late as 1979. So neither system appears especially suited to early identification of the nature of the problem.

On the second criterion—smoothness of transition—most outside observers give high marks to systems of the French sort. After reading the contributions of Lévy and Perrin-Pelletier, however, I fail to see why. The French transitions have not been models of smoothness. There has been a great deal of animosity, and the reason for it is obvious: any strategy that holds the promise of making companies more competitive entails substantial reductions in employment. In 1980 when I was on the Council of Economic Advisors, we studied the situation in steel. Our analysis was confirmed by Donald F. Barnett and Louis Schorsch: The ability to compete depends more on raising labor productivity than it does on reducing wages.[1] Given stable capacity, that implies substantial reduction in employment.

Reduction in employment at the company level will proceed smoothly only if macroeconomic policy delivers new jobs for displaced workers. Thus industrial policy is not the key to modernizing mature industries. With or without industrial policy, it is macroeconomic policy that will determine the smoothness of transition. As a result I do not believe that the French system of industrial policy permits better performance than does its American counterpart—at least on this criterion. Unfortunately, in the domain of macroeconomic policy neither economy has performed particularly well.

Although package deals have not sufficed to ensure smooth transitions in France, it is interesting to consider the form such deals might take in the United States. The closest thing in the United States to a fully negotiated, fully enforceable agreement is the consent decree in antitrust law. Consider, for example, the decree signed in January 1984 to settle the government's suit against American Telephone and Telegraph. A single, unelected individual, not responsible to public opinion, enjoyed the power to negotiate a deal of virtually unlimited dimensions with two powerful parties; he then had the power to impose execution of the agreement on both parties by force of law. This model is unlikely to be carried outside the unique domain of antitrust policy.

The final criterion for evaluating systems that deal with industrial decline is the extent to which they eventually generate competitive industries. If I understand Raymond Lévy's chapter correctly, the goal of French policy is not an internationally competitive industry but rather one that is capable of supplying domestic markets when imports arrive at a "normal" rate. So even if the policy is successful in its own terms, it will score poorly on my criterion. The United States will do better—not because government policies are enlightened but because market forces are about to erode the old order. Even if the U.S. steel industry succeeds in its twenty-year political crusade to block imports completely, the minimills, small mills that rely on scrap steel, are going to get them from behind. Only one or two technological innovations are required before

1. *Steel: Upheaval in a Basic Industry* (Cambridge, Mass.: Ballinger, 1983).

such mills can take over the entire steel industry, and those innovations will be achieved in the next two or three years. In spite of government policy rather than because of it, the U.S. industry will arrive at a position in which it meets the test of ability to compete internationally.

The case of automobiles is harder to analyze. After reading François Perrin-Pelletier's chapter, I cannot identify the goal of French policy. In the United States I continue to search for the analogue of the minimill. Robert Crandall claims it is Japanese ownership of plants in the United States. It might also be the opportunity of domestic producers to outsource.

The French system has not performed any better than has its American cousin. Nevertheless, I expect demands for adoption of such a system in the United States to continue. What kind of a future can be predicted for industrial policy in this country? I suspect the United States will muddle along its current path. It will espouse free trade and practice protectionism. It will proclaim the need for industries to stand on their own at the same time that it accords them backdoor subsidies.

If industrial policy does come to the United States, it will be brought from the Right not the Left. The Left will shy away from industrial policy because the labor movement in this country is too weak and the practice is fundamentally antidemocratic. On the other hand, recognizing the power of government and perceiving the message of automobiles and steel to be that government will deliver insulation from foreign competition without asking much in return, American industry might swing in favor of the practice. In fact we are seeing the first glimmerings of such a swing. Roger Porter will not admit it, but time will show the accuracy of this prophecy.

Part II

Directions for Reform

Martin Malvy

Modernization: The Industrial Policy of Laurent Fabius

FRANCE AND THE UNITED STATES currently appear to differ greatly in economic circumstance. During the decade following the first oil shock, however, the two countries have encountered similar economic problems: slow and irregular growth, serious inflation, swollen unemployment, and frequent corporate bankruptcies. To combat these problems, both countries resorted first to macroeconomic policy. As stagflation proved resistant to such treatments both sought new prescriptions for government policy. One such prescription is industrial policy.

Historically, the two countries are supposed to be opposites. France is said to rely on a powerful and knowledgeable civil service to compensate for a private sector obsessed with land-based, risk-free investments. The United States is said to rely on governments that govern little and entrepreneurs who energize the market system. France supposedly embraces industrial policy, while the United States allegedly treats it like the plague.

Although this caricature strays far from reality, it is true that the success of industrial policies will depend on the cultural, social, and historical environment in which they operate. For this reason it is useful to examine each country's experiences with industrial policy. A complete treatment of the French experience would require examination of a long historical tradition, ranging from the policies of Jean-Baptiste Colbert in the seventeenth century to the philosophy of Claude-Henri de Rouvroy, Comte de Saint-Simon, in the nineteenth to the economic planning of Jean Monnet after World War II. In this chapter, I first give a brief overview of French industrial policy during the recent government of Laurent Fabius, in which I served. Then I discuss the application of this policy to energy, the sector for which I was responsible.

The Policies of Laurent Fabius

Economic modernization was the major goal under former Prime Minister Laurent Fabius. The world is entering a new industrial age. The technological

115

revolution now in progress will prove to be as significant as those based on steam, electricity, and the internal combustion engine. To ensure that France will participate fully in this new industrial era, the Fabius government spent a great deal of money, despite severe budgetary constraints, on research and development. Much of the effort was focused on electronics—especially integrated circuits, data processing, telecommunications, aerospace, and robotics.

Modernization also requires reinforcing the adaptive capabilities of business enterprise. Adaptation requires investment on a scale usually seen only during periods of reconstruction after wars. But investment in turn requires mobilization of saving commensurate with business needs. The Fabius government attempted to facilitate such mobilization by granting large amounts of capital to public enterprises, by reducing certain taxes on business, by establishing new forms of saving, and by promoting increases in profit margins. All these measures met with some success.

Modernization requires adaptation by people as well as by companies. Every worker must be prepared to cope with technological and organizational change. Young people in particular must be trained for new industrial jobs. Throughout their professional careers workers must be helped to keep current in their education and training. Thus the government made a considerable effort in the field of manpower development.

Finally, modernization requires adaptation to social as well as technological change. Economic modernization offers an opportunity for new patterns of industrial relations, including flexible work schedules and flexible work weeks. As Prime Minister Fabius said, "We will not manage the gigantic changes of the present and future without taking account of their social requirements." Thus his government asked management to implement fully the legislation of 1981– 82 designed to promote social progress. In the words of Jean Auroux, the former minister of labor, this legislation constituted "a new code of conduct in which the balance between freedom and constraint is redefined to recognize the necessities of economic and social life by the standards of the late twentieth century."

Not all companies will be able to maintain their current activities, even if they seek to modernize. They will have to change fundamentally if they wish to survive. So will the workers they employ and the regions in which they are located. Not all will succeed in this venture. Recognizing this, the Fabius government undertook an ambitious policy of conversion to alleviate the adverse situations that develop as a result of structural change. Steel, coal, shipbuilding, basic chemicals, automobiles, and textiles are all industries that must continue to reduce employment substantially. They all received large doses of public assistance to facilitate their transformations. At the same time, in the spirit of national solidarity the government adopted exceptional measures on behalf of unemployed workers. Such measures were designed to bring new activities to regions threatened by the pursuit of modernization.

Modernization requires the support of all companies, public and private, big and small. Business must devise creative solutions to difficult problems if the government is to achieve the goals of its economic plan. Public enterprise in particular must take the lead in economic recovery and develop new approaches to industrial relations. Such novelty is an essential ingredient of the modernization process. Nevertheless, we must remember the words spoken by Fabius on July 24, 1984: "The French people tell us they no longer want a distant, indifferent, bureaucratic state. Nor do they want, as some suggest, a state weak and unarmed before the financial interests. The people want the state neither to prohibit nor to require, but rather to facilitate achievement of whatever is possible."

Energy Policy as a Case Study

The main themes of the Fabius industrial policy are clearly visible in the energy sector of the economy. As secretary of state for energy in that government, I came to know this sector very well. In France the state has always taken an active interest in energy because of the magnitude and the risk of investment, the length of the adjustment process, the strategic importance of the product, and the paucity of domestic energy resources. Even in the age of coal, France lacked energy. Its lack of energy explained in part the fragility of its diplomacy and the tardiness of its industrialization. French policy relies on control of all the major branches of energy by a set of technocratically managed public enterprises. During the 1950s and 1960s these enterprises enabled the country to develop an internationally recognized oil industry; during the 1970s they permitted it to develop nuclear power so successfully that no other country in the world can match its achievement. Currently France enjoys commanding expertise in all aspects of nuclear technology.

The performance of the energy sector is crucial to the modernization of French industry. As a result, in October 1981 Parliament adopted a major plan for energy. The basic goal of the plan was to reduce dependence on foreign energy. In 1973 domestic production of energy accounted for 22.5 percent of domestic energy consumption. Just ten years later, domestic production accounted for 38.4 percent of domestic consumption. The plan of 1981 calls for a 50 percent increase by 1990 in the extent to which domestic production satisfies domestic consumption.

One way to reduce consumption of foreign energy is to increase domestic production. France is poor in fossil fuels. Although it accounts for 3 percent of world consumption, it controls only 1 percent of world production and only 0.1 percent of world reserves. To compensate, it has developed nuclear power, which will provide a plentiful and cheap source of domestic energy. France must take good advantage of such power by ensuring efficient use of electricity in industry and by exporting surplus electricity to neighboring countries.

Another way to reduce consumption of foreign energy is to promote conservation. Since 1979 France has saved between 3.5 million and 4.3 million tons of oil equivalent each year. It must continue to effect such savings.

In addition to reducing dependence on foreign supplies in general, France hopes to reduce dependence on particular suppliers. As a result, it continues to seek new sources of supply. In 1981 the Middle East was the source of 68 percent of French oil imports. By 1983 the Middle East accounted for only 45 percent, and during the first quarter of 1984 it accounted for 35 percent.

Apart from reducing energy dependence, France shall attempt to promote exports of energy-related equipment. In 1981 France's foreign energy bill was equivalent to three months of export receipts. It hopes to increase export receipts of capital goods used by energy-producing companies. Production of such capital goods accounted for 10 percent of employment in the French power industry. Currently 90 percent of domestic production of oilfield equipment is exported. The corresponding shares for mining and for natural gas equipment are 60 percent and 60 to 80 percent, respectively. France will give priority to maintaining its lead in oilfield services and equipment. It already accounts for 10 percent of world exports of the latter. It will also promote exports of nuclear power plants, of gas equipment, and of equipment for processing nuclear fuel.

In short the aim of French energy policy under Laurent Fabius was nothing less than conversion of a national weakness into an element of strength. If it succeeds, it will be industrial policy, exercised continuously over a long time, that deserves the credit.

Henri Guillaume

Implications of the New Indicative Planning

JEAN MONNET, the founder of indicative planning, adopted industrial reconstruction and modernization as his top priorities. Ever since, industrial policy and indicative planning have been discussed in the same breath. Although planners continue to stress industrial modernization, often in Monnet's vocabulary, the realities behind the words have changed. The concept of modernization to be found in the Ninth Plan (1984–88) differs markedly from the one that appeared in the First (1947–52).

The early planners tended to think of modernization in very simple terms: the greater the rate of investment, they reasoned, the greater the rate of modernization. The plans they developed were national, sectoral, and operational—national in that all economic policy was formulated by the central government, sectoral in that particular policies were tailored to the needs of particular industries, and operational in that planners helped to allocate savings among investments.[1] Today, France emphasizes the qualitative dimensions of modernization. Planning is decentralized, horizontal, and hortatory—decentralized in that regional governments participate actively, horizontal in that policies are designed to be applied neutrally to all industries, and hortatory in that planners enjoy no powers other than persuasion.

In discussing the current relationship between indicative planning and industrial policy, I shall focus exclusively on the agency I headed during the government of Laurent Fabius, the Commissariat Général du Plan (CGP). The reader should not forget that in 1965 under Prime Minister Georges Pompidou and then again after 1981 under President François Mitterrand, the Ministry of Industry increased substantially its operational responsibilities in the domain of industrial policy. A complete picture of the relationship between planning and industrial policy would have to take account of these responsibilities.

---

1. During reconstruction, France experienced a scarcity of domestic saving in relation to investment needs. As a result it relied on the Marshall Plan to finance reconstruction. The planners enjoyed considerable say in the distribution of Marshall funds.

The Formulation of Industrial Policy

Indicative planning affects industrial policy in three ways. It provides medium-term forecasts of the future; it promotes cooperation among business, labor, and government; and it promotes coordination of economic policies among the several agencies of government.

Forecasting

The CGP constructs a series of five-year projections of the French economy. Initially these projections were strictly macroeconomic in nature, but recently they have been disaggregated to the point that particular industries are studied. Each projection embodies a different set of assumptions regarding the international economic situation and the policies adopted by the French government. Taken together, the projections offer a menu of choices to policymakers as well as some indication to the private sector of where the economy is headed.

Forecasting permits the government to spot in advance such weaknesses in the domestic economy as might develop during the planning period. For example, the forecasts of the Ninth Plan revealed two areas of particular concern: without policy attention, exports would not suffice to balance imports, and business cash flow would not suffice to prompt desired investment.

Consensus through Consultation

Government, business, and labor interact in a variety of settings, but those provided by the CGP remain the most important. The modernization commissions on which these interests sit have existed since the days of Jean Monnet. Hence all parties find the setting comfortable. Because the commissions engage in discussion but not in bargaining, the atmosphere is conducive to the development of consensus.

During the formulation of the Ninth Plan, the modernization commissions were joined by two new groups. The first (the Commission Nationale de Planification) was asked to draw general conclusions from the studies of individual industries conducted by the modernization commissions. France's regional governments were represented on this task force. The second type of newcomer (the groupe de stratégie industrielle, or GSI) was charged with the study of particular problems of industrial strategy. Some of the GSIs focused on particular industries (chemicals, mechanical equipment, transportation equipment), but many studied problems afflicting multiple industries (the computerization of French society, the need to upgrade the skills of the French labor force). The groups met for eighteen months. The length of the period ensured development of good working relationships. Views were expressed openly and information was exchanged. Although the GSIs were designed to promote sharing rather than harmonizing of views—and although they failed to achieve complete consensus—they did help eliminate some of the starkest differences of opinion that had existed before their formation. For example, most members of the groups came to agree that the traditional reliance on sectoral policy should be scrapped in favor of horizontal policy.

Consider the case of energy. After the first oil shock, most OECD countries decided to promote both energy conservation and nuclear power. Although all were quick to devise plans, few persevered in their implementation. As a result, many countries suffered as much from the second oil shock as from the first.

Not France. In 1974 the French government accelerated its development of nuclear energy by increasing its nuclear budget fourfold. In 1980 when the rate of economic growth declined, the temptation arose to curtail the expansion of nuclear power. Such curtailment could easily have weakened the heavy electrical equipment industry that supplies nuclear power plants. Fortunately, France did not succumb to the temptation. By 1984, ten years after its plan had been formulated, nuclear power accounted for half of all French electricity. By 1989 the corresponding share will be 75 percent. The cost of French electricity no longer depends on the prices of natural gas and petroleum, and its price is among the lowest in Europe.

Without the interactions institutionalized within the planning framework, it is unlikely that the nuclear project could have been sustained as long as it was.

Coordination of Government Policies

The several agencies of government have their own policy agendas. An important function of the Commissariat Général du Plan is to coordinate these agendas. To perform this function, the CGP develops a broad goal for economic policy and then adds a series of particular expressions of that goal.

The broad goal of the Ninth Plan is economic modernization—to be undertaken by all economic agents. In the words of the plan itself, "There are no doomed sectors; there are only outdated technologies or companies that have yet to adjust." In keeping with this general theme, the plan identifies a variety of issues worthy of special attention. Four deserve mention here.

—The importance of equity finance.   Companies cannot modernize unless they invest, and they cannot invest without access to savings. In the past, French companies have lacked the ability to generate equity funds. In part the lack of equity could be attributed to the poverty of profit margins. More important, however, was the lack of external equity finance. The owners of enterprise directed too large a fraction of their own savings toward real estate and speculation.

—The importance of small and medium-sized companies. Most people either blame large companies for job destruction or credit them with job creation. Neither view is accurate. Job creation seems to be the domain of small and medium-sized companies in industry and in business services. The Ninth Plan seeks to encourage the creation of new companies by cutting red tape and developing venture capital.

—The importance of the qualitative features of modernization. The concept of modernization means different things to different people. Some take a technological view, but the Ninth Plan argues otherwise. It asserts that changes that are limited to plant and equipment are unlikely to improve productivity: modernization requires a change of attitudes as much as a change of machines. Planners have tried to convince their colleagues in government no less than their partners in the private sector of the importance of this view, but it has proved a difficult task. Some assert that modernization inevitably works against employment; others insist that social change derives from rather than causes modernization.

—The importance of decentralized bargaining. Human beings are the key to modernization. The best way to harness their energy is to develop comprehensive negotiations between labor and management at the company or industry level. Unless collective bargaining is extended beyond its traditional boundaries of wages and working conditions to include such matters as the introduction of new technologies and modifications in the length of the working week, it is unlikely that human resources will be deployed efficiently. Comprehensive decentralized bargaining will require a major change in French habits. The CGP is encountering stiff resistance to its views on the matter.

Implementation of Indicative Plans

Between the 1950s and the 1980s French indicative planning lost some of its luster. The planners seemed to care more for lofty discourse and wishful thinking than for implementing their ideas. To some extent their penchants were understandable: the CGP lacks both administrative and financial power.

Because it cannot enforce directly the implementation of a plan, it must resort to persuasion. In 1982 the process of indicative planning was reformed. Although the commissariat continues to lack administrative and financial power, implementation of the plans has been facilitated. The message of the Fabius government was clear: "the Ninth Plan must be put into effect." Toward this end, once a plan has been adopted, the CGP devotes most of its attention to securing finance for priority programs, to observing negotiation of planning contracts between particular ministries, public enterprises, and regional governments, and to monitoring industrial developments.

—Priority programs (*programmes prioritaires d'exécution*, or PPEs). No matter how well it is designed, a plan is unlikely to achieve success on all fronts. Hence the importance of establishing priorities. The Ninth Plan announces twelve PPEs.[2] Each receives a commitment of funds from the government that extends over several years. As Christian Goux points out elsewhere in this book, such commitments are extremely rare in France. They signal resolve on the part of the government to realize its priority goals.

—Planning contracts (*contrats de plan*). The Fabius government was reluctant to impose its views on management, labor, and regional governments. It preferred negotiation to command. In transforming its own relationships from an authoritarian to a contractual footing, it hoped to transform the nature of relationships in society as a whole. Planning contracts were concluded most frequently with public enterprises and regional governments.

Public enterprises are now major factors in the French economy. In the industrial sector they account for roughly 25 percent of value added and investment. Their incidence differs among industries: they appear very frequently in heavy industry and electronics but only rarely in light manufacturing.

The nationalizations that occurred in 1982 changed the character of the public sector. Before President Mitterrand came to power, most public enterprises were utilities or banks. Such is no longer the case. Many public enterprises are now large manufacturing corporations; they compete against foreign rivals throughout the world.

This change in the nature of public enterprise required a change in the rules laid down by government for public managers. The basic rule, as emphasized by President Mitterrand, is managerial independence. To achieve it, public enterprises are subject to the standard rules of private law. On the board of

2. For example, the plan seeks to restore equilibrium in international trade, to increase expenditures on research and development, to increase productive employment, to catalyze the development of private enterprises, to reduce dependence on foreign energy, and to devise healthy relationships with developing countries.

directors, representatives of government must share power with representatives of labor as well as with people chosen for their expertise in technology or commerce. To the extent that it wishes to influence the behavior of the companies it owns, government must resort to bargaining and contracts.

Planning contracts are developed in three stages. First, each company establishes a three-year plan for its own behavior. Typically, government intervenes only marginally in the formulation of such plans.

During the second stage, government explores the extent to which the enterprise can contribute to the goals of the national plan. The results of these studies are included in each contract. It is important to recognize, however, that government never forces public enterprises to heed the results of the studies. Even in the domain of employment, enterprises are free to choose their own course of conduct. In the jargon of French administrators, the government imposes no constraint of public service on public enterprises in the competitive sector.[3]

These studies may not bind their subjects, but they do influence their behavior. Very often the studies show the companies how much they could contribute to the public interest without jeopardizing their ability to compete. In fact, in some cases the studies show that public and private interest coincide to a greater degree than the companies had believed. For example, public enterprises now recognize that R&D activity as well as stimulation of small and medium-sized suppliers and customers in the private sector serves to benefit appreciably the public enterprise itself.

The final stage of a planning contract establishes how much the government (as owner) will contribute financially to the company's projects and how much will be put up by the company itself.

In 1984 the government signed planning contracts with virtually all public enterprises in the competitive sector. Only in steel did government and business become embroiled in prolonged discussions.

Contracts have also been worked out with regional governments. Before 1982 local governments had neither the authority nor the budget to intervene in industrial affairs. The central government took great pains to preserve its power in this area. Since 1982 the situation has changed dramatically. Regional government does now impinge on industrial development through the planning contracts.

Contracts between central and regional governments date from the Planning

---

3. By custom, public enterprises that are not public utilities are said to belong to the competitive sector.

Reform Act of 1982. The stages of contracting are similar to those followed by public enterprises. During the first stage, each region is invited to formulate its own plan; it is not obliged to accept the postulates of the national plan. During the second stage the central government looks for regional objectives that coincide with the goals—especially the priority goals—of the national plan. Typically the two levels of government share equally in the funding of projects that meet the goals of each.

Given the regional implications of the current crisis,[4] the regional governments have eagerly embraced their new powers. Unfortunately, they have found it easier to become lightning rods for dissatisfaction than to receive accolades for the success of their interventions.

Despite these difficulties the regional planning contracts have achieved some success. Through their commitment to advanced technology, all the regions are promoting the future rather than prolonging the past. Equally important, they have created an environment in which decentralized initiative is flourishing. They emphasize helping others to help themselves. Each region has developed its own set of institutions for delivering such help. Some cooperate with private enterprise through local chambers of commerce; others have developed special associations of private enterprises; still others have created local committees to support growth.

Small and medium-sized companies benefit most from the decentralization of industrial policy. Many regional governments, for instance, have promoted the diffusion to small business of the knowledge generated in the large public and private research laboratories that lie within their boundaries. The region's universities and large companies may thus be able to contribute vigor to the whole of the region's economy.

The planning contracts therefore reveal a desire to break with the traditions of the past. Rather than devise detailed strategies at the national level for particular industries, the planners are trying to foster decentralized initiative. But the traditions of Colbert die hard in France, and decentralization has experienced its fair share of difficulty and disappointment. On balance, however, the experience has been positive; it augurs well for the future.

—Monitoring industrial developments.   The impact of the Ninth Plan on the French economy will be monitored in two ways. First, the CGP will review each planning contract every year and will report its findings to Parliament. Second, a national industrial commission has been formed to diagnose the sources of,

---

4. As Raymond Lévy points out in his chapter, many industries in which employment is contracting are heavily concentrated in single-industry regions. Dismissed workers find it difficult to land new jobs in other industries.

and propose solutions to, the problems confronting industry. It does not negotiate with affected parties. Already it has studied and reported on two major industries: motor vehicles and telecommunications.[5]

Conclusion

In one short chapter it is impossible to describe all the instruments of French planning. It *is* possible, however, to show that the Commissariat Général du Plan is a staff not a line organization. It enjoys no formal authority whatsoever. This is as it should be. Nothing will promote industry more than private initiative, and no one can hope to understand the imperatives of industrial strategy better than the people who run and work in business. The most government can do is to bring the principal participants together to ensure cooperation. Only in a very few sectors—where the magnitude of investment obliges government coordination and finance—is industry-specific policy still indicated. Elsewhere, the heart of the problem is the development of imagination and flexibility. It is to be hoped that French planners understand these needs and that they will retain the best of the past while adapting their style to the new realities of the industrial world.

5. The commission comprises forty-five members drawn equally from government, business, and labor. Currently it is chaired by François Dalle, president of L'Oréal. For information, the commision relies on the groupements de stratégie industrielle, described above.

Philippe Herzog

Public Enterprises Should Promote Social Efficiency

WHEN IT came to power in 1981, the stated goal of the French Left was industrial growth. Toward that end it nationalized a number of large industrial corporations and most of the banking sector. Unfortunately, the government failed to achieve its goals, and in 1983 it formally abandoned them. As long as public enterprises pursue the same goals they pursued when they belonged to the private sector, sustained industrial growth will not occur. Such is the lesson of the French experience since 1982. Neither neoliberalism nor state intervention will solve the problem. Instead France needs a decentralized approach to industrial problems, one in which workers take managerial initiative and in which new criteria of efficiency are established.

It would be a mistake to underestimate the plight of French industry at the end of the 1970s. Steel, textiles, machine tools, coal, shipbuilding, and parts of the chemicals sector were in full decline. Some 700,000 jobs had been lost. In rising industries such as electronics and industrial equipment, French companies were losing ground to foreign rivals. Their stock of physical capital was aging, expenditures on R&D were declining, and workers were beginning to look undereducated. (Not all sectors, of course, were weak. Some companies—especially the public enterprises engaged in nuclear power, telecommunications, aerospace, and transportation, as well as some small and medium-sized companies—were doing fairly well.)

The Left attempted to inject new vigor into industry. Its aim was to assist industries in difficulty and to attempt to increase domestic production. The government supplied substantial funds for investment in industry and devised plans for growth in a number of areas, including consumer goods, steel, machine tools, and electronics.

In spite of these efforts, however, employment in the industrial sector not only continued to decline but the decline accelerated. Even industrial output failed to grow. Part of the explanation lies in the failure to implement fully the strategies mentioned above—a failure that can be attributed to the contradiction between the goal of profitability on the one hand and of investment and employment on the other. Real expenditure on industrial R&D rose at only 4 percent a year. Workers were not trained sufficiently or in sufficient numbers. Although the plan for electronics included provisions to train 400,000 people, for instance, France is very far from realizing that goal. Industrial investment remained modest in volume; its recent recovery is unlikely to be sustained.

In 1983, as everyone knows, the Fabius government abandoned the ambitions embodied in the Left's initial industrial policy. It ceased to plan the development of whole vertical streams of production, it renounced the growth of capacity in coal and steel production, and it accepted massive reductions in employment. It initiated cuts of productive capacity in the automobile industry, in engineering, and at Creusot-Loire. It seemed to accept the view that competitive strength requires reductions of employment in the short term, that modernization depends primarily on profit, and that industrial policy should aim merely at the creation of a climate favorable to enterprise. Essentially its policy differed little from the one adopted by its predecessor, even though nationalizations and expansion of workers' rights gave it potential tools that its predecessor lacked. The failure of the Fabius government to use these tools effectively in the pursuit of full employment and growth was its principal deficiency. We should not be so naive as to think that the benefits of the Fabius reforms lie just around the corner.

The Case against Market-Based Criteria of Efficiency

How then can public enterprise be deployed in the public interest? The task, in effect, is to develop new criteria of efficiency for public enterprises, as established by the workers and their unions.

—The strategy of investing to maximize financial returns must cease. Such a strategy reduces labor cost but not capital or materials costs. From society's point of view, labor must be considered a fixed cost, a resource to be renewed and enriched.

Layoffs must no longer be viewed as panaceas. In the automobile industry, for example, the cost of labor accounts for only 20 percent of value added. The real cause of low profitability is increases in the ratio of capital to output.

The current revolution in technology is based on the capabilities of people not machines. It permits significant savings in materials and machinery per unit output, but it requires a substantial investment in human beings. That is precisely the type of investment that will not occur unless traditional financial profitability is abandoned.

Needless to say, people are not the whole story. People also need the right machines with which to work. Reliance on foreign parts and equipment puts French industry at a severe disadvantage and reduces substantially the volume of employment. Producers of electronic equipment, for instance, are burdened by the high cost of key foreign components. Similarly the automobile industry will never regain its strength unless it produces more of its own manufacturing equipment.

There is also too much competition between French companies in product markets. The elimination of competitors, with the unemployment it entails, is hardly desirable; cooperation among competitors is a preferable alternative. For example, Renault and Peugeot must learn how to develop jointly the production of equipment used to make automobiles. Thomson-Brandt, the Compagnie Générale d'Electricité (C.G.E.), and Bull must do the same in electronics.

—Under present circumstances, financial profitability does not always lead to sustained economic growth. During the past three years the financial situation of industrial companies has improved: profits are up and the growth of debt has decelerated. Government subsidies of investment and R&D have increased dramatically. Capital grants and loans to public enterprises are 82 percent larger in 1983 than they were in 1980. The financial instrument created to benefit industrial investment, the *compte de développement industriel* (CODEVI), has absorbed over Fr 54 billion in private savings since the beginning of 1984.

Unfortunately this improvement in the financial health of corporations has come at a price: in the public sector 100,000 jobs have disappeared, little investment has occurred, and the national debt continues to pose problems.

Not only has the price been high, but the benefits have been modest. Companies have been using their money less to increase plant and equipment than to buy positions in other companies. Their profits have come from their financial investments and from exports made possible by the strength of the dollar. That is why the capitalized value of the stock market has been rising even though national saving has been declining. Unless these trends are reversed, any improvement in the economy will be short lived indeed.

It is wrong, therefore, of management to intimate that excessive wages account for the decline of investment. The share of labor in value added is lower today than it was in 1973. More than 60 percent of the resources available for investment are used to buy securities rather than plant or equipment; 75

percent of all profit is earmarked for distribution rather than internal use.

—Consider now the international dimension of the current situation. With respect to manufactures, France registers a trade surplus with the third world and a trade deficit with the United States, Germany, and Japan. Every time the government stimulates the economy, the trade deficit with the latter grows. Admittedly, during the past few years, France's trade deficit with the United States has abated, but her deficits with other European countries remain large. The value of the franc is supported all too precariously by high rates of interest and capital inflows.

—Public enterprises were important to the growth of the French economy after World War II. Their purchases of plant and equipment, as well as their production at low cost of energy, transport services, and several other intermediate products, stimulated efficiency throughout the industrial sector. But the enterprises nationalized in 1982, if left to their own devices, may not participate in the economy as effectively. They are all multinational enterprises; they care as much about profit abroad as they do about profit in France. Thus C.G.E. hopes to become a world leader in the production of certain kinds of robots; it does not think of serving the needs of the mass of small and medium-sized companies that forms the aging core of the French economy. In fact, despite its priorities, C.G.E. has performed extremely poorly in the field of robotics.

What is the purpose of nationalization? Is it simply to improve relations between management and labor? Is it merely to allow citizens to observe the relations between management and government? Such goals hardly justify the amount of institutional change that nationalization represents. Unless the Left can improve radically upon its conception of the mixed economy, it is doomed to fail. The sad truth of the matter is that the injection of public funds that followed nationalization appears to have been used only to prepare the public enterprises for return to the private sector.

New Criteria of Efficiency

To end the current industrial crisis, the economy must be transformed from below. If social efficiency is to prevail, labor must be accorded an increased role in corporate decisionmaking. The social and political implications of such participation could be truly revolutionary.

—The goal of labor is to improve its real standard of living. This requires an increase over time in the difference between real value added and gross profit.

Unfortunately, at the present time value added is growing slowly, and the share of profit in value added is rising. The strategy of labor should be to reduce the ratio of capital to output and to select investment projects on the basis of their ability to increase value added.

—Labor should develop new forms of cooperation among business enterprises. It should try to reduce the impact of external constraints on domestic decisions by attempting to satisfy a larger share of domestic demand. Such an attempt should not be defensive, in the sense of merely trying to keep foreigners out by artificial means, but rather should consist of efforts to develop domestic production, especially production of those capital goods that are needed for the production of final goods. Specifically, labor should promote cooperation among producers to develop whole streams of production and all regions of the country. These might take the form of guaranteed purchases offered by buyers or guaranteed prices offered by sellers. For example, labor should advocate diffusion of electric power to reduce the cost of production in most industries; it should promote the production of basic chemicals to reduce the cost of producing specialty chemicals; it should urge development of the ability to produce electronic components to reduce the cost of producing electronic goods; it should favor production of agricultural and mining equipment to stimulate the production of food and coal; and it should work to expand production of steel and new materials to stimulate the production of more plant and equipment.

In effect, measures of this sort would reflect a refusal to accept a place in the international division of labor that is dictated by the domineering economies of the world. Let me stress, however, that these measures would not reflect a desire to insulate France from the world economy. On the contrary labor would welcome increased exchange, especially if it involved cooperation. Such cooperation should be based on three principles: each country must gain in output and employment from the trade, each must improve its balance of payments, and preference should be given to relations with developing and socialist countries.

—Labor should also seek modifications of the internal organization and the financial structure of business. Cooperation must be the order of the day. Together, companies can finance projects that none could undertake alone. The practice of reciprocity within a cooperative group could increase stability, reduce risk, and thereby facilitate efficient finance.

One of the most important goals of cooperation should be regional development. Groups of companies, as well as the nationalized banks, should be called upon to finance organizations specializing in retraining workers. They should also take responsibility for making sure that no jobs are eliminated without creating at least as many new ones. In this way regional problems would be solved not through preservation of existing inefficient structures of employment but rather by decentralized responsibility for a modernization designed to increase employment.

—A successful industrial policy requires an appropriate financial policy. If new employment could be financed, the current crisis could be ended. Toward that goal, labor should favor reforms of the banking and tax systems that encourage productive investment and discourage portfolio investment. For example, the return to capital should be taxed at a variable rate to promote investments that increase employment and output. In addition, worthy but risky projects should be financed jointly by multiple banks to keep the rate of interest charged as low as possible.

Conclusion

The primary goal of industrial policy should be to increase employment and output, not profit and capital. If labor were given a greater role in the decisions of business, employment would receive the attention it deserves.

The power of labor should come at the expense of both the state and private capital. The social inefficiency of government intervention under rules of the game established by multinational corporations is by now well known. Decentralization must occur if modernization is to succeed. In particular, both economic planning and corporate finance must be accomplished in a format of cooperative decentralization.

Why did the Fabius government not try these strategies? Clearly it refused to adopt them because it was guided by the criteria of capital—the views of the industrial and international establishments to which such a large segment of the French Left belongs. In this setting, the views of the Communist party are refreshing. They constitute an attempt that is both theoretically justified and pragmatically feasible to transform the nature of management. Were the Left as a whole to adopt them, it would no longer be obliged to renounce the goals that brought it to power. In fact, it would be able to achieve them.

François Lagrange

Industrial Policy Should Be Conducted at the Supranational Level

FRANCE IS OFTEN considered the promised land of protectionism, and until World War II, such a perspective was justified. Between the reign of Napoleon I and the fall of the Third Republic, trade liberalization occurred only once (under Napoleon III) and it lasted just a few years. Despite its historical legacy, however, France can no longer be considered a protectionist country. Since 1945 the government has sought to increase French exposure to the world economy. The biggest step, of course, was participation in the European Economic Community (EEC): in signing the Treaty of Rome, France committed itself to long-term freedom of trade. After that, industrial policies differed in detail, but they all took free trade as given.

The strength of the new belief in free trade is apparent in recent events. In 1981 the parties that had dominated the French political landscape throughout the Fifth Republic were swept from power. Even so, in the face of serious economic crisis the French government retained its commitment to free trade. In June 1983 Minister of Industry Laurent Fabius declared that protectionism offered no solution to problems of structural change; it merely offered business the illusion of security. As a result of this belief, the Mitterrand government stressed modernization and adaptation to technological change. It attempted to stimulate investment, and it expanded the government budget for research and development.

Belief in the desirability of change is not enough. For a country like France, modernization will require increased cooperation with foreign countries. Given Europe's lag in technology vis-à-vis the United States and Japan, such cooperation must extend beyond as well as within the borders of Europe.

Structural Change

Both the European Coal and Steel Community (ECSC) and the EEC were created for political reasons. Nevertheless, both organizations have had major

133

Table 11-1. *Incidence of International Trade on the French Economy, 1963, 1973, 1983*
Percent of GDP

Year	Exports	Imports
1963	10.8	11.7
1973	18.2	17.6
1983	25.5	26.8

economic consequences. Not only did they achieve free movement of goods within the European Communities, but they also reduced tariffs on products imported from the rest of the world. As a result the incidence of international trade on the French economy grew dramatically (see table 11-1). As of 1983 the exposure of France to international trade appeared similar to the corresponding exposure of Germany, Italy, and the United Kingdom (see table 11-2). It exceeded that of Japan and the United States by a substantial margin.

The rise of imports and exports required the transformation of French economic structure. Between 1960 and 1980 the purpose of French industrial policy was to adapt the home economy to the exigencies of international competition. Toward this end the government promoted research and development, investment, economic infrastructure (first transportation, then telecommunications), and business education. Most important, however, the government promoted the creation of large industrial enterprises and the development of technological expertise.

Table 11-2. *Incidence of International Trade on the Large Industrial Economies, 1983*
Percent of GDP

Country	Exports	Imports
France	25.5	26.8
Germany	32.2	29.8
Italy	26.2	25.5
Japan	14.3	12.2
United Kingdom	26.7	25.5
United States	10.1	10.4

Large Companies

Except for Michelin and a few others, at the end of World War II none of the world's largest corporations were French. In the mid-1960s the government detonated a merger movement of major proportions. Most of the companies that dominate French industry today—Saint-Gobain–Pont-à-Mousson, Peugeot, Renault, Thomson, Elf-Aquitaine, CFP-Total, Aérospatiale, Banque Nationale de Paris, Union des Assurances de Paris, Assurances Générales de France, Groupe des Assurances Nationales—were involved in extraordinarily large mergers at that time.

In 1982 many of these companies were nationalized. Nationalization produced few changes in corporate structure, but in some cases product lines were concentrated in a single company by means of swapping assets among public enterprises. Thus Thomson ceded its telecommunications activities to the Compagnie Générale d'Electricité (CGE), while CGE sent to Thomson its capacity to build mass-produced consumer goods. Similarly, both Thomson and CGE ceded some of their information-technology subsidiaries to Bull. In chemicals a few assets traveled between Pechiney Ugine Kuhlmann, Rhône Poulenc, Elf-Aquitaine, and CFP-Total.

The mergers of the late 1960s and early 1970s merit two observations. First, despite the volume and the value of acquisitions, France still accounts for few of the world's largest companies. According to a recent *Fortune* listing of the 500 largest corporations outside the United States, 33 are Canadian, 38 French, 58 German, 87 British, and 136 Japanese. Only in banking is France represented well: of the world's 12 largest banks, 4 are French. Although size does not correlate perfectly with ability to compete, these figures must be considered revealing.

The second observation is that the merger movement was insular. Almost none of the mergers involved foreign companies. The attempt to create a European computer company failed;[1] the rapprochement between Fiat and Citroën never proceeded very far; Thomson's attempt to acquire Grundig failed. Only two major mergers involved companies of different nationality: Hoechst's acquisition of Roussel-Uclaf[2] and Thomson's purchase of Telefunken.

Technology

For twenty-five years now, France has attempted to develop its technological expertise in a variety of sectors, most importantly in petroleum and nuclear

---

1. In 1969 Bull, Siemens, and Philips formed a joint venture called Unidata. By 1975 cooperation among the three had ceased.
2. Although Roussel-Uclaf was nationalized in 1981, Hoechst retained a 49 percent interest in the company.

power. Elf-Aquitaine was formed to find and extract Algerian oil. The Commissariat à l'Energie Atomique and Electricité de France were given joint responsibility for developing expertise in nuclear power. In 1984, 55 percent of French electricity was of nuclear origin; ten years earlier, the corresponding figure had been only 10 percent. Nuclear power represented 20 percent of primary energy in 1984, compared with 2 percent a decade earlier. In addition to nuclear power and petroleum, France has focused on telecommunications, aerospace, and information processing.

Technological Cooperation at the European Level

In September 1983 the French government sent to each member of the EEC a memorandum titled "A New Stage for Europe: Cooperation in Research and Industry."[3] The memorandum warned of a growing gap in technology between Europe on the one hand and the United States and Japan on the other. It argued that Europe could take full credit for the first industrial revolution and substantial credit for the second, but so far no credit for the third—the one now occurring in electronics. Except in telecommunications and industrial electronic equipment, it continued, European companies are frequently outclassed by their American and Japanese rivals. Unless something is done to reverse the trend, it concluded, Europe will have to admit for the first time in its history that it does not account for most of the global advances in science and technology.

The logic of the French memorandum can be supported readily. In electronic components American and Japanese companies account for over 60 percent of the European market. In 1982 the United States produced twelve times, and Japan four times, as many integrated circuits as did the EEC. In numerically controlled machines a single Japanese company, Fujitsu-FANUC, supplies 50 percent of the world market. Some 70 percent of Japanese exports of machine tools involve numerical control; the corresponding figure for the EEC is 16 percent. As for robots, 50 percent of those now in use in Europe come from Japan, 25 percent come from the United States, and only 17 percent come from the EEC itself. In information-processing equipment, European companies account for only 10 percent of the world market; indeed, they account for only 40 percent of their own market. Eight of ten personal computers purchased in the EEC are imported from the United States, and nine of ten videocassette recorders are imported from Japan. Apple, the computer company formed

3. "Une Nouvelle Etape pour l'Europe: Un Espace Commun de l'Industrie et de la Recherche."

only in 1977, already exceeds the sales of France's largest computer company (Bull). Neither Siemens nor Bull has attained the size of Hewlett-Packard, even though Hewlett-Packard ranks only fifth among American manufacturers of information-processing equipment.

The macroeconomic consequences of these patterns are plain for all to see. Between 1971 and 1980 industrial employment in the EEC declined by 0.9 percent a year. During the same period it rose by 1.5 percent a year in the United States and by 0.7 percent a year in Japan. Since the end of 1982 the gap has widened. Recovery in the United States has stimulated investment, while European industry continues to age.

The major reason for Europe's weakness is the fragmentation of its markets. Many electronics goods are destined for purchase by governments. And yet each government of Europe maintains a separate system of procurement. Tailoring products to multiple national requirements serves to dissipate the research efforts of European producers. No wonder Europe spends more than Japan on R&D, while it accounts for just one-quarter of the Japanese number of patents and licenses.

Toward a New Industrial Policy for Europe: The French Proposal

Until recently, the European Communities did not engage in much industrial policy. Only in steel did they impinge forcefully on market structure, conduct, and performance. Today, as a result of the French memorandum, industrial policy at the EC level is receiving a new impetus. Although the development of European industry depends most importantly on the behavior of industry itself, the governments of Europe can facilitate such development by creating the appropriate environment. And the key feature of a favorable climate is cooperation. The French memorandum describes five areas in which cooperation would bear especially sweet fruit:

—Research. Currently, the research budget of the EEC represents less than 3 percent of the total budget of the Commission of the EEC and less than 2 percent of the combined research budgets of member states. To foster cooperative research, a greater share of public funding should occur at the EEC level. Cooperation should extend beyond finance to research itself. Scientists should be encouraged to circulate freely and frequently among member states. Joint research projects should be undertaken.

—Technical standards. When technical standards are set at the national level, competition is reduced. Without vigorous competition or the opportunity to realize economies of scale, European companies will never be able to catch their American and Japanese rivals.

—Trade policy.   The EEC is a very open market. Almost 50 percent of the goods it imports pay no duty whatsoever. Japan imports one-fifth the amount of industrial goods that France does. It is time to use trade policy in the service of industrial policy. Although France must honor its international commitments and recognize the benefits of free trade, it must also permit its own industries to develop to the point that they can compete in world markets.

—Joint ventures.   European companies must learn to cooperate in research, production, and marketing. To facilitate such cooperation, the antitrust laws of each country should be amended to state explicitly that the dangers of economic concentration must be evaluated at the EC level rather than at the national level.

—Economic infrastructure.   A variety of projects, including a tunnel under the English channel and networks of high-speed trains, fiber-optical cables, and data banks, would certainly prove beneficial to European industry.

The Current Status of European Cooperation

In February 1984 the EEC established ESPRIT, the European Strategic Program of Research and Development in Information Technology. ESPRIT is patterned on both Japanese and American organizations (for example, the Semi-Conductor Research Corporation and the Micro-Electronics and Computer Technology Corporation). Its goal is to reinforce European cooperation in research on information technology. The research in question is basic. It occurs before the stage at which competition would develop among companies. As a result it does not jeopardize the quality of competition in product markets.

The specifics of the program have been established cooperatively by the Commission of the EEC and by twelve interested companies.[4] The commission finances projects in advanced microelectronics, software, advanced information processing, office equipment, and automated factory equipment. Normally the commission finances 50 percent of each project it approves.[5] All types of research organizations—universities, government laboratories, and private en-

4. Three of these are British (General Electric Company, International Computers Limited, and Plessey), three are German (A.E.G., Nixdorf, and Siemens), three are French (Bull, C.G.E., and Thomson), two are Italian (Olivetti and STET), and one is Dutch (Philips).

5. Small and medium-sized companies can expect more; projects to which national governments contribute can expect less.

terprises—are eligible to receive funds. Every project, however, must involve organizations in at least two member states.

All European companies will have access to the knowledge produced by ESPRIT. The terms of access will depend on the degree to which the relevant project was financed by the commission.

ESPRIT was launched experimentally in 1983 and formally in 1984. Some 11.5 million ECUs (European currency units) were spent on pilot projects; during the first five years of its operational life, the program will enjoy a budget of 750 million ECUs (roughly $600 million). With such a budget, ESPRIT should help to begin the standardization of European equipment. Alone, however, it will hardly suffice to create parity between European companies and their rivals.

Cooperation in biotechnology research is also being encouraged. During the first quarter of 1984 France and the Commission of the European Communities proposed increased training of biotechnologists, creating a European data bank on biotechnology, harmonizing national regulations of biotechnological products, developing legal definitions of biotechnological property rights, and stimulating the production of agricultural raw materials employed in biotechnological production.[6] The commission is currently elaborating the details of this program.

Cooperation is also needed in telecommunications. In 1984 the commission urged national governments to open their procurement processes to companies from other member states. It also urged them to launch joint research projects (for example, in videocommunications). The French and German governments have already responded by agreeing to joint procurement of mobile telephones. Similarly, the French have proposed to the British a scheme for reciprocal opening of the market for central exchanges.

The Results

Many joint programs—Ariane, Airbus, and the European center for nuclear research (CERN)—can already be considered successful. Ariane, for example, is able to launch civilian satellites at one-third the marginal cost of the American space shuttle. During its first year of commercial operation, it attracted nearly $1 billion in orders, including five launchings for General Telephone and Electronics.

6. On account of the Common Agricultural Policy, European companies in biotechnology must often buy their raw materials at prices well above world market levels.

Other programs have yet to demonstrate their results. These include joint ventures in nuclear fusion, information processing, memory cards, mobile telephones, fast trains, a transonic wind tunnel, and a synchrotron. Some of these ventures involve only governments; others involve business enterprises. The nationalities of the partners tend to vary among projects.

Unfortunately, much remains to be done. Especially lacking are cooperative initiatives in the private sector. Most European companies are devoting the bulk of their efforts to American and Japanese markets. Their behavior is attributable in part to the rapid growth of those markets and in part to the heterogeneity of Europe's fiscal, financial, and legal environments. Nevertheless the most important reasons for European attention to meta-European markets lie elsewhere. In the first place, European companies believe they have more to learn from American and Japanese enterprises than they do from other European companies. In the second place, European companies are accustomed to fighting each other for supremacy in European markets. In addition, European governments are unaccustomed to surrendering leadership in particular markets. Under these conditions, cooperation among European companies poses severe psychological problems.

European industry now suffers from two problems: the research and development it undertakes is fragmented, and the scale of its companies is national not European in scope. Goods do move freely within Europe; but the ownership of capital, which affects the ability of companies to export, remains unwilling or unable to migrate easily. At a time when the United States and Japan are rationalizing their productive capacity on the basis of enormous domestic markets, the continued fragmentation of European industry poses a major threat to Europe's ability to compete.

Cooperation beyond the European Economic Community

Cooperation within Europe does not preclude cooperation with other developed nations. In fact, any attempt to avoid contacts with the most advanced economies would destroy European efforts to become competitive in world markets. Europe in general and France in particular must continue to base economic policy on increasing exposure to foreign competition. Such exposure will require cooperation. Thus France should increase its involvement in direct foreign investment as both a source and a host country. It should also foster joint research activities involving French and non-European organizations.

Direct Foreign Investment

Foreign investment in France still requires the approval of the French government. Nevertheless, for several years now the government has been favorably disposed to such investment. In fact it has subsidized foreigners willing to invest in undeveloped or depressed regions of the country.

Currently, foreigners are investing in France at the rate of $2.5 billion to $3 billion a year. Of this amount the industrial sector accounts for $1 billion. Of the total, companies from the EEC account for roughly one-half, and those from the United States account for roughly one-quarter. In 1983, for example, American companies invested $550 million in France; $315 million of this was in the industrial sector. Since 1981 Japanese investments in France have taken off. Currently Japanese interests own thirty industrial companies in France; before 1981 the number of such companies was insignificantly small.

Foreign-owned companies now occupy an important place in the French industrial structure. Measured in relation to population, the rate of direct foreign investment in France is twice as high as the corresponding rate in the United States. In 1983 foreigners controlled 2,326 French companies.[7] These companies accounted for 20 percent of value added and employment in French industry. Subsidiaries of American corporations accounted for 523 of the 2,326 companies, 37 percent of their sales, and 33 percent of their employment. IBM is the second largest taxpayer in France.

France wishes to be a source as well as a host of direct investment. Until recently, most French investment abroad fell in the energy sector (and understandably so, given France's lack of domestic petroleum). Now, however, France is investing in a wide variety of sectors. Since 1981, investment abroad has been exceeding foreign investment in France. Currently, 400 French companies own subsidiaries in the United States; 150 are industrial enterprises. In 1983 French companies invested $700 million in the United States—$300 million in industry and $140 million in energy. The most visible of recent investments are the purchase of Texas Gulf by Elf-Aquitaine and of American Motors by Renault. Other important French companies with assets in the United States are Pechiney, Saint-Gobain, and Schlumberger. Nevertheless, France still ranks only eighth among foreign direct investors in the United States.[8]

7. Foreign control occurs when foreigners own at least 20 percent of a company's equity.
8. Behind Great Britain, the Netherlands, Canada, the Dutch Antilles, Japan, West Germany, and Switzerland.

Research and Development

Despite efforts to develop European cooperation in R&D, it remains the case that French scientists spend more time in the United States than they do in the rest of the world combined. More French scientists work in California alone than in all European laboratories outside France. These scientists tend to specialize in research on outer space, the ocean, and nuclear energy.

The United States is also a major partner in industrial research, much of it in electronics and information-processing equipment. Matra, Bull, and Thomson have all signed numerous agreements with American companies.

For the moment, scientific cooperation between France and Japan remains spotty. The governments of the two countries must take steps to overcome the obstacles of distance and culture.

Conclusion

France has always found it difficult to balance its external trade. Until the 1970s the agreements of Bretton Woods and the structure of French trade permitted France to achieve equilibrium through devaluation. Given the importance of inelastic imports such as energy, not to speak of floating exchange rates, France no longer enjoys such freedom. In fact it is external balance that constrained the Mitterrand government so uncomfortably as it attempted to cope with slow growth and high unemployment. Unlike the United States, France is not the issuer of a reserve currency. It cannot use such status to finance its commercial deficits.

Despite the problems it has posed, the exposure of the French economy to world competition has been an extraordinary catalyst of progress. The French standard of living and level of technological expertise would never have grown as they did had French enterprise not been subjected to the forces of foreign competition.

Despite the discomfort of exposure, then, France should maintain its international presence. Such presence will require modernization at home and cooperation abroad.[9]

9. This chapter is based on a speech delivered in 1984, and several of the situations it discusses have evolved significantly since then. In particular, French investment in the United States has not only increased but has also begun to involve medium-sized companies as well as larger ones. Moreover, microeconomic cooperation among the European countries has increased, especially within the framework of Eureka.

Paul Mentré

The French Economy Should Be Deregulated

TO THE TRUE LIBERAL the very concept of industrial policy is anathema. The affairs of business should be left in the hands of business itself. Profitability should determine which new products to develop, which investments to undertake, and how many people to employ. With very few exceptions, activities in need of subsidy are activities that fail to serve the public interest.[1]

Economic liberalism grows poorly in French political soil. Under the weight of its interventionist past, France is unlikely to deregulate its economy either quickly or completely. Nevertheless a basis for optimism does exist. Philosophically speaking, deregulation should be congenial to political parties of the right. Unfortunately as long as those parties inhabited the corridors of power, they were reluctant to abstain from intervention. But their absence from power between 1981 and 1986 should have forced them to appreciate the importance of deregulation. Perhaps they are now prepared to embrace two propositions: that industrial policy is no substitute for sound macroeconomic policy and that the only valid industrial policy is one that relies primarily on companies and markets.

The Record of Selective Intervention

Since World War II, French microeconomic policy has displayed three distinctive features: a large number of public enterprises, a large number of regulations at the industry level, and a large number of government subsidies. The regulations date from the German occupation; the subsidies are supposedly coordinated within the framework of indicative planning.

---

1. Even believers in the market recognize, of course, the importance of government intervention in the presence of externality.

According to those who believe in industrial policy, this mix of various kinds of government intervention deserves credit for the successes of several French industries—those that produce equipment for nuclear power, aerospace, and telecommunications, for example. A quick look at these industries, however, reveals the real reason why public policy has "succeeded": in each case government has bought most of the industry's output. Once government committed itself to the purchase of specific products and ignored the business cycle in its temporal pattern of procurement, the steady growth of these industries was ensured.

Unfortunately most goods are not bought primarily by government. Even in such advanced industries as electronics, information processing, biotechnology, and energy, consumption decisions are made by large numbers of heterogeneous economic agents. Government cannot control the preferences of such a hodgepodge.

Most countries have reacted to decentralization by deregulating their economies. The rationale for their behavior is compelling: deregulation develops the flexibility of an economy. In France, however, the early decisions of the Socialist government ran counter to this global trend. For example, in 1982 the government nationalized five large industrial companies and most of the commercial banks it did not own already. Together with their subsidiaries, the newly nationalized companies raised the public share of industrial output from 18 to 32 percent. Among companies employing at least 2,000 people, the government now controls 47 percent of industrial output (compared to 19 percent in 1980).

The government believed that microeconomic interventions in the form of nationalizations would help it improve the performance of the economy.[2] Specifically it hoped that stimulating the public sector would entail the growth of the economy as a whole. The government based its hope on the conviction that private shareholders had been failing to invest sufficiently in their enterprises.

In retrospect the government's position can be seen to have depended on two faulty premises. First, the government misconstrued the role of large industrial corporations in a modern economy. Such corporations contribute primarily by their development of a vigorous coterie of smaller enterprises. This development requires the large enterprises to rely heavily on subcontractors and it also requires them to leave the securities market to their smaller brethren. In other words, large enterprises should not be expected to grow rapidly,

2. Undoubtedly, ideology as well as economics played a role in the nationalizations. The Socialist and Communist parties have always advocated nationalization. Their joint platform of 1972 awarded high priority to the practice.

and they should finance such growth as they achieve with internal funds. Unfortunately the government chose to finance the large nationalized corporations from its own budget. The resulting government debt has crowded those issuing private securities out of the capital market.[3]

The government's second faulty premise involved the connection between France and the world economy. The government seemed to believe that the existence of world market prices would not prevent the newly nationalized companies from adopting "social" goals.[4] Unfortunately, once the government decided to continue to participate in the European Communities and the European Monetary System, as it properly did in 1983, isolation from the world market became impossible.

By 1983 the government recognized the errors of its ways. To its credit it took steps to improve the financial condition of private enterprise, but the results of this change in policy have remained modest. Internal finance now plays the role it did just after the second oil shock, and that role is far too small.

Creating a Favorable Business Environment

The best way to promote industrial development is not to intervene in particular industries but rather to create a favorable environment for business enterprise. Such an environment consists of macroeconomic equilibrium and microeconomic competition.

The Importance of Macroeconomic Policy

In an economy as open as that of France, macroeconomic policy must ensure external balance. Unfortunately France has not achieved such balance in recent years. In 1981 and 1982 the government embarked upon a strategy of consumption-led growth. By 1982 that strategy had resulted in a commercial deficit of Fr 100 billion (2 percent of GDP). Recognizing the problem, the government reversed direction and curbed consumption. Nevertheless, despite a series of devaluations, external balance will be difficult to achieve. Worse, France will have to devote much of its saving to service of the public debt. According to the Institut National de la Statistique et des Etudes Economiques

3. In 1983 the amount spent by government to finance public enterprise was roughly equal to the government's budgetary deficit.
4. The Communist economists in particular have demanded new directions for public enterprise. See, for example, the chapter by Philippe Herzog in this book.

(INSEE), the debts of the past will condemn France to grow at a rate 1 percent below that enjoyed by other industrial countries. In the past, France was able to grow faster than did those other countries. Thus it is not without pain that the French have learned that external balance requires investment-led rather than consumption-led growth.

Balance must also be achieved in the labor market. Over the past ten years, GDP has grown at roughly similar rates in Europe and the United States. Nevertheless, European employment has stagnated, while employment in the United States has grown by 2 percent a year. Undoubtedly, many factors must be taken into account to explain this contrast. The most important, however, are the comparative evolutions of labor productivity and labor price. Real wages cannot be allowed to rise more rapidly than does labor productivity. To allow for growth of the former, the latter must be stimulated.[5] Alternatively the government must prevent the explosion of wages. To do so, it should abolish all indexation, with the exception of the minimum wage.[6] Unfortunately, despite government efforts to question automatic increases in wages in 1982 and 1983, France has not been able to secure equilibrium in the labor market for over a decade.

Macroeconomic balance should allow for steady economic growth. The key to growth is productive investment by the private sector. Such investment is stimulated most effectively by reducing government taxes and expenditures,[7] maintaining a moderate budgetary deficit, substituting a macroeconomic for a selective monetary policy, and moderating wage increases in the public sector. These policies will prevent the crowding out of private investment and will dampen adverse movements in wages and prices.

The Importance of Competition

Industrial policy is not the only microeconomic policy available to government. Stimulating vigorous competition is another. In the French context, stimulating competition would consist of deregulation, privatization, and the development of a strong antitrust law. Let us see how these principles might be

5. Contrary to popular opinion, increases in productivity do not entail increases in unemployment. See the report of France's Conseil Economique et Social, "Productivité, Croissance, Emploi," *Journal Officiel de la République Française* (August 14, 1984).

6. Similarly, only need-based welfare programs should be allowed to increase benefits automatically with the cost of living.

7. Some 45 percent of French national income passes through the hands of government. This percentage is too high. Special priority should be given to the reduction of payroll taxes born by business. After that, the taxation of corporate income should be lightened.

applied in four broad sectors of the economy: energy, transportation, telecommunications, and finance.

Energy. In 1928 the government granted itself a legal monopoly for importing petroleum. It delegated this monopoly jointly to petroleum companies willing to behave as the government desired. It established a regime in which all producers had to receive authorization before they could build refineries and pipelines, import crude oil, stock petroleum products, build gasoline stations, or change prices. The government used its authority to ensure that French refining companies could grow and prosper in a world dominated by the big Anglo-Saxon companies.

This system is no longer adapted to the realities of petroleum markets. The French petroleum industry is no longer a tender infant. More important, since the first oil shock the major problem of Western oil companies has been to develop the flexibility necessary to adjust to rapidly changing conditions. The welter of regulation prevents such adjustment in France.

Not only are the French regulations outmoded, but they are also costly to consumers. According to a government commission formed in 1974 to study the petroleum industry, from 1960 to 1974 the prices of petroleum products in France exceeded the corresponding prices in Germany by 10 percent.[8] In Germany such prices are not controlled, and competition is relatively free.

Among the developed market economies, France alone has established a legal monopoly for importing natural gas, a monopoly delegated to Gaz de France (GDF). Such a monopoly lacks economic justification. Any company should be allowed to purchase natural gas, whether for its own use or for resale to other French companies. At most, GDF should retain a monopoly of the distribution of gas to individual households.

Legal monopolies also exist in the importation, transport, and distribution of electricity. To some extent technology justifies the creation of such monopolies. Nevertheless markets are used less fully than they might be. Large industrial users of electricity should be allowed to import electricity themselves, the natural-monopoly elements of Electricité de France (EDF) should be kept separate from those that fail to display increasing returns, and marginal cost pricing should be adopted wherever possible.

Finally, a legal monopoly exists in the importation of coal. Delegated to the Association Technique d'Importation Charbonnière (ATIC), it should be terminated entirely.

Once these legal monopolies have been limited, the prices of energy to

8. *Sur les Sociétés Pétrolières Opérant en France: Rapport de la Commission d'Enquête Parlementaire* (Paris: Union Générale d'Editions, 1974).

French industries should no longer deviate from world market levels. Given the continuation of monopolies in the distribution of natural gas and electricity, government intervention in the prices facing households must continue to exist in some form.

Transportation. Transportation is another sector in which market forces should be unleashed. The most serious problem currently lies in trucking. Since the 1930s the government has sought to protect the French national railways (SNCF) from the competition of trucks. Under a law passed in 1949 the traffic of each trucking company is limited by quota. During the 1970s the government of the day sought to change this system. In fact the report of the Guillaumat Commission urged the abolition of quotas, price controls, and legal restrictions of entry into the market.[9] Unfortunately in 1982 a new government opted once again for quotas.

Freedom to enter the market, to choose one's routes, and to select one's prices should be granted not only to truckers but also to river barges and to domestic airlines. Such deregulation would, of course, require major changes on the part of the SNCF.

Telecommunications. France is the only large industrial country that monopolizes postal, telephonic, and telegraphic services as well as the dissemination of television programs.[10] At one time technology justified these monopolies, but that time is now past. Rather than deregulate accordingly, the French government has sought to extend its monopolies, to control the producers of telecommunications equipment, and to decide what types of R&D should be undertaken in this area. As a result it has retarded the development of initiative outside the government's orbit.

The government should promote private television to ensure competition for the public networks. It should also foster competition in long distance telecommunications, for example, by creating private telecommunications satellites.

Financial services. French monetary policy is microeconomic in nature. It is based on discrimination by the Bank of France both in discount rates and in quantitative controls on the offer of credit. In addition to such discrimination the financial authorities have ensured the survival of a wide variety of channels linking ultimate savers and ultimate investors. The terms of borrowing tend to differ enormously among channels.

France must join the deregulation of financial services that is sweeping the United States, Japan, and even the United Kingdom. Financial intermediation

---

9. *Orientation Pour les Transports Terrestres* (February 1978).

10. France now permits limited competition between public and private radio stations. Late in 1985 it awarded rights to operate one private television channel, and it was considering awarding rights for another.

must be reduced. Financial enterprises must be forced to compete not simply among themselves but also with other forms of connection between savers and investors.[11]

Promoting Competition

These four sectors of activity merely illustrate a general need for competition. What can government do to promote competition throughout the economy?

First, with the exception of natural monopolies the government should sell all of the enterprises it owns to private interests. Because the French stock market can absorb only Fr 10 billion or so of new issues each year, privatization cannot be accomplished overnight. Nevertheless recent British experience confirms the feasibility of the strategy. The French government might wish to offer tax incentives to some or all of those who subscribe, and it might wish to take upon itself the obligation to repay some of the debt of the privatized companies.

Second, the government should terminate its control of prices. Continuously since 1945 the French government has enjoyed the authority to fix prices, and it has not hesitated to use that authority. Whether partially or completely, the government has controlled the prices prevailing in the economy. The ordinance of 1945 that enables this must be repealed.

Third, the government should strengthen the agencies charged with enforcing competition law. In 1977 the government did move to fortify the Commission de la Concurrence, but the commission remains weak. France must adopt a system comparable to that now found in Germany.

Fourth, the government should put its weight behind creation of a genuine common market in Europe. Toward this end it should favor harmonizing technological norms, deregulating sectors like agriculture, abolishing discrimination in. public procurement, and reinforcing European antitrust law. It is time for Europe to acknowledge the connection between American economic dynamism and American antitrust legislation.

Finally, the government should examine the effects of its own actions on competition—the effects, for example, of professional licensing, limitations on large-scale retailing, deliberate obstruction of imports, and exemption of certain vertical restraints from prosecution under the antitrust laws. In so doing the government would be following in the footsteps of the Armand-Rueff Commission, which drew France's attention to the importance of competition a quarter of a century ago.

---

11. Government should be allowed, however, to establish fiscal incentives for savings destined to finance certain types of investment.

Conclusion

Industrial policy is not the way to promote industrial development. In fact selective intervention by government is justified in very few cases. The most important of these is investment in knowledge. After all, the social value of information is likely to exceed its private value. Not only is information a public good, subject to the free-rider problem, but the appropriate rate of discount for investments in information lies below the privately determined rate of interest. For both reasons the private sector will invest too little in knowledge.

If research and development in France and the United States are compared, there is some similarity in both the amount spent on research in relation to GDP and the amount spent by government in relation to the private sector. What distinguishes the two countries is the degree to which research is actually conducted by business enterprise. In comparison with the United States, France (like Europe) spends little of its research money in the private sector. This tendency should be reversed. Government should offer more tax advantages to companies that finance their own projects. In addition, without ignoring the importance of basic research it should spend more of its own money in the private sector.

But R&D is the exception that proves the rule. Further development of the French economy requires that the government recognize the value of competition. Only in a regime of competition will French companies develop the ability to compete.

Statistical Appendix

Table 12-1. *Average Annual Percentage Increase in Civilian Employment, by Country, Selected Periods, 1968–82*

Country	1968–74	1974–80	1980–82
United States	2.3	2.3	0.1
Japan	0.7	0.9	0.9
West Germany	0.4	-0.2	-1.2
France	1.0	0.2	-0.4
United Kingdom	0.2	0.1	-3.4
Italy	0.2	0.9	0
Canada	3.1	2.6	-0.3

Source: Conseil Economique et Social, "Productivité, Croissance, Emploi," *Journal Officiel de la République Française* (August 14, 1984), p. 25.

Table 12-2. *Average Annual Percentage Increase in Real Gross Fixed Capital Formation (Machinery and Equipment), by Country, Selected Periods, 1960–80*

Country	1960–68	1968–73	1973–80
United States	7.5	6.2	3.7
Japan	14.6	12.2	3.2
West Germany	3.9	8.0	3.2
France	8.6	9.8	2.9
United Kingdom	4.9	3.9	2.5

Source: Conseil Economique et Social, "Productivité, Croissance, Emploi," p. 55.

Table 12-3. *Average Annual Increase in Total Factor Productivity, by Country, 1971–73 and 1974–82*
Percent of GDP

Country	1971–73	1974–82
United States	2.3	−0.1
Japan	4.2	2.4
West Germany	2.3	1.3
France	3.4	1.6
United Kingdom	3.5	0.9

Source: Conseil Economique et Social, "Productivité, Croissance, Emploi," p. 105.

Table 12-4. *Average Annual Percentage Increase in Real Value Added in Industry, by Country, Selected Periods, 1960–83*

Country	1960–68	1968–74	1973–79	1979–83
United States	4.9	3.4	1.6	−1.1
Japan	13.1	12.2	4.3	6.6
West Germany	4.4	5.2	1.6	−0.7
France	6.9	7.0	2.4	−0.8
United Kingdom	3.1	2.2	0.6	−6.0
Italy	7.1	5.2	2.3	1.9
Canada	6.3	5.8	2.3	0.5

Source: Conseil Economique et Social, "Productivité, Croissance, Emploi," p. 50.

Figure 12-1. *Evolution of Industrial Employment, Selected Countries, 1960–81*

Thousands of people
Logarithmic scale

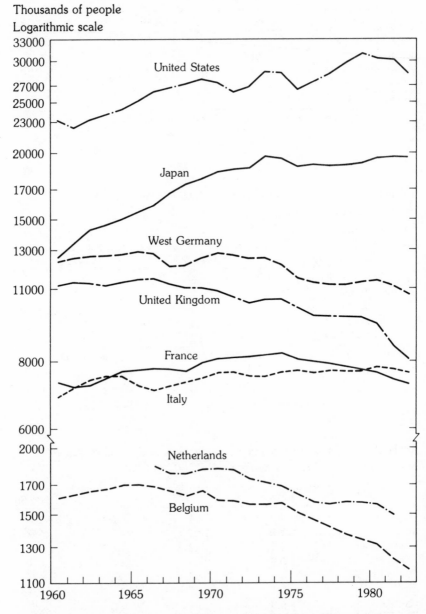

Source: Counseil Economique et Social, "Productivité, Croissance, Emploi," *Journal Officiel de la République Francaise* (August 14, 1984), p. 26.

Figure 12-2. *Importance of Internal Finance to French Corporations, 1959–82*

Rate of internal finance[a]

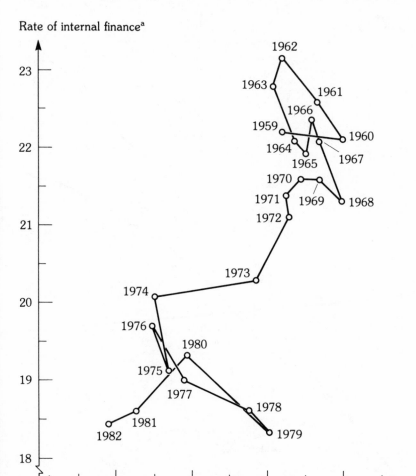

Rate of investment[b]

Source: Conseil Economique et Social, "Productivité, Croissance, Emploi," p. 58.
a. Gross saving of corporate and quasi-corporate enterprises divided by their gross capital formation.
b. Gross fixed capital formation of corporate and quasi-corporate enterprises divided by their gross value added.

Figure 12-3. *Factor Productivity in France, 1959–81ª*

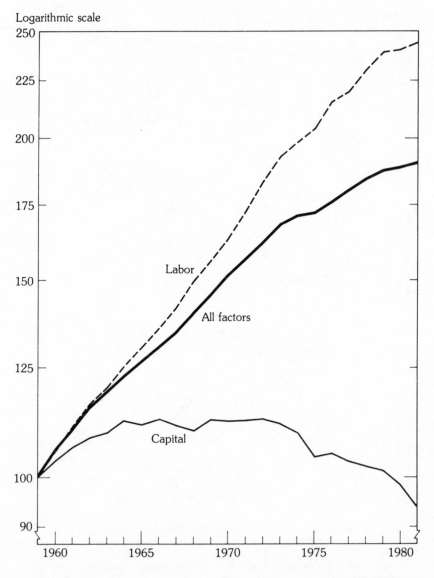

Logarithmic scale

Source: Conseil Economique et Social, "Productivité, Croissance, Emploi," p. 99.

a. Labor productivity is measured as the volume of GDP divided by the number of hours worked. Capital productivity is measured as the volume of GDP divided by the stock of gross fixed assets at the beginning of the year.

Figure 12-4. *Relationship between Investment and Employment in France,
1959–73 and 1974–81*[a]

Average annual percentage
increase (decrease) in employment

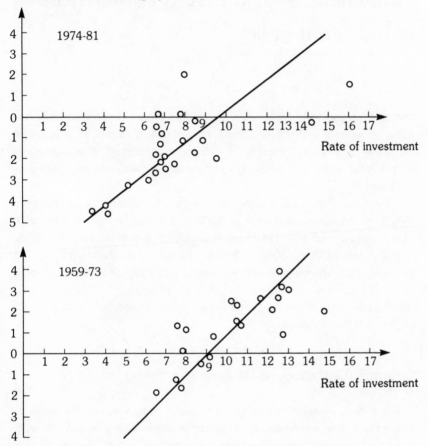

Source: Conseil Economique et Social, "Productivité, Croissance, Emploi," p. 115.
a. Each observation represents one industry. For 1959-73 the industrial sector is broken down
into twenty-one industries. For 1974-81 it is broken down into twenty-four industries. The rate of
investment is measured as total investment divided by the stock of gross assets at the beginning of
the year.

Christian Goux

Parliament Should Play a Larger Role in Industrial Policy

IMPLICITLY or explicitly the United States, like France, engages in industrial policy. American antitrust laws and trade legislation, as well as government procurement, impinge forcefully on industrial structure. The dismantling of AT&T is but one of many examples of industrial transformation inspired by government.

If France and the United States both engage in industrial policy, however, they do so in very different ways. In the United States the legislative branch is able to play a major role in the process.[1] Such is not the case in France. Although former Prime Minister Laurent Fabius, when minister of industry, proclaimed it "inconceivable that a matter as important as industrial modernization should be absent from parliamentary discussion,"[2] it remains the case that the executive branch dominates the formulation, execution, and evaluation of French industrial policy.

Structural Limitations on Parliamentary Power

The French constitution establishes a hybrid political system. In some respects the system is presidential; in others it is parliamentary. In most respects, however, it favors the executive over the legislative branch. The president of the republic is elected directly on the basis of universal suffrage. This confers on him substantial leverage over the prime minister—the nominal head of government. From the birth of the Fifth Republic in 1958 until the parliamentary election of 1986, the prime minister and the president represented the same political viewpoint. As a result the government and the president—the two elements of the executive branch—presented a united front vis-à-vis Parlia-

1. See the chapter by Donald Riegle in this volume.
2. Statement of the Government on Industrial Policy, October 11, 1983.

ment. And because the parliamentary majority also shared the political views of the president, Parliament was reticent to criticize the executive branch. Constitutionally, legislative powers are enumerated rather than residual. Legally, the executive branch sets the agenda of the legislature. It can force Parliament to vote for a bill by attaching the implication of no confidence to a negative vote. Furthermore, the budgetary powers of Parliament are tightly circumscribed. Under Article 40 of the constitution and the Ordinance of January 2, 1959 (relating to finance bills), members of Parliament can neither cut government revenues nor create or increase government authorizations to spend. Thus Parliament cannot substitute its own budgetary choices for those of the government even if aggregate expenditures would not rise.

Parliament is also limited in its expertise. Until recently it has been composed almost exclusively of doctors, lawyers, and civil servants. The greatest ambition of the civil servants has been to migrate to the executive branch. Under such circumstances it has been difficult to develop the economic skills necessary for Parliament to engage in industrial policy.

The political system is not the only source of parliamentary weakness. The structure of French industry is very complicated; so, therefore, are French industrial problems. The complexity of French industrial structure is illustrated by the number and scale of industrial companies. As of January 1, 1983, the national institute of statistics (INSEE) counted 2,801,389 companies operating in France. Of these, 1,855,394 were unincorporated and 922,511 registered fewer than five salaried employees. During January 1984 alone, 6,064 companies were formed and 1,950 disappeared.

Whatever the scale of the company, the problems encountered in dealing with it are industrial and scientific. Unfortunately Parliament is poorly equipped to consider such problems. Parliament is perfectly capable of evaluating the desirability of a law that makes certain behavior a crime, but it cannot evaluate easily a law that promotes one method of rolling steel at the expense of another. Thus Parliament lacks the information as well as the judgment to decide issues of this sort. Most of its information comes from the executive branch, even though Parliament is supposed to provide an independent source of insight. (The one exception to Parliament's lack of involvement in industrial affairs is its immersion in the military budget and therefore in military procurement, a major component of French industrial policy.)

Not only does Parliament fail to participate in formulating policy, it is not even able to follow the extent to which the budget it votes for has been executed faithfully.

The chief means available to Parliament to deal with industrial policy is the submission of written and oral questions to the government. Rarely, however, do such questions provoke genuine debate. In the case of French nuclear policy, for example, Parliament was utterly silent. It said nothing when the government abandoned the graphite-gas process developed in France, in favor of Westinghouse's technology. It said nothing when the government and Electricité de France decided in 1974 to accelerate the development of nuclear power. It has watched as the executive branch has decided where to build nuclear power plants. And nuclear policy is not a special case. The same lack of participation occurs in regulating communications, another sector subject to pervasive industrial policy.

Unfortunately Parliament's powers of investigation are limited. Other than asking questions of the government, it can deploy its six standing committees (commissions permanentes), it can create select committees (commissions d'enquête), and it can also ask the authors of its committee reports (rapporteurs) to study the execution of the budget.

In principle the rapporteurs of the finance committee are empowered to obtain all necessary financial and administrative documents from the executive branch—including those designated as confidential. But although such power is available at all times, it is exercised primarily during budget season.

Parliament has frequently used its power to create select committees. It has used them to study the petroleum industry (1974), energy policy (1974), the aerospace industry (1976), and the textile industry (1981). To take advantage of procedural flexibility, it has also created some quasicommittees—the factfinding boards (missions d'information). One has studied the issue of nuclear safety (1979), while others have studied energy policy (1981), the automobile industry (1981), and the paper and board industry (1983).

Nevertheless Parliament faces difficulties. Budgets are hard to follow because of the way they are constructed. Their divisions can be misleading and the government's tendency toward funding broad agencies such as the Fonds de Développement Economique et Social (FDES) or the Fonds de Modernisation Industrielle (FMI) also complicates the process. Regrettably, subsidies can flow to given recipients through many channels, and it is difficult to reconstruct them all. As former Prime Minister Fabius said when he was still minister of industry, "the system is extraordinarily complex. No one—certainly not the owner of a small or medium-sized business—can be expected to orient himself within it."[3]

The total absence of parliamentary control over the credit policy of the

3. Statement of the Government on Industrial Policy, October 11, 1983.

government is also critical. Government influence on the banking system is a key element of French industrial policy.

Finally, even when Parliament gets some of the information it needs, the information is often out of date. Not until mid-1984, for instance, did it receive the report of the FDES for 1981–82.

The Future

I am optimistic that Parliament will begin to exercise more control over the behavior of the executive branch. First, the American experience suggests that an office of technology assessment controlled by the legislative branch can be very useful indeed.[4] Given the institutional differences between France and the United States, however, Parliament did not choose to adopt the American machinery without modification. A law passed on July 8, 1983, created a permanent joint committee of the Senate and the National Assembly. The committee comprises eight representatives of each body and is advised by a commission of nineteen eminent scientists. The chairman of any legislative committee or the chairman of any political bloc within one of the chambers may ask the committee to investigate a matter within its jurisdiction. The committee enjoys the same fact-finding powers as are available to other legislative committees.

Without such a committee, as Jean-Yves Haberon warned, there can be no real discussion of the issues, no informed choices, and no evaluation of past decisions.[5] Nevertheless, such an organization cannot be considered a panacea. In the words of Senator Jean-Marie Rausch:

> One cannot expect an office of technology assessment to alter decisionmaking overnight. Although it can reinforce the Parliament's ability to oversee the executive branch, it is no substitute for genuine democratic control of technological choice. It is at the level of individual citizens that the environmental impact of new industrial organizations must ultimately be decided.[6]

Parliament has also begun to devote more time to major debates on important economic issues. In 1981 it debated energy policy; in 1983 it focused on industrial policy. I expect more such debates in the future.

In addition Parliament is gaining some control over the process of economic planning. It was responsible for amending the Ninth Plan to include a major

4. See National Assembly Report No. 1743 for 1983.
5. AJDA, October 20, 1983.
6. Senate Report No. 82 for 1982.

project: cooperative industrial policy within the European Communities. It has also accorded five-year budgets for the four programs of high priority that constitute the core of the plan. Such medium-term strategies will facilitate oversight of the plan and increase cooperation between Parliament and the Commissariat Général du Plan.

Finally, Parliament has been successful in revising the budgetary process. It is now making three-year projections of revenues and expenditures. It has also revised the system by which it grants subsidies, and it has altered the system of budgetary authorizations—a system subject to much experiment over the past few years.

Conclusion

In periods of economic crisis citizens turn to Parliament for help. In France Parliament has tried to gain some control over the budget it nominally approves. I hope it will be successful. Without a broadly based industrial policy, France may find itself without an industrial sector. It is impossible to have a modern industrial system without a modern political system.

François de Combret

What Can the United States Learn from the French Experience?

DURING the presidential campaign of 1984 industrial policy became a major issue in the United States. The Democrats proposed creation of a government investment bank similar to Franklin Roosevelt's Reconstruction Finance Corporation; the Republicans opposed not only such a bank but virtually all forms of industrial policy. Why was industrial policy suddenly on the American agenda? In the United States as in other developed countries, the industrial sector is undergoing tremendous transformation. Some industries that have been important for a century are now collapsing. Others, especially those in electronics and biotechnology, are emerging and developing rapidly. Competition from the third world merely intensifies the resulting structural dislocation.

Dislocation causes pain and suffering, especially in declining industries and regions. Those who suffer are searching for wonder drugs, policies that might heal the wounds of threatened industries, avoid bankruptcies, accelerate the birth of new industries and new technologies, and protect the country against the competition—always unfair, it seems—from Japan and the third world. It has come to be felt that industrial policy might be a wonder drug, that it might work in the United States as it is supposed to have worked in countries like France. No wonder the Brookings Institution is examining the implications of French industrial policy for a potential American counterpart.

What does the French record show? Does it support the confidence of the Democrats, or does it confirm the fears of the Republicans? I shall argue that the French experience has neither positive nor negative implications for the United States. Industrial policy depends heavily on the institutional as well as the economic environment in which it operates. The institutional environments of France and the United States differ so radically that the experience of one country cannot be applied to the other.

Differences between the French and American Environments

During the past several years I have observed industrial policy in France and the United States in both the public and the private sector. For more than ten years I participated in the formulation of industrial policy within the French government. For the past three years I have been involved in industrial policy of a different sort: the mergers and acquisitions arranged by a large investment bank in New York.

Experience has taught me that every developed country engages in industrial policy. The United States is no exception. When the American government spends money on research and development, when it procures military equipment, when it offers tax incentives for investment, when it provides special loans for regional development, it is behaving very much like its French counterpart. The question then is whether the French system of coordination and organization of policy could be adopted with profit by the United States.

However successful it might have been, French industrial policy is so deeply rooted in French culture that it is difficult to see how it could be transferred to another country. Three features of the cultural environment are especially important in this regard.

The first is the French system of education. At the top of this hierarchical system lie a few elite schools—the Ecole Polytechnique, the Ecole Nationale d'Administration, and the Ecole Normale Supérieure. It is not surprising that all of the French speakers at this conference come from these schools, for these educational institutions train people to become high-level civil servants. In practice only the weakest graduates head immediately to the private sector. The private sector is considered a demotion. The American system leads in the opposite direction. It inculcates the belief that public service is certainly not the only and probably not the best choice of career.

The second major difference between the French and American environments relates to the relative importance of technocratic and commercial values. In France technology is king. The French are very proud, and justifiably so, of their capabilities in the civil and military branches of nuclear technology. They are also very proud of the supersonic transport, the Concorde, even though it has proved to be a tremendous financial failure. Beyond these well-known projects, I could cite color television. The French believe they invented the best system of color television in the world. Unfortunately, in spite of the quality of the picture, other countries chose other systems on which to base their technological standards. As a result the French system is difficult to export. But that, to the French mind, is a detail. The important thing is the satisfaction that comes from believing one's product is best in the technological sense.

Given the technological perspective, it is hardly surprising that public administration also occupies a privileged position in the pecking order of professions. Not only does basic research and engineering require strong government support, but the choice of technological standards becomes a decision of major importance.

In the United States, emphasis is placed not on technology and its administration but rather on commerce and money. Take the case of IBM. IBM is a commercial but not a technological wonder. The Apple computer may be innovative technologically, but it has not suffered commercially: although it was created less than ten years ago, Apple is now worth more than $1 billion. No wonder a recent issue of *Forbes* contained an article about the 400 richest people in the United States. In France, if one is rich, one is expected to be ashamed of his status.

The final major difference between France and the United States relates to size. Geographically the United States is almost a continent, while France is merely a country. Demographically there are five Americans for each Frenchman. At current exchange rates, American GNP is ten times as large as its French counterpart. Comparisons of this sort are easy to make, but they fail to convey fully the difference in perspective that results.

When I arrived in the United States, Texaco was in the process of buying Getty Oil for $10 billion. But Getty ranks only fifteenth among American petroleum companies, and many American deals now involve more than $10 billion. To a Frenchman, however, this acquisition appeared absolutely astounding. When one considers that the French government recently nationalized many of the largest industrial corporations as well as several large financial institutions, all for the same price of $10 billion, one can appreciate the sense of wonder.

From the standpoint of industrial policy, scale breeds flexibility. In the United States there are many companies in the electronics business. When one goes bankrupt, the existence of the industry is not jeopardized. The disappearance of Osborne Computer, for example, had virtually no impact on the structure of the American market. In France, however, the number of important companies in each sector is very limited. If Bull had gone bankrupt, the future of the entire French electronics industry would have been placed in doubt. Hence the need to rescue companies in trouble.

Rescue can come from public or private sources. In the United States private sources may be adequate. Every day the *Wall Street Journal* reports another acquisition or merger worth at least $100 million. When large companies run into trouble, there are many potential rescuers. In France, however, the market for large corporations is extremely thin. If such corporations are to be saved, the government must often intervene.

Differences in Industrial Policy

To appreciate the way a public financial institution of the sort proposed by the Democrats would function in the United States, one cannot merely examine the performance of its French analogue. Public investment banks comprise merely the tip of France's industrial policy iceberg. The performance of such banks depends on the policies in place for other parts of the economy. In this section I shall describe just a few of the supporting policies that distinguish France from the United States.

Control of foreign investment. Recently I read in the newspaper that Nestlé had bought Carnation—a company worth $3 billion. Nestlé was able to effect this acquisition without asking anyone in the American government. To a Frenchman such behavior is astonishing. In France, even under relatively market-oriented regimes, such acquisitions would be impossible without prior approval of the government.

Control of credit. The French financial system is aptly described as capitalism without capitalists. The government owns virtually all of the banks. Savings and loan associations funnel the savings they collect to the Treasury Department. Can anyone imagine such a system in the United States?

The government's control of credit is especially important in France because the stock market is very small. Indicative of the weakness is the manner in which France evaluates its companies: it merely examines sales revenue, an indicator of company size. Compare this with the approach taken in the United States. Here, the principal criterion is earnings per share. Use of such a criterion presupposes concern with reputation in the stock market, and such reputation matters only in a system characterized by a multitude of shareholders.

Taxes. At the educational institutions where French civil servants are trained, the best possible tax system is defined as the one that allows the government to pluck the chicken without making it scream. As a result, the French invented the tax on value added. Unlike the U.S. system, which offers strong incentives to invest via the system of credits on direct taxes, the French system guarantees substantial revenue to government. A great deal of national income flows through the government in France; in the United States it flows directly from households to business enterprises.

Welfare state.   In France the government makes it very difficult for a company to reduce its number of employees (Raymond Lévy has attested to that in his chapter, and Jacques Calvet, the chairman of Peugeot, could have done the same). Such is not the case in the United States. In my capacity as a New York investment banker, I was given the task of restoring the financial health of an American steel company. I promise you that layoffs can be accomplished much more easily in the United States than in France.

Antitrust laws.   The French government is skeptical of the value of competition. At the same time that AT&T was being dismantled in the United States, the French government was creating a monopoly in the telephone business.

Conclusion

I could continue at length this discussion of differences in policy environment between France and the United States, but my point should now be clear: a public financial institution would find itself surrounded by complementary instruments of policy that differ markedly between the two countries. That is why one cannot infer much from the French record about the prospects of such a bank in the United States. Whether the French system is good or bad is beside the point. The French system is for France; the American system is for the United States.

Roger B. Porter

Industrial Policy and the Role of Government in the Economy

IN RECENT YEARS scores of conferences have been held on the role of government in the economy in general and on industrial policy in particular. Two developments fueled much of the discussion.

First, the U.S. economy seemed to perform poorly during most of the 1970s. Not only did it experience two bouts of double-digit inflation, but it also suffered from historically high levels of unemployment. As the growth of labor productivity and real GNP declined, the conviction arose that economic policy needed a new direction. Macroeconomic policy, some argued, would have to be supplemented with microeconomic policies aimed at specific industries. Such policies would improve macroeconomic performance. Because they would consist primarily of improved coordination and enhanced cooperation, their social cost would be small. Relatively painlessly, it seemed, industrial policy could improve the allocation of economic resources and raise the level of economic prosperity.

A second development was the performance of the Japanese economy. During the 1970s, labor productivity in manufacturing rose more rapidly in Japan than in the United States. Although the Japanese started from a low base, their rate of economic growth was impressive. Much of the increase in output was attributed to the Ministry of International Trade and Industry (MITI). According to its admirers, MITI assisted specific industries to become more competitive; particularly during the closing years of the decade, the ministry focused its efforts on the high-technology industries.

Some of the interest in the Japanese model was stimulated by those who argued that the future belonged to flexible, decentralized systems of production rather than to mass production techniques. Because the Japanese were considered adept at the new forms of production, borrowing from their experience would help U.S. companies to compete successfully in an era of high technology.

The Themes of Industrial Policy

Whatever the sources of their belief, virtually all advocates of industrial policy share the conviction that U.S. mechanisms of resource allocation have failed. Although the programs they propose differ markedly, it is possible to discern several common themes.

Foremost among them is an active role for government in the economy. Some proponents of industrial policy believe government should expand its role, for example, by creating a national development bank to finance new industries or technologies. Others argue that government should coordinate more effectively the myriad programs it already sponsors. Few if any argue that government should do less than what it does now. Most contend that government should intervene frequently and purposely.

A second theme is that government should intervene selectively as well as generally. It should target resources to specific sectors and industries. Some advocates want funds focused on industries with the potential "to be strong international competitors." Others want assistance for "industrial sectors and regions that particularly need help."[1]

A third element in most formulations of industrial policy is the desire to bring about "a strategic consensus among government, industry, and labor as to the basic directions in which the economy ought to move."[2] Adversarialism would give way to cooperation.

While the relative importance of these themes may vary among advocates, most believers in industrial policy favor an active role for the government, concentration of benefits on those with great potential or those with great need, and collaboration between government, business, and labor.[3]

A Critical Assessment

Having identified the elements of industrial policy, it is worth evaluating briefly the assumptions on which they are based.

1. Robert B. Reich, "Why the U.S. Needs an Industrial Policy," *Harvard Business Review*, vol. 60 (January–February 1982), p. 75; and "Rebuilding America: A National Industrial Policy," *AFL-CIO American Federationist*, vol. 90 (October 22, 1983), p. 3.

2. Lester Thurow quoted in Simon Lazarus and Robert E. Litan, "The Democrats' Coming Civil War over Industrial Policy," *Atlantic Monthly*, vol. 254 (September 1984), p. 92.

3. The debate over industrial policy has been burdened by several loaded terms and phrases. Proponents cast the debate in terms of cooperation instead of adversarialism. Opponents cast the debate in terms of central planning instead of responsive decentralized markets.

Targeted Assistance

The essence of industrial policy is targeted assistance from government. Rather than adopt across-the-board measures that rely on the market to allocate resources among industries, industrial policy programs would provide benefits to selected industries. Some proponents such as the AFL-CIO call for aiding basic smokestack industries. Others would focus assistance on emerging high-technology industries. The common element is a selective rather than a general approach.

Whether one attempts to pick winners, assist losers, or both, the common assumption is that this approach is preferable to a market allocation. But because advocates of industrial policy base their claims for it more on economic efficiency (an expanding pie) than on redistribution (cutting the pie differently), they must demonstrate that the entity that decides who gets what can increase the size of the pie more effectively than can the market.

An efficient capital market means that on the basis of currently available information, all productive investment opportunities within the limits of the savings available to the economy have been exhausted. In an efficient market an agency that targets investment must substitute investments with lower returns for investments with higher returns.

The capital markets of the United States are generally recognized as the most efficient in the world. How then could the relatively small number of people in control of industrial policy be expected to do better than the market? There is no compelling reason to believe that such a group would allocate resources more efficiently than does a capital market that reflects the judgment of millions of individuals and businesses.

Whatever term one uses—the 1984 Democratic platform called for "appropriate financing mechanisms" in an attempt to stay a safe distance from the concept of a bank—if targeted assistance means anything, it means that some industries will fare better in the scramble for scarce resources than they would under a market allocation, and others will fare worse. Proponents of industrial policy often ignore this opportunity cost. In their desire to promote promising ideas that the market does not fund, they seem to forget that such intervention will mean less for someone else. Interestingly, industrial policy schemes focus on who will get more, not on who will get less. Presumably the development bank would decide who gets more and let the market decide who gets less.[4]

4. The opportunity cost of such a policy is made even more clear if one imagines a development bank financed by a tax on all new issues of corporate bonds and stocks, as well as on retained earnings.

The obvious implication of all this is that government officials possess information unknown to the market or judgment superior to that of the market. There is no evidence to support either claim. There is no reason to believe that government has better information about the potential of newly emerging industries or the potential for revitalizing old ones than that available to the scientists, engineers, entrepreneurs, managers, marketing analysts, venture capitalists, bankers, and investment analysts that constitute the market. Indeed the government's ability to forecast does not inspire great confidence. Looking back over the past decade, one can conceive of an industrial development bank promoting a supersonic transport, the breeder reactor, and synthetic fuels (coal gasification technology). Each would have been a financial disaster involving significant amounts of capital.

Enhanced Collaboration among Government, Industry, and Labor

A second element in most industrial policy proposals is the concept of enhanced collaboration among government, industry, and labor. The origin of this notion lies in what many have characterized as a tradition of adversarialism in our business-labor-government relationships, and a fundamental misunderstanding of the coordinating role of the market.

To improve these relationships, tripartite councils have been proposed to bring industry, labor, and government to the same table with a common purpose. Together, the theory goes, they can develop a sound program for revitalizing an old industry or developing a newly emerging field.

Most advocates envisage each partner as bringing something to the table. Labor and management would agree to act in specific ways—to reduce the rate of increase in wages, to increase certain types of investment, to rationalize production in certain ways. Government would encourage such behavior through protection against imports, loans at subsidized rates, loan guarantees, grants, relief from regulation, or some other targeted preference. In fact government assistance would be conditional on certain actions by industry and labor. This approach was adopted by the Democratic candidate for president in 1984. During the campaign, he announced that he would create a tripartite committee to "hammer out a plan that will give us a modern and competitive steel industry that we must have. I will tell the committee that everyone must contribute. . . . " He emphasized that "management and labor must do their fair share, too."[5]

5. "Steel Import Cut Proposed by Mondale," Baltimore *Sun*, September 18, 1984. It is worth asking who in such arrangements represents steel users. Presumably one answer is the government. Others would argue that steel users should have a specific representative in such discussions.

Much of the impetus behind this thinking is a concern that government appears to be giving away benefits without getting anything in return. Enthusiasts of industrial policy do not object to providing targeted benefits to the private sector. Quite the contrary. They want to use them to direct the behavior of labor and management toward more productive paths.

There is a superficial attraction to conditionality and the notion of not giving away something for nothing. But those who endorse this notion should remember two things.

First, imposing conditionality puts government on a very slippery slope leading to imposition of a detailed plan for managing an industry. While the process would presumably begin with an industry seeking to advance an "acceptable" plan, it could quickly lead to increasingly detailed negotiations over who would do what. The underlying assumption is that those in government know more about what is good for an industry than do those in the industry itself. This assumption is questionable at best and dangerous at worst.[6]

Second the government would have to monitor and implement whatever conditions are agreed to. Suppose that in exchange for import relief a dozen companies in an industry submit plans regarding what they intend to do if the relief is granted and that the government agrees those plans represent a reasonable response on the part of the industry. Suppose also that after a year or two, two-thirds of the companies have fulfilled their obligations while one-third have not. Can or should the government withdraw import relief from those that have not fulfilled their obligations? Do we want the government to impose sanctions on those that do not meet their stated goals?

The Search for "Coherent," Coordinated Policies

Supporters of industrial policy frequently point to the panoply of contradictory, ad hoc government policies affecting business and assert that they must be replaced with a coordinated and coherent approach. The Rohatyn report states that "What is often lacking . . . are efforts to coordinate or even to recognize the effects of all these different policies on a particular industry. The auto industry, for example, is subject to an array of industrial policies . . . from tax provisions [and] import restrictions [to] environmental and fuel economy regulations, some of which clearly work at cross-purposes."[7]

6. For example, some "appropriate" conditions for the steel industry might include a wage freeze to last until steel wages equal the average for all U.S. manufacturing, eliminating dividends and dedicating the retained earnings to investment in new plant and equipment, and reducing state and local property taxes on steel facilities with the funds going into new investment.

7. Center for National Policy, *Restoring American Competitiveness: Proposals for an Industrial Policy* (Washington, D.C.: CNP, 1984), p. 10.

There is no question that one can find many examples of federal policies working at cross-purposes. Nevertheless the existence of inconsistency does not result from a lack of strategic thinking on the part of government officials. Seemingly conflicting policies are no accident. They have two sources.

First, policies are designed with many objectives in mind—a clean environment, a safe and healthy workplace, nondiscriminatory hiring practices, special benefits to assist the economically disadvantaged, and so forth. Conflicting policies often reflect competing goals that may be worthwhile in and of themselves but that cannot be pursued simultaneously.

Second, conflict reflects the strength of contending political interests. Public policies are fashioned in the political marketplace. They result from the give and take of our political process and reflect the inevitability of compromise in a democracy composed of separate institutions sharing power. It is remarkable that some people argue that inconsistency in policy would be reduced rather than increased by a shift of even more economic decisions to the same political system.[8]

In every political system some officials, usually at the center, spend a great deal of time attempting to fashion coherent, comprehensive, and consistent policies. They seek to reconcile competing interests and eliminate duplication in light of their sense of national priorities. Their task in part is to marshal support for the program they have developed and to guide it through the multiple stages of our political processes. Some are more skilled and successful than others. Our attention is drawn more frequently to situations in which they fail to achieve coherence than to situations in which they succeed.

The culture and institutions of the United States reflect the diversity and pluralism of its society. Public policies are made in the political marketplace, which, like the economic marketplace, admits a broad array of interests. And properly so. Americans do not want to delegate decisionmaking to a small group even if this would hold out the promise of more coherent and consistent policies.

An Appropriate Role for Government

No one has summarized more succinctly the conclusions of a broad spectrum of economists on the question of industrial policy than has Charles L. Schultze:

---

8. Depending on the power granted the new agency, one might argue that industrial policy proponents want a shift away from the present political system toward more central and less pluralistic control.

America is *not* deindustrializing. Japan does *not* owe its industrial success to its industrial policy. Government is *not* able to devise a "winning" industrial structure. Finally, it is *not* possible in the American political system to pick and choose among individual firms and regions in the substantive, efficiency-driven way envisaged by advocates of industrial policy.[9]

Nevertheless the debate over industrial policy has been healthy. It has forced Americans to identify the real problems facing their economy as well as the types of policy most likely to solve them. If industrial policy is not the answer, the question remains: What is the appropriate role for government in the economy? Let me outline briefly the three roles that I consider to be desirable.

Pursuing Sound Macroeconomic Policies

Sound monetary and fiscal policies are indispensable. There is simply no substitute for sustained noninflationary growth—the primary objective of macroeconomic policy. Failures of macroeconomic policy are responsible for much of the interest in industrial policy; sound macroeconomic policies are by far the best cure for industrial maladies.

Since World War II, monetary policy has generally been both procyclical and inflationary. The procyclical effect reduces the average rate of capacity utilization; the inflationary effect increases the effective tax on income from capital because depreciation allowances are not indexed to inflation.

Likewise, large deficits in the federal budget reduce the availability of funds for private investment. To some extent these deficits have been fueled by the proliferation of federal subsidies—many of which favor the nonindustrial sectors of the economy. Reducing such subsidies would thus help industry in two ways rather than one.

Maintaining a Climate for Entrepreneurship

Government also has an important role in establishing and maintaining a climate for entrepreneurship. Much of the creation of such a climate involves putting a set of incentives in place that will unleash the innovative forces in an economy. Among the most important incentives are those relating to saving and investment. The current tax system favors consumption more than investment. One positive step for the United States would be to move to a tax system that is neutral with respect to consumption and saving. The entrepreneurial climate is also influenced by whether policies favor the short term, favor the long term, or

9. "Industrial Policy: A Dissent," *Brookings Review*, vol. 2 (Fall 1983), p. 4.

maintain neutrality between the two. Investments should not be distorted by tax shelters that direct savings to projects with low social returns.

A vibrant industrial sector requires adequate investment and research and development. New investments are most likely to be undertaken when those making the investments are persuaded there is a healthy prospective rate of return *and* when they are reasonably confident that conditions affecting their investment will not change dramatically. The more uncertain the climate, the shorter term the investments and the faster the return investors look for. Stable public policies—keeping the rules of the game reasonably constant—can contribute to a healthy entrepreneurial climate. This stability involves regulations, tax policy, and those practices that affect competitive relationships between and within sectors of the economy.

The entrepreneurial spirit is also encouraged by the ease of creating new companies. Ease of entry can spur innovation. Government should ensure that its regulatory structure permits rather than prevents entry and thus enhances competition.

A healthy relationship between labor and management can also contribute to the entrepreneurial climate and a nation's economic performance. The principal task of government in this area is to establish a framework of balanced collective bargaining in which neither management nor labor is advantaged and in which governmental interference is minimized.

The entrepreneurial spirit and an innovative society are also characterized by mobility of labor and capital. One cannot allocate resources efficiently if those resources are immobile. In the United States, flexibility in the allocation of labor resources, in the form of mobility between academic, industrial, and government research laboratories, as well as through effective dispute-settlement arrangements, has served to increase employment and stimulate technological change.

Entrepreneurship is also enhanced by antitrust policies that strengthen competition and avoid monopolistic practices. But the antitrust laws must be employed wisely. High concentration is not necessarily associated with high prices. The government must not use the antitrust laws to protect weak competitors at the expense of effective competition. Entrepreneurship also depends on patents and copyrights that effectively protect property rights.

Dealing with Externalities

A final role for government relates to three types of investments involving genuine externalities or public goods. First, some investments are important for the long-term health of the economy as a whole and yet would not be undertaken by a single private firm. Basic research is perhaps the clearest and most important example.

Second, government appropriately pursues certain noneconomic objectives such as worker safety, a clean environment, and nondiscriminatory economic opportunity, for which there are not clear ownership rights. Pursuing these objectives, normally through regulations, often imposes economic costs. What is important is that these costs are identified and weighed to ensure that the benefits to society match or exceed the costs being imposed.

Third, some major infrastructure investments require government to play an active role. The U.S. interstate highway system is one good example. Where there are identifiable beneficiaries, such as those who travel on the highways, user fees can help ensure that the level of investment is related to the contribution the investment makes.

These roles for government reflect an underlying conviction that markets are more efficient than are government planners at allocating economic resources. Recognizing the danger of protectionism and government interference in the garb of industrial policy, Adlai E. Stevenson, the former senator from Illinois, concluded well in saying that "the best industrial policy for the United States would be to get the government out of the market, not more deeply into it."

Donald Riegle

American Industrial Policy: Building on the Chrysler Experience

AFTER SEVERAL DECADES of remarkable economic growth, the developed market economies must contend with enormous changes in the nature of international competition. These changes are just now being perceived and are yet to be fully understood. I, of course, see the challenge most clearly as it confronts the United States. Our industries are up against a new kind of competition. Given the ease of technological and capital transfer, such mature products as automobiles can be produced in virtually any country, regardless of its standard of living. So how can plants in the developed countries compete? No matter how much our plants are automated, it will be difficult to reduce labor costs to Korean, let alone to Pakistani, levels. If the gimmicks used by some nations to create artificial competitive advantages through subsidies are also considered, the task of achieving an effective competitive position appears more difficult still. No wonder the unemployment rate in Michigan was 11.5 percent at the time of this conference. No wonder that rate had exceeded 10 percent for fifty-five consecutive months. No wonder the industrial base of the state is eroding.

Most thoughtful members of the American business community sense the severity of the new challenge. Many are worried that their country is not adapting its attitudes and practices to the new economic realities. This lack of adaptation has several causes. For one, American public attention has been distracted by the good news of the recent recovery. For another, little leadership on the issue has been forthcoming from our two most recent presidents. Arriving from the statehouse of Georgia, Jimmy Carter lacked the personal experience to understand the issues, to articulate them, and to develop a team to deal with them (although he fortunately had the good sense to place Robert Strauss in charge of international trade). Ronald Reagan has been even less effective than Carter. Not surprisingly, his perspective derives from California movie society, and his economic philosophy evolved during the years of public relations speeches given for General Electric and Twenty-Mule-Team Borax.

Frankly speaking, the Reagan White House shows less sensitivity to the problems of basic industry than any I have seen during my two decades in Congress. As a result of factors of this sort, Americans have not simply failed to develop a national industrial strategy; they have failed even to initiate a real national debate on the subject.

In searching for alternatives to the status quo in this country, some Americans have looked with envy at the ability of France and other industrialized nations to build cooperation among government, industry, and labor, and to harness that cooperation on behalf of national strategies for industrial competitiveness. I share their conviction that adversarial relations may have served us well in the past but provide no model for the future. Nevertheless, on the basis of my experience in the Senate trying to shape a coherent American response to the plight of basic industries, I doubt that the American political system is likely to incorporate much of France's system of national planning. We must devise our own blueprint for interaction among business, labor, and government, one that lies between central planning and combative confrontation. Some corporate executives, people like Lee Iacocca, John Young, and Felix Rohatyn, have broached the right subjects; but no one has yet developed a national strategy that is economically sound and politically compelling.

Perhaps the best way to approach reform of the American system is to examine a specific case of how that system has worked in practice. Given both its importance and my personal involvement, I shall examine the American government's decision in 1979 to rescue Chrysler Corporation.

Chrysler was not the first troubled enterprise to obtain government support. As of late 1979, when Chrysler knocked on government's door, Congress had already approved several large financial assistance packages, including those for the Penn Central railroad, for Lockheed Corporation, and for Conrail (not to speak of its efforts on behalf of New York City). In fact, at this time, the federal budget shows $250 billion in outstanding loan guarantees—including over $18 billion for small businesses, the maritime industry, the steel industry—and other forms of economic development.

The Chrysler situation was distinctive only in that the corporation and the crisis were so large. In 1978 Chrysler was America's tenth largest manufacturing firm with sales of $13.6 billion and employment of 140,000. It purchased goods and services from 20,000 suppliers, thereby supporting another 180,000 jobs. It sold cars and trucks through 4,800 dealerships that employed another 100,000 people. By itself, Chrysler accounted for 1 percent of all income of the American black community.

Early in the fall of 1979 it was clear that an economic disaster of unpredictable proportions was imminent. Chrysler required $40 million in cash every day. Expert analysis indicated that by February 1980 the cash would run out. Because the U.S. economy was already in a weakened condition, no one could say when or where the damage of a Chrysler collapse would end. Many solid, vigorous companies would have experienced lasting financial weakness. Several industrial cities would have borne the major brunt of the collapse. According to official estimates, the failure of Chrysler would have increased the federal budget by $2 billion to $6 billion. Spending on unemployment benefits, pension benefits, and trade adjustment assistance would have increased, while tax revenues would have dropped.

The choice was between rapid federal assistance and total corporate collapse. There simply was no realistic alternative. Some observers suggested glibly that Chrysler could solve its problems through bankruptcy. They claimed Chrysler could use the new bankruptcy law to reorganize, sell off some assets, and continue as a smaller but healthier company. Experts in bankruptcy law made it clear that such a position was nonsense. If the corporation filed for bankruptcy, its entire operation would be shattered within days. Machinery and other assets would be tied up in court battles for years.

The intense legislative battle that finally ended just before Christmas 1979 revealed several things about the ability of the United States to deal rationally with industries under challenge.

—The crisis at Chrysler highlights the utter lack of coherence in the myriad federal policies affecting business. Certainly government cannot be blamed for all of Chrysler's problems; but a number of government actions conflicted with one another such that their combined effect served to weaken Chrysler significantly.

Three sets of auto regulations gave quite different signals to auto manufacturers. Fuel efficiency standards encouraged production of small cars; safety standards prompted production of large cars. The combination of standards for fuel efficiency and pollution control enhanced the desirability of major technological breakthroughs, but antitrust policies prevented U.S. companies from cooperating in R&D. These conflicts, together with federal efforts to keep the retail price of gasoline low and the disastrous gasoline allocation system adopted after the shah of Iran fell, imposed heavy costs on U.S. auto companies. Chrysler, as the most vulnerable company, was a disaster waiting to happen.

It might amaze a foreign observer that the federal government had developed no mechanism for coordinating the activities of the several agencies charged with administering these policies. In April 1979, I chaired a hearing on government regulation of the auto industry. One panel included key officials of three major agencies regulating the auto industry—the National Highway Traffic Safety Administration, the Environmental Protection Agency, and the Department of Energy. The thrust of the testimony of each was that the regulations of his agency placed no undue burden on the auto companies. One witness even testified that his department believed that Chrysler could finance the heavy capital costs associated with rapid downsizing of its cars. That was just three months before the company announced the largest quarterly loss in history and teetered at the edge of an abyss. The important point here is that each agency was discussing Chrysler as if its own regulations were the only ones the company had to meet. Each ignored the burdens imposed by the other agencies. In fact, I discovered during the hearing that these three officials had not even met each other before their appearance on Capitol Hill that day.

—The Chrysler case demonstrates the U.S. government's lack of knowledge regarding even major U.S. industries. For weeks after the Chrysler problem surfaced, members of Congress found it very difficult to obtain independent information about the structure, operations, and financing of the auto industry. That is a remarkable failure, since the industry provided one out of every twelve manufacturing jobs and generated a large share of the demand for such basic goods as steel, aluminum, copper, iron, and rubber.

Eventually, one senator received a leaked copy of a devastating report on the regional economic impact of a Chrysler collapse. It had been prepared by a small research bureau of the Department of Transportation in Cambridge, Massachusetts. This was the one place in the entire federal government that had been analyzing this key industry as a productive and financial system.

Ironically, the studies of this office had been launched almost by accident. When the federal fuel economy bill was enacted, one member of Congress inserted language requiring that standards be economically practicable. The regulatory agency charged with oversight of the program faithfully undertook the relevant analyses but regularly suppressed results that conflicted with its viewpoint. It was later learned that the staff in Cambridge had accurately identified Chrysler's potential financial problem one year before it occurred. But its report on the subject had been ignored. The office that produced it has since been disbanded.

To his credit, Commerce Secretary Malcolm Baldrige created within his department the capacity to continue this type of industry-specific analysis. But there still is no evidence that such information affects decisionmaking in the top levels of the administration.

—The legislative fight to rescue Chrysler was shaped by the deep mutual suspicions between government and big business in the United States. These suspicions stemmed from the adversarial relationship established early in this century when the federal government was small.

The auto industry had long been the most powerful and profitable industry in the United States. Therefore, when the environmental protection movement expanded in Congress, the industry was a tempting target. With the industry protesting the cost of proposed regulation, environmental policy was thrashed out in intense legislative battles. The auto industry's lobbying effort, which resulted in some significant victories, was long remembered bitterly by key members of Congress who had been on the opposite side.

Therefore, when Chrysler had to ask for federal assistance, many in Congress and the executive branch took considerable pleasure that the mighty had fallen. Many members of Congress saw Chrysler primarily as a domestic policy adversary. It was difficult for them to move beyond that and see Chrysler as a significant national asset, a major part of the country's capacity to produce fuel-efficient cars and engines. For three months, thousands of local auto dealers, suppliers, and auto workers had to visit members of Congress to help personalize the crisis. It was a massive effort that only a company of Chrysler's size could have mounted. The success of that effort depended on a unique set of political and economic circumstances. It undoubtedly could not be replicated today.

—The Chrysler legislation built solidly on the experience of Congress and the executive branch with Lockheed, Conrail, and New York City. That experience demonstrated the wisdom of granting substantial powers to the Loan Guarantee Board to give it the flexibility needed to respond to unforeseeable events and to implement a successful rescue effort.

Drafters of the legislation consulted with some of the nation's leading financial experts to devise new ways to compensate the government fully for its risk without placing an unbearable burden on the corporation's cash flow. The law authorized an exchange of stock warrants that permitted the taxpayers to participate in the subsequent success of the corporation.

Provisions were included that required all parties of interest to make sacrifices needed to help ensure the long-term success of the rescue effort.

—Legislative success was very difficult to achieve. The rules of the Senate are structured to give each senator considerable power over legislation. The Chrysler bill came to a final vote in the closing hours of the Ninety-sixth Congress. In actuality, any one senator could have killed the bill. The fact that no opponent moved to do so shows that virtually every senator recognized that the impending collapse of Chrysler entailed unacceptable risks.

As a result, the federal government was able to provide a safe umbrella under which Chrysler and thousands of other parties were given the chance to cooperate in a massive rescue effort. Within a year or so, Chrysler was a much different corporation with modernized plants, new lines of products that proved popular in the marketplace, and greatly reduced costs. The guaranteed loans were repaid seven years early, and the government gained $340 million through fee income and the sale of warrants.

The dire warnings of opponents did not come to pass. Chrysler proved not to have been a hopeless case, as some had claimed. And the decision to assist Chrysler did not encourage numerous other companies to seek government aid.

In spite of the apparent success of the Chrysler rescue, I fear that public attitudes have not been changed. If Chrysler came to the government for help today, I doubt that it would receive any. Ronald Reagan opposed the rescue legislation. Without an administration as helpful as that of Jimmy. Carter, Congress would not even have reached first base in its effort to save a major company.

So Americans still have much to learn from the Chrysler experience. They must explore ways to deal more generally with the problems of major industries adapting to sweeping changes in world competition. Unless they come to grips with the manner in which the world trading system is pressuring the standard of living in developed countries, the democratic institutions of the United States will be placed under severe stress. No one should underestimate the fragility of democracy. As I watched the mass hypnosis that occurred during the presidential campaign of 1984, as I watched the American people choose the path of brass bands and balloons and flags rather than the path of serious contemplation of the issues, I could not help but feel that we are living dangerously. Before long our leisure to debate the issue of how to increase our ability to compete in world markets will expire; we must devise specific policy alternatives, and we must do so now.

Robert S. Strauss

Comments

THE MERITS OF INDUSTRIAL POLICY used to be debated under the heading of French-style economic planning. So let me begin with two observations on that subject. First, after World War II the French relied heavily on economic planning to restore the health of their economy. The successes of that planning, in particular the creation of a modern economic infrastructure, were obvious to all. The history of American economic policy contains no similar experience. As a result, economic planning enjoys more support in France than it does in the United States. Second, planning in France has evolved. It no longer resembles the variety used just after the war. Although the French continue to target industries, and to do so most successfully, French policy is far less coherent than most people in the United States realize.

In the United States one now hears a lot about industrial policy, but different people mean different things by the term. Certainly among Democrats there has been no single position.

But although the definition remains unclear, many elements of industrial policy already exist in American economic life. The internal revenue code favors some kinds of investment over others. The defense program entails expenditure of tremendous sums on research and development as well as equipment. In both cases the efforts of government may be poorly coordinated and the amount of planning may be negligible, but the impact on the economy is still selective.

The major reason why Americans cannot seem to coordinate the actions of government is, of course, political. As soon as the government announces a desire to plan the allocation of resources, public policy becomes intensely political. Politicians begin to speak on behalf of the interests they represent. In a democracy such representation of special interests is appropriate, but at times the general welfare suffers at the expense of special interests. Such, perhaps, is the price one pays for living in a democracy. In this country the deliberate selection of economic winners and losers is not now and will not become a power of government.

What then should be the role of government in industrial affairs? First, government should attempt to develop institutions that facilitate cooperation among the leaders of business, labor, and government. As long as these institutions can be structured in a manner that minimizes the direct intervention of government, they should not be anathema to those who oppose government intervention in the market. The creation of such institutions would coordinate the positions of key interest groups and hence create some political muscle on behalf of cooperation within Congress.

Second, government must retard the buildup of negative, protectionist forces within this country. It must decide how to react to foreign targeting and foreign subsidies, and how to aid domestic industries subject to acute foreign competition. In this sense trade policy must form a central part of any sensible industrial policy.

The Reagan administration has already made its choices in trade policy. Its steel decision of September 1984 has, for reasons that remain a mystery, succeeded politically. It is not clear, however, that this approach will succeed in keeping the protectionist forces of this country at bay. It would seem to do just the opposite.

It is critically important that the United States continue to debate industrial policy in its broadest terms. A few years ago when the economic crisis appeared most acute, Americans were doing just that. Every day some congressional committee was holding hearings or some newspaper was writing an editorial on the subject. As economic conditions improved, however, the debate on industrial policy was forgotten. Without a crisis, it is impossible to interest the public in reform. And yet temporary improvement of the economic climate permits Americans to debate the subject more intelligently, more objectively, and more meaningfully. Now is the time for a bipartisan quest of economic policies to repair the very obvious weaknesses in America's domestic economic fabric.

General Discussion

WALTER ADAMS   As Roger Porter spoke, there were times when I thought I had discovered an ideological and philosophical soul mate—times when I wished Mr. Porter were a candidate for high political office. And yet I must confess to certain reservations about his analysis.

Porter distinguishes between planning effected by governments and planning effected by markets. The reason for the distinction is the belief that markets are competitive and competition permits decentralization. In real economies, however, including that of the United States, markets do not always conform to textbook models of competition. Therefore Porter's conception of the difference between governments and markets may be inaccurate. Which is preferable, industrial planning done by the big three producers of automobiles, or government planning in the form of industrial policy? Planning by a lethargic oligarchy in steel or planning by government bureaucracy? On the basis of market performance in concentrated American industries, the answer to this question is hardly obvious.

Porter's analysis assumes a tinge of unreality when it assigns markets to one hermetically sealed category and governments to another. In practice, governments and markets interact pervasively. Economic power often translates into political power. Government is not always the autonomous agency that it is sometimes supposed to be. In fact the greatest danger associated with government planning is the possibility that big government, big business, and big labor will end up conspiring against the public.

ROGER PORTER   I appreciate your expression of political support, however qualified it may be. As you might suspect, few in Washington have encouraged me to seek political office.

American markets are indeed less than perfect. Anyone who suggests otherwise is out of touch with reality. Nevertheless, in recent years American companies have been subjected to intense foreign competition. The big three producers of automobiles think at least as much about foreign competition as they do about each other. International trade serves to perfect somewhat the state of competition.

I also agree that government and markets interact and that such interaction does not always serve the public interest. Those who lobby government tend to focus on a particular industry. They tend to be enthusiastic about the industry's importance and future. Either they think the industry is performing well and must be helped to expand or, if things are not going well, they think the situation can be turned around with just a little support from government. These enthusiasts fail to take account of the impact of their proposals on other parts of the economy and on the economy as a whole. Markets do register such general equilibrium effects; the same cannot be said of governments.

Economic power does often yield political power. Unquestionably economic size and power enable certain groups to exercise disproportionate political power. The more government intervenes in the economy, the more advantageous this power will be. The big will get bigger, and the strong will get stronger. No one thinks about how to allocate scarcity; that is to be left to the market. When people think of industrial policy, they focus on the allocation of benefits.

FRANÇOIS LAGRANGE   Roger Porter argues that some activities should be conducted by government while others should be conducted in the marketplace. And yet many of the activities he would assign to one compartment could be and in fact are being conducted in the other. For example, in France some industrial enterprises undertake basic R&D and some public highways are privately financed. In the United States, on the other hand, the use of a tremendous amount of land in the form of national parks is determined by government rather than in the market. This is truly a socialistic achievement. France has nothing like Yellowstone or the Grand Tetons. So where is the boundary between public and private, between a market-oriented economy and its administratively controlled alternative?

ROGER PORTER   I certainly do not oppose private provision of basic research, highways, or natural parks. I merely believe that such activities would be supplied in suboptimal quantities by a market system. Private enterprise selects projects with great or sure rewards. Not all projects of the sort identified by François Lagrange, not even all of public interest, will meet the profit test.

It is very difficult, of course, to determine how much basic research, how many highways, and how many parks should be supported by government. All we can do is stumble toward a determination when, in the budgetary and political processes, government funds get allocated among uses.

The actual process of allocation is far from optimal. In the United States the pendulum effect is at work. When someone makes a convincing case that some class of project has been underfunded, the pendulum swings and the project is overfunded. Similarly, when it is decided that a project has been funded to excess, it is often cut back too much. Expenditures on defense offer a good example of this phenomenon. During the past two decades defense expenditures have gyrated wildly. When defense spending was at 10 percent of GNP, Americans decided it had climbed too high. Now that spending has dropped to 5 percent, many people feel it should go up to 7 or 8 percent. In practice, then, the pendulum swings constantly, permitting frequent reassessment of what is best.

PHILIPPE HERZOG   Roger Porter suggests that business managers know better than government bureaucrats what should be done in particular companies and industries. By his logic, employees of the companies should know at least as much as management. Does he believe that participation by employees in the decisions of a company would improve the efficiency of business enterprise?

According to Mr. Porter, the United States has chosen a market economy while France has selected an administered alternative. In a real market economy, however, private enterprise bears the losses as well as the profits that result from market behavior. Such is not the case in the United States. The magnitude of the American budgetary deficit reveals the full extent to which the losses and wastes of the American private sector have been socialized. Indeed the size of the deficit in international trade shows that foreigners are obliged to bear a large fraction of the resulting burden.

Mr. Porter fails to consider one important justification of government intervention in the economy. Purely financial investments now earn a much higher rate of return than do investments in research, in plant, or in equipment. Unless the government takes steps to reverse this ranking, the market system will be unable to modernize itself.

ROGER PORTER   Mr. Herzog argues that government can enlist employees of the private sector to help it evaluate industrial policies. As a result it can reduce its informational handicap. However plausible this view, it does not get to the heart of the problem. The danger of industrial policy is not that government lacks information; the danger is that government does not know how to say "enough is enough." Unless their own money is at stake, those who invest may throw good money after bad. In a market economy the financial system is generally flexible enough to cut out unsuccessful projects. Financial enterprises constantly weigh alternatives and redeploy money to their best advantage. The federal government has no such mechanism.

Mr. Herzog also argues that the United States is exporting the results of its waste and inefficiency to the rest of the world. To the extent that this is true, it is a problem that requires macroeconomic policy not industrial policy. The strength of the dollar and the height of real rates of interest in the United States should not be blamed on any failure to adopt industrial policies.

DONALD RIEGLE   I foresee a pattern of increasing chaos in the world trading system. The chaos manifests itself in a proliferation of ad hoc responses to policy problems. In the United States the steel decisions announced during the fall of 1984 as well as the automobile decisions of the spring of 1985 illustrate the kinds of responses I have in mind.

If the automobile quotas are lifted, I have been led to believe that Japan could increase its share of the American market from 22 percent to 40 percent within twelve months. The Japanese have the capacity to produce, the marketing network in the United States, the cost advantage in production, and the quality of product to accomplish such a feat.

From my perspective as a legislator, I wonder how we can avoid protectionism while dealing with the problems that free trade would create. The same type of problem must exist in France. How is it dealt with there?

CHRISTIAN GOUX   I believe the world trading system will disintegrate into a series of blocs. One bloc will consist of the extremely poor countries—most of them located in Africa. They will continue to depend on foreign aid. A second bloc will consist of the Communist and Asian countries. They will be aligned more on Japan than on the West. Although we tend to think of Japanese dominance in terms of cost advantage, the real reason why Japan will lead this group is cultural affinity. In fact the importance of oriental culture is likely to lead to new forms of capitalism in this bloc.

Europe will constitute a third bloc. Europe is special because political institutions have fallen so far behind industrial realities that they might never catch up. Its fragmentation prevents its adjustment. Europeans speak different languages, employ different institutions, and continue to have to deal with the German problem that has afflicted them throughout this century.

A final bloc will include the United States and its several allies in the Western Hemisphere. These allies are linked economically as well as politically to the United States. I fear that this bloc will detach itself from the others. Although the United States has enjoyed two or three years of prosperity, it too will encounter major industrial problems over the next few years. Europe tends to ignore the American prospect, thinking that American prosperity will last forever.

JEAN-LOUIS GERGORIN   Senator Riegle has asked a fundamental question. Unfortunately, it is not a question to which Europeans pay much attention because they focus more on problems of debt than on problems of trade.

The day is not far off when Europe will have to confront the issue of trade. When it does, it will find itself poorly suited to the task. Bilateral bargaining and voluntary restraints will become the order of the day. Given its fragmentation, Europe will find it difficult to engage in such negotiations. At every European meeting, agreement must now be secured among twelve people, each of whom represents an entire nation. It takes twelve times ten minutes merely to propose the agenda for a meeting. The European Commission is still very timid because some member states fail to recognize the importance of appointing commissioners whose political stature matches their intellectual ability.

If Europe is to survive in the economic order of the future, it must develop institutions like the American special trade representative. It must do so in trade, but it must also do so in antitrust policy and public procurement. Without the political courage to delegate authority to a supranational body, Europe will not be able to develop an economy that fosters technological change.

FRANÇOIS DIDIER   Many of those present appear to believe that the business environment in the United States differs appreciably from that in France. In the former they see a market system; in the latter they find a system of government promotion and control. The divergence has, however, been exaggerated.

In France the spirit of enterprise cannot be totally absent. After all, the term in English for commercial vitality is entrepreneurship not unternehmenship or undertakership. More seriously, in the United States the market is not the only arbiter of choice. Some twenty-five years ago I was head of the Paris airport authority and got to know the president of Air France very well. At the time, many airlines were introducing Boeing 707s. Unable to do the same, my friend lamented the subsidies received by the American airlines to buy the planes. Currently the same thing is happening in the competition between the American space shuttle and the European Ariane. After the technological and economic evaluations are made, military considerations often dictate the choice of Boeing or McDonnell-Douglas equipment.

DONALD RIEGLE   In some sectors of the U.S. economy—sectors such as aircraft and electronics—government support over a long period of time has been essential to the development of global preeminence. In this sense the United States does indeed have an industrial policy.

Until recently, however, such policies have been limited to industries of military interest. The private economy, the entrepreneurial economy, flourished with minimal involvement of government. I do not believe that such success will continue. I do not mean to imply that entrepreneurship has lost its importance but merely to suggest that as markets become truly global, international differentials of the sort one now observes will prevent exclusive reliance on laissez-faire. Sectors of the economy other than those that supply the military will have to develop cooperative relationships with government. Such cooperation has paid big dividends when it has been employed. It is time to expand its scope.

Cooperation is not central planning. In all probability cooperation should take the form of joint ventures. Chrysler is a good model of how to handle a discrete case but it does not reveal much about how to handle major industrial transitions.

Voluntary import restraints of the sort applied by the United States to steel are not what I have in mind either. Such restraints cannot substitute for crafting an adjustment policy that holds the promise of a stronger competitive position. The same is true in automobiles. With the elimination of import restraints the Japanese could take 40 percent of the American market. If they did, the health of the American automobile industry would change dramatically. The United States must devise positive adjustment policies; otherwise it will experience a great deal of turmoil.

FRANÇOIS PERRIN-PELLETIER   Let me attempt to respond to Senator Riegle's question regarding what will happen upon termination of the voluntary restraint of Japanese exports to the United States.

No nation is prepared to accept a major decline in its production of automobiles. The industry employs so many people and contributes so much to technological change that it will continue to remain a major force in each country. Competition will become a battle between nations rather than a battle between companies.

As a result I do not believe that exports from Japan will come to account for 40 percent of the American market. Either the Japanese will continue to limit their exports or controls will be placed on them. One way or the other, international trade will not be liberalized entirely.

I do not share Senator Riegle's conviction that Japanese exports threaten the health of American producers. The Americans make their money on expensive automobiles—not because the Japanese fail to produce such cars but rather because market supply currently falls behind market demand. With or without quotas, expensive Japanese cars will be in short supply in the United States. Hence the financial health of American producers will remain intact.

We should not forget the impact of the American quotas on the European market. Although they did not admit it, the Germans accepted a voluntary restraint on Japanese exports only because the United States had already done so. It will be interesting to see whether the Germans withdraw their support for the European scheme now that the United States has terminated its arrangement with Japan.

DONALD RIEGLE   Japan does produce automobiles in the Buick range, does it not?

FRANÇOIS PERRIN-PELLETIER   Yes, it does.

DONALD RIEGLE   If it wants to, then, it could export a large number of such automobiles to the United States.

FRANÇOIS PERRIN-PELLETIER   That is where we disagree. For the moment, the Japanese strength lies in mass production. Even the Europeans— Mercedes, BMW, Peugeot, Audi—find it difficult to sell cars of this size in the United States. They certainly are trying to do so. In three to five years, perhaps, but not next year.

DONALD RIEGLE   I hope you are right.

FRANÇOIS LAGRANGE   Senator Riegle makes a strong plea for a dialogue among business, labor, and government. I wonder how the senator envisions this dialogue. What would be its framework? What would be its issues? Should debate focus on macroeconomic policy or should it extend to microeconomic policy? One of the most important lessons to be learned from a conference such as this is the narrowness of the line that separates macroeconomic from microeconomic policy. Macroeconomic policy pursued beyond a certain point is nothing more or less than industrial policy.

DONALD RIEGLE   In the United States the debate over nuclear weapons is commensurate with the magnitude of the nuclear problem. By that standard Americans have failed miserably to generate high-quality debate on trade and macroeconomic policy.

In describing the American and the French political systems, Christian Goux stressed the differences between a parliamentary and a presidential system. In a parliamentary system, he argued, legislators exercise little independent control over economic policy. Consider, however, the current situation in the Senate. Because the party that controls the White House also controls the Senate, the Senate operates much like a parliament. All chairmanships of committees and subcommittees are held by members of the president's party. If the president does not wish to launch a debate on macroeconomic or industrial policy, then the Senate will not launch such a debate either. The lead of the White House is followed; there is no desire to rock the boat. I can think of one or two exceptions to this rule, but an issue as esoteric and complex as industrial policy is not, and cannot, become one of them.

Let me provide a concrete example. I am the ranking minority member of the Subcommittee on Economic Policy of the Senate Banking Committee. "Economic policy" is about as broad a mandate as a subcommittee can have. Surely industrial policy could have been discussed within such a forum. And yet during the first two years of the Reagan administration, Senator Armstrong, the chairman of the subcommittee, called no meetings on industrial policy. In fact he called no meetings of any kind.

The House is a livelier place. Belonging as it does to the opposition party, it has begun to consider industrial policy. Two or three proposals have been developed. They reflect some thinking and some ideas. Nevertheless they certainly could not pass for sweeping master plans.

So how does the United States generate a serious debate? One possibility is President Reagan. Unquestionably the president is a sensational communicator. When he gets interested in an idea, he wants to present it to the American people. He does a very good job of that. As a result I would like to figure out how to get these issues on his radar screen, especially because he has time left in his second term to act. Unfortunately I am not optimistic. On the basis of what I know about his predispositions on this issue, I do not think I can rely on him to launch the debate.

Felix Rohatyn is another possibility. He has been beating this drum. Frankly, however, his are sounds in the wilderness. He gives a speech and people come, but there is no real takeoff in terms of media exposure.

I suspect it will take a crisis to force the issue. As a nation, the United States finds it difficult to catch up to complex and amorphous issues at the boundaries of government, business, and labor until the pressures of the situation are so severe that it has to act.

I am very troubled by the prospect of waiting for a crisis to evoke action. If Americans procrastinate to the point that they can act only after the fact, they may find themselves very limited in terms of what can be done, how it can be done, and how it will dovetail with all the other things the United States must do around the world. I am frustrated by the limits of my own ability to elevate this issue to national prominence.

BRUCE MACLAURY   Senator Riegle's concern with the U.S. system's inability to deal with amorphous problems except in periods of crisis fits in very well with what Robert Strauss said earlier, namely that industrial policy seemed a more important issue during recession than it does during recovery. If Christian Goux is correct and the United States is headed toward crisis then issues such as industrial policy are likely to become much more lively in the United States.

I do not share the pessimism of Mr. Goux. The United States still has time to reform macroeconomic policy to the point that industrial and other microeconomic policies will appear much less urgent than they do today. Improvements in macroeconomic policy will permit entry into a sustained period of prosperity.

The discussion on which we have embarked is precautionary. The problems of Michigan, of Ohio, and of Pennsylvania justify such discussions. They should not be construed as proof positive, however, that the United States should proceed immediately with implementation of industrial policies.

WALTER ADAMS   The very fact that we debate industrial policy in the context of international trade serves to illustrate the maxim that industrial policy is a stepchild of economic crisis.

When he describes the problems associated with competing in global markets, Senator Riegle emphasizes the importance of wage differentials between rich and poor countries. I disagree with his point of emphasis. Even if American wages failed to exceed those in Asia, the American steel industry as currently constituted might not be able to compete effectively in world markets. Management has been hopelessly lethargic and technologically backward. Wages are not simply above levels to be found in Asia: they exceed the American average for manufacturing by roughly 80 percent. Although the industry has been protected since 1969, it is no more vigorous today than it was then. This is a case of self-inflicted injury; and yet the government is asked to bail the industry out.

The protection awarded to steel has affected other industries adversely. One of these—automobiles—is as dear to my heart as it is to that of Senator Riegle. As long as Japanese producers of automobiles buy steel at world market prices while American producers buy steel at protectionist prices, the American industry is bound to be the less competitive of the two. As Alfred Marshall once said: "If there are three balls in the bowl and if you touch one of them, the other two will move too." We have never fully appreciated Marshall's wisdom.

I do not wish to suggest that the automobile industry is free of blame. It too has allowed wages to exceed the American average in manufacturing by a hefty margin. It has allowed product mix and product quality, as well as product price, to become unresponsive to market forces. In large measure the problems of the automobile industry, like those of the steel industry, should be viewed as self-inflicted.

For these reasons it is very dangerous indeed to advocate collusion—a better term than cooperation—among business, labor, and government. There has been too much not too little interaction—for both the health of the industry and the public interest.

DONALD RIEGLE   I agree with much that Walter Adams says. Like others who studied at Michigan State University, I was heavily influenced by his lectures. Nevertheless on several points my position differs from his.

I will not dispute the argument that labor and management should take full responsibility for the greed they have expressed while exercising their monopoly power. But we should not blind ourselves to other dimensions of reality. The industrial base of this country is shrinking rather dramatically. In large measure no doubt this shrinkage is necessary and efficient, but I find it difficult to look ahead and to say that everything will end happily, that things will be good for Americans, for America, and for the West. I am deeply worried about the impact of industrial crisis on the stability of the system the West has enjoyed since World War II.

I look at the McDonald's hamburger people. They pay the minimum wage of $3.35 an hour. On the basis of working a forty-hour week even a single person cannot live on such a wage. And yet McDonald's now employs more people than does General Motors. The United States has been replacing high-income jobs in manufacturing with low-income jobs in services. How will people afford the standard of living associated with a rich country?

I do not oppose adjustment. Obviously it is impossible to take a snapshot of an economy and preserve forever the structure observed. Major adjustments must, however, be managed. Given the deficits in merchandise trade and the government budget, the inadequacy of national saving, the defaults on foreign loans, and the budgetary requirements of national defense, free-market sophistry as espoused by the leaders of my own government is not enough. The president thinks everything will work like a charm if only the country stays the course. He says as much with a cock of his head as he gets into his helicopter. I do not share his optimism. It looks to me as if American industry will experience substantial turbulence unless Americans select an awfully good pilot or an awfully good navigational plan. Some type of collective decisionmaking is required—not central planning but something new to the history of American institutions. Inevitably it will involve interaction among business, labor, and government.

BRUCE MacLAURY   The comparison of General Motors with McDonald's is certainly dramatic. It might be misleading as well. By and large the people who staff McDonald's are people who would not otherwise be in the labor force—teenagers and women who work part time. During the 1970s these jobs did not displace highly paid positions in industry. Rather they permitted the United States to increase employment substantially under difficult macroeconomic conditions.

JOHN WATTS   As I read the works of Robert Lawrence and Charles Schultze, I come away with the impression that compared with other developed countries industrial employment in the United States has not shrunk. It has merely shifted among particular industries. Unlike Senator Riegle, then, I do not see a reason for alarm.

Let me turn the discussion for a moment from industry to finance. Given his varied experience, I wonder if Mr. de Combret shares the opinion of a very persuasive partner at Lazard Frères, Felix Rohatyn, to the effect that the health of American industries—sunrise and sunset alike—requires development of new financial institutions linked in some way to the federal government?

FRANÇOIS DE COMBRET   I am not convinced that the United States needs new financial structures. For evidence let me return to the steel company that I described earlier. After studying the company's market, we concluded that it could not survive for very long. As a result, we decided it should file for reorganization and then for bankruptcy. The company did just that, and the owner was able to recover $35 million. We placed these funds in a high-tech company from Silicon Valley. That company is doing very well, and our client is happy with the situation.

This example demonstrates clearly that existing American institutions are capable of transferring resources from sectors of low productivity to sectors of high productivity. They can do so just as a textbook might prescribe. In this case I fail to see what government intervention could have added.

When Mr. Rohatyn advocates industrial policy, he has in mind what he did for New York City. He did not create a new financial institution; rather he forced labor, bankers, and politicians to sit at the same table and get to know each other. It is conceivable that coordination of this sort would help, but the financial institutions already exist in this country. The capitalist system works well. It creates jobs. I do not see how government intervention would improve the situation.

DONALD RIEGLE   During the past year, under the leadership of Ted Kennedy, a group of Senate Democrats has been studying industrial policy. One of the issues that came up was whether the United States needed a governmentally sponsored bank for industry. The group decided not to advocate such a bank in spite of the arguments put forth on its behalf by Mr. Rohatyn. Not only did we doubt the political wisdom of the project, we also doubted the need for a single new mechanism of finance. Instead, the group recommended establishing a pool of money that the federal government could distribute to the states. Combined with state funds, this money could be used to influence decisions at the margin—to encourage promising activities that would develop slowly if at all without aid.

GEORGE KRUMBHAAR   Many of the specific policies suggested by advocates of industrial policy have already been implemented at the state and local levels. A recent survey of the National Governors Association reveals that every state has engaged in some such policy, examples of which include abatement of taxes on particular activities, construction of research parks, and encouragement of agreements between public universities and local industry. This may show that industrial policy is already alive and well in the United States. It may also show that industrial policy is appropriately handled at the state level, where healthy competition is assured. North Carolina is not a natural mecca for high technology; and yet not by coincidence does it enjoy a low rate of unemployment. Successive governors have worked hard to ensure that citizens could find jobs if they wished to work.

Does anyone agree with me about the importance of state and local policies? Is there a French counterpart to decentralized industrial policy?

CHRISTIAN GOUX   François Mitterrand is committed to the idea of decentralization. Under his leadership several powers have been delegated to the regions. Given the importance of employment, the regions have attempted to exercise these powers in the economic sphere. In principle every region now has its own industrial policy.

I am not sanguine, however, about the prospects of regional industrial policy. Most problems of employment involve migrations of large industrial enterprises. The larger the enterprise, the greater the likelihood that government policy will be set in Paris. The very fact that most regional policies are still devised in Paris serves to underscore the impotence of the regions.

It is important to recognize that economic concentration, no less than political concentration, accounts for the importance of Paris in the French system of government. Genuine decentralization of the political process will be difficult to achieve as long as the economy is controlled by a few large companies.

ROBERT LAWRENCE   Contrary to widespread opinion, the industrial base of the United States is expanding not contracting. To the extent that industry is creating problems of unemployment, the cause is geographical displacement of employment opportunity, not the absence of such opportunity. It is time to recognize that the problem now faced by the United States is declining regions, not declining industries.

If we continue to view the problem as one of declining industries, we will inevitably adopt the wrong set of policy tools. For example, concern about unemployment in Michigan should not lead to protection of the entire automobile industry regardless of where it produces. The textile industry of New England provides a good case in point. During the 1960s we were concerned about unemployment in Massachusetts, so we protected the entire textile industry. Today a rather profitable industry is located in the South. Given the migration of the industry, it is not clear that protectionism was the best approach to the regional problem of Massachusetts. Clearly the concept of industrial policy is merely diverting our attention from what I think is the more fundamental question of why some regions decline while others rise.

Because America's problems are regional rather than industrial, it is appropriate to develop policies at the state level. Federal coordination could be improved, but the states must play a larger role.

What should the states do? Many people advocate legislation that inhibits closure of plants. Data suggest, however, that plant closures occur about as frequently in rising regions as they do in declining regions. The major difference between the two types of region involves the birth of new companies. Regional policy should focus on the determinants of business creation, especially in declining regions.

Bruce K. MacLaury

Concluding Comments

SEVEN RECURRING THEMES emerge from the papers and discussions in this book. The first three relate primarily to the French experience; the rest apply more directly to the United States.

—Since World War II the French economy has performed even better than have the economies of France's neighbors. At issue is the extent to which industrial policy deserves the credit for this achievement. Other factors, such as the shift from agriculture to industry, the rise of international trade, and the reliance on devaluation to neutralize inflation, also played important roles. It remains to be seen how the relative contributions of the various factors can be appraised.

—Industrial policy is closely tied to indicative planning. Both have changed rather markedly during the postwar period. Early in the postwar years the French government emphasized the construction of a modern industrial base. In so doing, it enjoyed broad support among the French people. During the 1960s the government engaged in a good deal of targeting: it focused its favors on a few companies in a few industries—on corporate national champions. The successes of targeting have been confined to sectors that sell a large share of their output to government. Where private parties buy the bulk of output, targeting has been of doubtful value. More recently, France has moved away from targeting. In policy jargon it has attempted to substitute horizontal for selective policies. In other words it has attempted to improve the business environment throughout the economy rather than to promote specific companies or products.

—The policies of the Fabius government were attacked from both the Left and the Right. On the Left there was disenchantment regarding the emphasis on profitability. In particular the Left wished to develop criteria other than profitability for use in public enterprises. In contrast the Right urged privatization and a general reduction of government interference in the microeconomy.

—French industrial policy is just one manifestation of government interven-

196

tion in the French economy. Such intervention reaches deeply into French history. No such tradition exists in the United States. On this side of the Atlantic, industrial policy has nothing to build on.

—Economic conditions differ substantially between France and the United States. For example, the dollar is a reserve currency, and the American market constitutes a major slice of the world market. As a result even if France were obliged to resort to industrial policy, it does not follow that the United States would face a similar imperative. The United States can survive its current resort to inappropriate macroeconomic policies by borrowing heavily from the rest of the world. The same cannot be said of France.

—In the context of mature industries, industrial policy should not take the form of protection from foreign competition. Even though it constituted just one component of a comprehensive package, protection did not restore the health of the French steel industry. In the United States, devoid as it is of coordinated planning, protection would be less valuable still.

—We must be careful to distinguish rhetoric from behavior. In France industrial policy is discussed quite vociferously. In the United States it is not. Even so the United States does engage in such policy. Voluntary restraints on steel imports provide one example. Others include the rescues of Chrysler and Continental Illinois, the funding of R&D activity, and the design of tax laws to foster investment. The United States exhibits many of the elements of an industrial policy without the phraseology.

If industrial policy is defined broadly, it can encompass a wide variety of activities now pursued by the American government. For example, the United States has consciously modified its antitrust policies in order to take account of international competition. In the computer field companies have been allowed to cooperate in research if not in development to a point that would not have been authorized in the past. Moreover, the movement to deregulate transportation, telecommunications, and finance must be viewed as microeconomic policy with a sectoral focus. To evaluate policies of this importance would require other conferences of this magnitude.

Christian Stoffaës

Postscript

MOST OF THE PAPERS in this book were written during the summer of 1984. As a result it was difficult for their authors to place the policies of President Mitterrand in perspective. In this postscript I shall focus on the industrial strategies of the Left during its five years in power.

The Setting

The year 1981 clearly opened a new phase in French industrial policy. Not only did the world economic environment undergo substantial change, but in May, François Mitterrand was elected president, and in June a Socialist-Communist majority was elected to the National Assembly. Never since the creation of the Fifth Republic in 1958 had the Left been called upon to govern.

The International Economic Environment

For a number of reasons, from the French perspective, the international economic situation deteriorated between 1981 and 1986. Following the second oil shock of 1979 the world economy suffered a deep depression that lasted until 1983. Foreign competition—from Southeast Asia in light consumer goods and from Japan in automobiles, mechanical equipment, and electronics— intensified. The electronics and information-processing industries experienced technological revolutions the effects of which spread at a rapid pace to the rest of the economy. American economic policy resulted in high rates of interest, massive revaluation of the dollar, and financial strains in developing countries. In France these developments increased the difficulties of such troubled industries as steel, shipbuilding, automobiles, and textiles. Employment in manufacturing generally declined and exports of capital goods to OPEC and the third world fell. Thus the Left was immediately confronted with a deep, pan-European recession. In a sense, the Left was not lucky to come to power in the early 1980s.

Macroeconomic Policy

During these five years, French macroeconomic policy underwent dramatic changes. Before taking power in 1981 the Socialist and Communist parties argued that economic policy should be geared toward fighting slow growth, rising unemployment, and excessive inequality. They considered reflation the policy of choice for increasing growth and employment, and they advocated increased taxation, increased expenditure on social programs, and work sharing to reduce inequality.

When the Left came to power under Prime Minister Pierre Mauroy, it attempted to implement the policies it had backed during its years in opposition. The government budget for 1982 entailed a 27 percent increase in spending over the previous year. During the summer of 1981 alone, 55,000 new jobs were created in the public sector; another 60,000 were budgeted for 1982. Minimum wages and social benefits were increased sharply and new taxes struck high incomes and great wealth. The working week was reduced legislatively to thirty-nine hours, and a fifth week was added to annual vacation time.

By mid-1983, however, the policy of reflation was clearly in trouble. The government's strategy proved to be totally countercyclical with respect to the world economic environment. Although unemployment was stabilized and modest growth was achieved, an enormous trade deficit appeared (Fr 93 billion, or 3 percent of GNP, in 1982), the budget deficit rose to 3.5 percent of GNP, and the rate of inflation rose relative to the OECD benchmark. The result was three devaluations of the franc in quick succession. In March 1983, in the wake of the third devaluation and the defeat of the Left in local elections, economic policy underwent a radical transformation. Although urged to increase interventionism, spending, and protectionism, President Mitterrand chose a policy of wage and price controls, budget tightening, and tax increases. The new policies improved the balance of trade and the balance of payments, and reduced the rate of inflation (to 5 percent in 1985). At the same time, however, unemployment resumed its sharp rise, reaching 2.5 million people by the end of 1985. And the number of layoffs and industrial bankruptcies increased sharply.

Ideology

The Left came to power with an idealized vision of industrial policy, believing it to be a powerful tool that could alter profoundly the structure of French industry as it solved high unemployment, slow growth, and national economic dependence. Supply-side policies, including increased intervention in the industrial sector, were viewed as necessary complements to reflation of demand—both to cure *la désastreuse gestion antérieure* (the mistakes of the previous administration) and *pour sortir de la crise* (to restore prosperity).

During its years in opposition, the Left had severely criticized the industrial policies of the government of Raymond Barre. It argued that Barre's strategy of moving French industrial structure toward narrow technological niches (*créneaux*) in which France was supposed to be able to achieve commanding advantages would lead to massive unemployment, disindustrialization, and the sacrifice of entire industrial sectors and regions. Similarly, it attacked Barre's efforts to promote exports on the grounds that such a strategy merely increased France's dependence on foreigners. Although it agreed with Barre that productive investment was needed to end France's structural and cyclical problems, it argued that such investment required nationalizations and government intervention rather than economic liberalism.

The rationale for an extensive program of nationalization was essentially political. Nationalization appeared to be the key common element in Socialist and Communist ideologies, an element that therefore permitted the two parties to agree on a joint platform (the *Programme Commun de Gouvernement*) in 1972. In essence, French socialism became definable as social democracy plus nationalizations. Nationalization also permitted the government to control economically and to neutralize politically the economic forces that in principle were hostile to the Left: the very rich (the *mur d'argent*), the banks, the large corporations, and the trade associations (such as the Conseil National du Patronat Français). Nationalization was also supposed to reinforce the power of labor unions because in the older public enterprises the unions had been given substantial de facto power of codetermination. Despite these political motivations, however, economic arguments were used to justify the actions: nationalization would permit economic policy to eliminate what was perceived as an excessively fatalistic response to cyclical and structural problems. Early in the period of Socialist rule, the rhetoric surrounding the nationalizations was positively lyrical in quality. The nationalized companies would each serve as a *fer de lance* (spearhead) or *socle* (foundation) in the effort to achieve a *rupture avec le capitalisme* (a break with capitalism).

Industrial Policy during the Honeymoon Period (1981–83)

Just as the macroeconomic policies of the Left can be separated into two periods—the honeymoon (*état de grâce*) of 1981–83 and the austerity (*rigueur*) of 1983–86—so the industrial policy practiced by the Left underwent profound transformation. During the honeymoon period, government implemented the proposals contained in the platform developed in common by the Socialists and Communists.

Most objectives of the Left's industrial policies differed sharply from those of its predecessors. They included:

—creating jobs in manufacturing, or at least reversing disindustrialization.

—rescuing industries in trouble, following the principle that "there are no doomed industries, only outmoded technologies."

—developing an investment policy that was sufficiently activist (*volontariste*) to assure countercyclical investment behavior.

—promoting investments in research to develop new technologies and products.

—promoting whole vertical streams of production (*filières*) rather than specific niches (*créneaux*). According to this view, no niche is viable on its own; it depends on the viability of upstream and downstream industries. Increasing the specialization of French industry is undesirable: the ability to compete effectively in the world economy depends on the capacity of the industrial sector to satisfy the bulk of domestic needs and on the existence of a tightly knit and diversified industrial fabric. The government should thus intervene wherever necessary within each vertical stream of production.

—promoting attempts by French companies to reduce the share of imports in domestic consumption (*la reconquête du marché intérieur*). Rather than continue unlimited promotion of exports, the government should attempt to reduce the role of trade in GNP.

—expanding trade and creating new types of relations with developing countries (*codéveloppement*).

Nationalizations

The tools used to achieve these objectives were as radical as the objectives themselves. A program of nationalization more ambitious than any ever undertaken in France or abroad was begun. Five major industrial conglomerates (Saint Gobain–Pont-à-Mousson, Rhône-Poulenc, Pechiney Ugine Kuhlmann, Compagnie Générale d'Electricité, and Thomson), two steel companies (Usinor and Sacilor), two high-technology companies specializing in military products (Dassault and Matra), three subsidiaries or affiliates of foreign-based multinationals (Compagnie Générale de Constructions Téléphoniques, CII-Honeywell-Bull, and Roussel-Uclaf), thirty-six commercial banks (with the exception of the

Crédit Commercial de France and Crédit Industriel et Commercial, all were small or medium-sized), and two major investment banks (Suez and Paribas) became owned by the state. Whereas public enterprise already dominated such sectors as transportation, communications, energy, banking, and insurance, the public sector now accounted for a dominant share (60 percent) of basic industry (metallurgy and chemicals, for example), a dominant share of high-technology industry reliant on government procurement (aerospace, electrical equipment, telecommunications, electronics, computers, pharmaceuticals), and a major share (30 percent) of capital goods industries (automobiles, mechanical equipment, and so forth). Public enterprises now employed 750,000 people in France alone (and 250,000 abroad), produced 25 percent of industrial output, and accounted for more than 50 percent of production in industries displaying great producer concentration, capital intensity of production, large expenditures on research, and a high propensity to export. Some Fr 47 billion was spent to compensate shareholders adequately (with government bonds). Of the total, Fr 18.5 billion was used to compensate shareholders of the industrial enterprises that were nationalized. With very few exceptions, by 1982 the old managements of the new public enterprises were replaced with people selected by government.

Financing and Restructuring the Nationalized Corporations

The public enterprises received important capital grants from the government's budget: Fr 8 billion in 1982; Fr 14 billion in each of 1983, 1984, and 1985; and Fr 10 billion in 1986. Moreover, they were allowed to issue long-term bonds and nonvoting stock (titres participatifs) as well as to receive loans from the nationalized banks. A clear effect of the nationalizations was to break, or at least to relax, the financial constraints imposed on large French corporations by the underdevelopment of French capital markets.

In 1982 an ambitious investment program was launched in the steel industry with the objective of stabilizing production capacity at 24 million tons. Another ambitious investment plan had been adopted in 1981 for the coal industry. Under the plan, Charbonnages de France, a public enterprise, received increased government subsidies (up from Fr 4 billion in 1981 to Fr 7 billion in 1983–84). The goal of the plan was to reverse the former government's policy of capacity reduction so as to increase production from 23 million tons in 1981 to 30 million tons by 1990. In high-technology industries, strategy focused on electronics. In July 1982 the government decided that the sector as a whole should invest Fr 140 billion between 1983 and 1987. Information processing, components, electronic consumer goods, professional electronics, and telecommunications were to be emphasized. In this investment program, the public enterprises of the electronics and computer industries were supposed to play major roles as permitted by their increased receipt of subsidies and capital grants from government.

Most of the government's money was used, however, to avoid bankruptcies and cover losses in depressed sectors. For example, some 40 percent of the capital grants for public enterprises (Fr 25 billion) went to the steel industry, which suffered cumulative losses of about Fr 50 billion between 1981 and 1985. About 40 percent went to chemicals, nonferrous metals, and automobiles—also to cover losses and to allow the cleansing of balance sheets. Only 20 percent went to research and investment in such growth industries as electronics.

Although the government had said in 1981 that it would never treat its enterprises like Tinker Toys (that it would never engage in *Mecanno industriel*), it did attempt to reorganize and rationalize the public enterprises. Using the word *pôle* to represent the old concept of national champion, it began to take lines of business or subsidiaries from one public enterprise and place them under the control of another—the intent being to locate all activities of a given type in the same public enterprise. Thus most of the steel companies (Ugine Aciers, Métallurgique de Normandie, and Pompey, for example) were absorbed by Usinor and Sacilor. Petrochemicals, fertilizers, and other heavy chemical activities were concentrated in Elf-Aquitaine and CDF-Chimie. Pechiney Ugine Kuhlmann returned to its original specialization in nonferrous metals. With the absorption of Thomson-Télécommunications, Compagnie Electro-Mécanique, and Framatome, the Compagnie Générale d'Electricité achieved a virtual monopoly in telecommunications and electrical equipment. Saint-Gobain abandoned computers and electronics. Thomson specialized in military electronics, electronic consumer goods, and electronic components. Bull became the sole national producer of computers and information-processing equipment.

Rescue Policies and Sectoral Plans

Industrial policy developed along similar lines in the private sector. The Comité Interministériel pour l'Aménagement des Structures Industrielles (CIASI) was reinvigorated under a new name (Comité Interministériel pour les Restructurations Industrielles, or CIRI). Its mission was to coordinate financial support for failing companies to save jobs in troubled industries. Pressure was exerted on the banks to contribute to the rescue efforts. The Treasury employed both old and new mechanisms to finance lame ducks. In particular, it created or expanded various financial intermediaries designed to mobilize saving for use in industrial companies. These intermediaries raised money mostly by floating bonds guaranteed by the state itself on various securities markets.[1]

Comprehensive policies for specific industries (plans sectoriels) were launched in such troubled sectors as textiles, clothing, machine tools, and pulp and paper. Boussac in textiles, La Chapelle Darblay in pulp and paper, and Intelautomatismes and Machines Françaises Lourdes in machine tools were the most notable examples of companies that became the objects of rescue plans designed to prevent bankruptcies, save jobs, and curb imports. The sectoral plans involved government subsidies, loans at preferential rates, restructuring of companies, and exemptions from social security taxes. Shipbuilding also received enormously increased subsidies (Fr 4 billion in 1984, compared with Fr 1.5 billion in 1981). Renault, a public enterprise since 1945, was encouraged to create jobs.

Government expenditures on research increased sharply. The goal of the Loi d'Orientation de la Recherche et de la Technologie, enacted in April 1982, was to raise the share of GNP devoted to R&D from 1.9 percent in 1981 to 2.5 percent by 1986. The law was written after a major conference of scientists and policymakers, organized by the minister of research, Jean-Pierre Chevènement, was held in February 1982.

Budgets and the number of personnel at the major government research laboratories and agencies were increased. Public enterprises were encouraged to develop their research expenditures. Companies in the private sector received research subsidies and tax exemptions. New agencies were created and existing agencies were given greater budgets. Examples included the Agence de l'Informatique (ADI), the Centre Mondial pour l'Informatique and the Agence Nationale de Valorisation de la Recherche (ANVAR).

A cabinet-level post of minister of energy was created and attached to the Ministry of Industry. Although some in the Socialist party and the Socialist trade union (the Confédération Française Démocratique du Travail, or CFDT) sought a moratorium on the construction of nuclear power plants, the Communist trade union (the Confédération Générale du Travail, or CGT), operating

1. The intermediaries were Société Française de Participations Industrielles (SFPI) for the public enterprises, Caisse d'Amortissement pour l'Acier (CAPA) and Fonds d'Investissement Sidérurgique (FIS) for the steel industry, and IDI-Sofaris and Crédit National–Compagnie Financière de Développement Industriel (CFDI) for other private companies and for Renault.

through its branch at Electricité de France, secured continued if slower expansion of the system. As noted above, an effort was made to redevelop domestic coal. An ambitious policy to conserve energy and develop new energy sources (through the Agence Française pour la Maitrise de l'Energie, or AFME) was also launched.

An important natural gas contract with Algeria, which had been blocked by the previous government, was signed under terms very favorable to Algeria. Another was signed with the USSR. The Algerian contract was the only significant implementation of the policy of codevelopment.

In order to effect these policies, the regulatory and financial roles of the Ministry of Industry and of the Ministry of Research and Technology were increased. Pierre Dreyfus, former chairman of Renault, the alleged prototype of successful nationalization, was chosen minister of industry, serving from June 1981 until June 1982, while Jean-Pierre Chevènement, leader of the left wing of the Socialist party (the CERES group), became minister of research and technology. In June 1982 the two ministries were merged and placed under Chevènement's control.

Industrial Policy during the Period of Austerity (1983–86)

After the critical redirection of macroeconomic policy in March 1983, industrial policy also changed dramatically. Employment was no longer an objective of industrial policy. The importance of the home market and the need to occupy all stages of each stream of production were no longer mentioned. Instead, modernization became the goal. Companies had to become more competitive because the economy would remain open to foreign competition. Public enterprises had to become profitable, even if they needed to lay off workers. These enterprises were encouraged to withdraw from unprofitable activities and to cooperate whenever necessary with foreign multinationals.

The radical change in policy was symbolized by the resignation of Jean-Pierre Chevènement as minister of research and industry in March 1983 and his replacement by Laurent Fabius. In July 1984, under Edith Cresson, the ministry was renamed the Ministry of Industrial Redeployment and Foreign Trade— a symbolic, semantic change. At that time the departure of the Communists from the government, as well as the resignation of Pierre Mauroy and his replacement by Fabius as prime minister, confirmed the triumph of the new approach to industrial policy.

Major Revisions: Coal, Steel, Shipbuilding, and Automobiles

Budgetary constraints became the major impetus for change in industrial policy. They struck first in four industries targeted by the policy of 1981. In November 1983 a ceiling was placed on the budget of Charbonnages de France that entailed abandoning the ambitious investment plan adopted in 1981. Several inefficient coal mines were closed, 30,000 layoffs (50 percent of the workforce) were announced for the ensuing five-year period, and the production forecast for 1990 was reduced to 13 million tons. The change in policy provoked the resignation of the Communist chairman of the Charbonnages.

In April 1984, in accordance with the Davignon Plan of the European Coal and Steel Community, limits were placed on capital grants to the steel industry. This action led to revision of the plan of 1982. Some 25,000 jobs (30 percent of the workforce) were to be cut over a three-year period, and several plants were to be closed, especially in Lorraine. That decision, announced by President Mitterrand himself, engendered strong reactions, especially from the Confédération Générale du Travail and from the Communist party.

In shipbuilding, subsidies from the government were capped, and the five major shipyards were reorganized into two companies (Nord-Med and Atlantique). Plans were laid to cut employment in the industry, and oversight of the industry was transferred from the Ministry of Transportation to the Ministry of Industry.

In January 1985 the revelation of an enormous financial loss for 1984 at Renault (Fr 12.5 billion) led to the dismissal of its chairman, Bernard Hanon, and to his replacement by Georges Besse. At his previous post (Pechiney), Besse had acquired the reputation of being a tough manager and a job cutter. A plan to abolish 30,000 jobs at Renault and to have the company withdraw from peripheral activities was announced. Sharp and open conflict developed between management and the Confédération Générale du Travail, which had long enjoyed the reputation of being the co-manager of this "model" public enterprise. The purge at Renault was probably the most symbolic reversal of industrial policy.

Modernization and Industrial Conversion

Instead of trying to cover up the dramatic reversal of industrial policy, the government emphasized the change, hoping thereby to shock public opinion in general and its electorate in particular as well as to rally business leaders to the new policy. Speeches by members of the government became full of references to modernization, innovation, entrepreneurial spirit, and even profit. Refer-

ences to economic and social inequalities, worker participation, and full employment were no longer heard. The microeconomic austerity practiced in the
public sector was thus extended. The sectoral plans were slowed down or
abandoned. Under pressure from the EEC Commission, the textile plan disappeared. The role of the CIRI diminished. Major job cuts were authorized at
Peugeot-Citroën-Talbot, a large textile firm (Boussac) was sold to a private
financial group, and the government refused to rescue a major engineering
group (Creusot-Loire), which was subsequently dismantled and sold piecemeal.

The government did not shed all of its activism, of course. To cope with the
decline of traditional industries, it reinforced its regional policies. To attract new
investment in depressed areas, it created fourteen priority development areas
(*pôles de conversion*) in March 1984, and direct investment, especially on the
part of Japanese companies, was encouraged in these regions. Ironically, the
special conversion plan for Lorraine bore a strong resemblance to the policies of
the Barre government as embodied in the Fonds Spécial d'Adaptation
Industrielle (FSAI). In general, the government moved away from economic
nationalism and encouraged international joint ventures, especially within the
framework of the Eureka project.

As for activism in the high-technology industries, the government paved the
way for continued intervention by attaching the Ministry of the Post Office and
of Telecommunications to the Ministry of Industry. In so doing, it will be able to
finance its electronics and space policies from the vast profits generated in
telephone services. More generally, the one area in which government continues to pursue its early strategy is the promotion of research. Although government expenditures on research have not increased, austerity has not resulted in
their decline. The objective of spending 2.5 percent of GNP on R&D has not
been attained, but a ratio of 2.3 percent will nevertheless be reached in 1986.

Before closing, I should say something about the contribution of the banks to
industrial policy. According to the political rhetoric, the banks were nationalized
so that they could be placed at the service of industrial development. Smaller
banks have been regrouped around the Crédit Commercial de France and the
Crédit Industriel et Commercial, thereby creating some regional networks. But
with the exception of some arm-twisting by the Treasury, designed to force
certain banks to prop up lame ducks, banks have not been used as major
instruments of industrial policy. Under Pierre Bérégovoy, the minister of finance, financial markets have been substantially deregulated. And new ideas
have been implemented in these markets—nonvoting shares in public enterprises, a new type of listing on the stock exchange for medium-sized companies
(the *second marché boursier*), leveraged buyouts, and tax exemptions for venture capital and stock ownership. These reforms have, however, little to do with

public financial enterprise. Ironically, it is the Left that will have liberalized a sector that for forty years had been rigidly cartellized under government guidance.

The Industrial Policy of the Left in Perspective

It is too early to judge the effects of these policies comprehensively. Industrial policy can be evaluated only in the long run. The strategies of today's government will ripen, for better or worse, only in the reign of its successors. Even so, a few things can be said at this time.

The Left has generally failed to fulfill its own objectives. Industrial policy has not been a panacea for the structural and cyclical problems of the French economy. Economic planning has not been rehabilitated either as a major determinant of the allocation of savings among investments or as a major forum for social dialogue. Public enterprise is drowning in red ink. The combined net losses of public enterprises, old and new, in the industrial sector have increased sharply—from Fr 11.8 billion in 1981 to Fr 20.7 billion in 1982, Fr 17.6 billion in 1983, Fr 28.5 billion in 1984, and Fr 12.2 billion in 1985, for a five-year total of Fr 90.8 billion. Recent improvements in the results of the five major companies nationalized in 1982 do not outweigh the steep deterioration of the steel companies, of the basic chemical companies, and of Renault. The difficulties of these companies should be attributed both to the macroeconomic recession and to inadequate adaptation by the companies thereto.

Following a slight slowdown in 1982–83, the reduction of employment in manufacturing has resumed at an average annual rate of 150,000 jobs. The level of productive investment stagnated between 1981 and 1984, even though it began to increase sharply in other OECD countries in 1983. Public enterprises reduced their workforces in the same proportion as the rest of manufacturing (a contraction of 8 percent between 1981 and 1984) and have only moderately increased their rates of investment. The French share of world markets diminished from 10 percent in 1980 to 8.5 percent in 1984, while imports have grown. Not much can be said regarding reconquest of the domestic market or the buttressing of whole vertical streams of production. Except in electronics, where a new policy initiative has been taken, "reconquest" has remained no more than a political slogan.

Although failing by its own criteria, the industrial policy of the Left might have beneficial effects in the long run. Since 1981 the structure of French industry has changed radically. The restructuring of heavy industries—steel, basic chemicals, nonferrous metals—was certainly in order. Accumulated debts did have to be written off, obsolete plants did have to be retired, and investments in modernization did have to be coordinated. Nevertheless, these efforts have placed a heavy burden on the budget. And precious time was wasted during the reflationary period of 1981–83.

In the high technology industries the increase in government expenditure on research will also prove useful in the future. Still, a large part of this spending has been devoted to basic research and public laboratories, with only indirect effects upon industrial development. Also, the wisdom of the policy of national champions is open to question: it certainly increases the likelihood that French companies will grow big enough to compete in world markets; but it also creates sheltered monopolies supported by public procurement and insulated from international joint ventures.

Perhaps the clearest positive result of the new industrial policy has been a durable change in ideology. After being the cement of the union of the Left during the 1970s, industrial policy has become the major cause of the split between the Communists and the Socialists. Only the Communists now advocate nationalizations, sectoral plans, coercive planning, and protectionism. And their electoral weight is vanishing. Marxist ideology, very influential among French intellectuals and politicized labor unions until quite recently, has suffered major defeats. Through repudiation of its own ideology, the Left has helped French public opinion to convert itself to such modern economic values as free trade, profit, and entrepreneurship. It is not yet clear what the verdict on Socialist industrial policy will be. Perhaps it will appear to have been a necessary stage in the adaptation of French industry to a new world environment. Or perhaps it will become the critical ingredient of a major new political consensus. Perhaps, however, it will appear in history as the tombstone of the Left.

The extremism of economic policy during the early 1980s engendered strong adverse reactions from a large segment of the public. At the same time, the neoliberal and deregulatory wave born in the United States of Ronald Reagan and the United Kingdom of Margaret Thatcher reached French soil. As a result, economic liberalism—never a strong component of French ideology—has gained in popularity. It is an essential plank in the political platforms of the neo-Gaullist Rassemblement pour la République (RPR) and the Union pour la Démocratie Française (UDF). Since the parties of the center-right returned to government in March 1986, industrial policy is likely to change appreciably. Deregulation of finance, transportation, and telecommunications; abandonment of price controls and layoff controls; and denationalization of banks and industrial companies will become major items on France's policy agenda. Still, it remains to be seen whether such policies will be implemented in a manner that signals major change in the historical course and the sociocultural tradition of French industrial policy. The continuities may prevail, just as they prevailed between 1981 and 1986 despite the revolutionary slogans of 1981. But this should not be surprising. Already in 1856, in his book *l'Ancien Régime et la Révolution*, Aléxis de Tocqueville argued that the more France appears to change, the more it stays the same.

Authors' Biographies

WILLIAM JAMES ADAMS is associate professor of economics at the University of Michigan and an affiliate of the Foreign Policy Studies program at the Brookings Institution. A specialist in comparative industrial organization, he is currently writing a monograph for Brookings titled *Modernization of the French Economy Since World War II.*

HENRI AUJAC is scientific counselor to the president and former director-general of the Bureau d'Information et de Prévisions Economiques, a research institution affiliated with the Commissariat Général du Plan. He has worked for the High Authority of the European Coal and Steel Community and for the forecasting department of the Ministry of Finance. He teaches economics at both the Ecole Polytechnique and the Ecole Pratique des Hautes Etudes.

BELA BALASSA is professor of political economy at the Johns Hopkins University. He advises the World Bank, the Organisation for Economic Cooperation and Development, and many agencies of both the United Nations and the U.S. government. A leading authority on international trade, economic integration, and economic development, he has written numerous articles on the French economy.

ROBERT BOYER is a member of the Centre d'Etudes Prospectives d'Economie Mathématique Appliquées à la Planification, a research institution associated with the Commissariat Général du Plan. Earlier in his career, M. Boyer worked in the Direction de la Prévision of the Ministry of Finance. Currently, he teaches at the Ecole Pratique des Hautes Etudes.

FRANÇOIS DE COMBRET is a general partner at Lazard Frères et Cie., Paris. Before assuming his present duties, he spent three years as an associate at Lazard Frères and Co. in New York. Between 1971 and 1981, he advised President Valéry Giscard d'Estaing, first at the Ministry of Finance (1971–74) and then at the presidency (1974–81). Apart from his duties at Lazard, M. de Combret is conseiller référendaire at the Cour des Comptes.

FRANÇOIS DIDIER is vice-president for strategic planning, Société Nationale Elf-Aquitaine. Before assuming his present position, he directed first the refining/ marketing and then the exploration/production arm of Elf-Aquitaine. At the time of its construction, he was chief engineer of Paris-Orly airport.

GEORGE C. EADS is dean, School of Public Affairs, University of Maryland. Between 1979 and 1981 he served on President Carter's Council of Economic Advisers. He was the U.S. delegate to the OECD's high-level group on positive adjustment policies and chaired the interagency review of industrial policy undertaken by the Carter administration. Dr. Eads is the author of numerous books and articles on regulation.

MICHEL FREYCHE is president, Banque Française du Commerce Extérieur. He has occupied a wide variety of positions in the French civil service, including chief of the Direction des Relations Economiques Extérieures of the Ministry of Economic Affairs and financial counselor of the French embassy in the United Kingdom.

CHRISTIAN GOUX is representative of the Fourth District of the Var and chairman of the Committee on Finance, the Economy, and Economic Planning, in the French National Assembly. In 1981 he served as chairman of the national commission to reform economic planning. Earlier in his career, he directed international studies for the European Communities, counseled the European Development Fund, and worked for a variety of research organizations engaged in economic forecasting. An engineer and economist by training, a professor by profession, M. Goux is also mayor of Bandol and the author of *Où en Sommes-Nous: Sortir de la Crise* (1978).

HENRI GUILLAUME heads the Commissariat Général du Plan. Before presiding over French indicative planning, he served on the staff of Prime Minister Pierre Mauroy. He is professor of economics at both the University of Lille and the Ecole Centrale de Paris. With others, he is the author of *La Rationalisation des Choix Budgétaires* (1971) and *Le Modèle D.M.S.* (1978).

PHILIPPE HERZOG is chief economic spokesman and a member of the political department of the French Communist party. A professor of economics at the

University of Paris-Nanterre, M. Herzog has written widely in the fields of macroeconomic forecasting and industrial policy. His books include *L'Economie à Bras-le-Corps* (2d ed. 1984).

FRANÇOIS LAGRANGE is deputy chief executive officer of the Crédit National. Earlier in his career, he served as special adviser to a large number of cabinet ministers, as deputy commissioner of the Commissariat Général du Plan, and as staff director of the national commission charged in 1974 with reform of French corporation law. Apart from his other duties, M. Lagrange is a member of the Conseil d'Etat.

RAYMOND LÉVY is chairman of the board and managing director of Cockerill Sambre S.A. Before joining Cockerill Sambre, he was chairman of the board and chief executive officer of a number of important public enterprises in the steel and petroleum sectors of the French economy, including Usinor and Elf France. He also served as vice-chairman and president of the Société Nationale Elf-Aquitaine.

BRUCE K. MACLAURY is president of the Brookings Institution.

MARTIN MALVY was secretary of state for energy in the Fabius government. His other political positions have included member and vice-president of the National Assembly and mayor of Figeac.

PAUL MENTRÉ is inspecteur général des finances. He has occupied a wide variety of posts within the ministry of finance, including deputy chief of staff for the minister, Valéry Giscard d'Estaing. Between 1975 and 1978 he was délégué général à l'energie. Before that he was financial counselor in the French embassy in Washington and a member of the boards of directors of several public enterprises. M. Mentré is the author of *Gulliver Enchainé* (1982).

FRANÇOIS PERRIN-PELLETIER is counselor to the president of Peugeot S.A. He is also secretary general of the Committee of Common Market Automobile Constructors in Brussels.

ROGER B. PORTER is professor of government and business at the John F. Kennedy School of Government, Harvard University. Under President Ronald Reagan, he was deputy assistant to the president for policy development. His earlier government posts include special assistant to the president and executive secretary of the President's Economic Policy Board (1974–77), and secretary to the presidential transition team in August 1974.

DONALD W. RIEGLE is U.S. senator from Michigan. He serves on the Banking, Budget, Commerce, Science and Transportation, and Labor and Human Resources committees. Before entering the Senate, he completed five terms in the U.S. House of Representatives.

CHRISTIAN STOFFAËS is deputy director of the Direction des Industries Electroniques et de l'Informatique of the French Ministry of Industry. A graduate of the Ecole Polytechnique and Harvard University, M. Stoffaës has occupied a number of posts within the ministry, including director of policy planning. He also serves as professor of economics at the Institut d'Etudes Politiques in Paris. His many books include *Nationalisations* (1977), *La Grande Menace Industrielle* (1978), *Cours de Politique Industrielle* (1984), *Une Economie Mondiale* (1985), *Fins de Siècles* (1986), and *Industrie: Sortier du XXème Siècle* (1986).

ROBERT S. STRAUSS is a partner in Akin, Gump, Strauss, Hauer & Feld. He was special trade representative of the United States during the Tokyo round of multilateral trade negotiations. He also served as President Carter's personal representative to the Middle East peace negotiations and as chairman of the Democratic National Committee. In 1981, Mr. Strauss was awarded the presidential Medal of Freedom.

BERNARD VERNIER-PALLIEZ was French ambassador to the United States from 1982 to 1984. Before his diplomatic service he was managing director, president, and chairman of the board of the Régie Nationale des Usines Renault.

JOHN ZYSMAN is director of the Berkeley Roundtable on the International Economy and associate professor of political science at the University of California, Berkeley. He has served on a panel of the Office of Technology Assessment and advised the Presidential Commission on a National Agenda for the 1980s. His writings include *Political Strategies for Industrial Order: State, Market, and Industry in France* (1977) and *Governments, Markets, and Growth: Financial Systems and the Politics of Industrial Change* (1983).

Conference Participants

Walter Adams
Professor of Economics and Past President, Michigan State University

Raymond J. Ahearn
Specialist in International Trade, Congressional Research Service

Barry Ames
Legislative Assistant, Office of Congressman Les Aspin

Mark A. Anderson
International economist, AFL-CIO

Patricia P. Bailey
Commissioner, Federal Trade Commission

William E. Barreda
Director, Office of International Trade, Department of the Treasury

Edgar Beigel
Economic and Military Adviser, Office of Western European Affairs, Department of State

E. Marvin Belden
Senior Policy Analyst for Europe, International Trade Administration, Department of Commerce

Sheridan Bell
Desk Officer for France, U.S. Information Agency

Bertrand Bellon
Professor of International Industrial Organization and Industrial Policy, University of Paris-Villetaneuse

Douglas J. Bergner
Director of Program Development, Public Affairs Council

Brian J. Blood
Economic Officer, European Regional Political and Economic Affairs, Department of State

Joshua B. Bolten
Associate, O'Melveny & Myers

Robert R. Bowie
Dillon Professor of International Affairs Emeritus, Harvard University

Myles Boylan
Policy Analyst, Division of Policy Research and Analysis,
National Science Foundation

Daniel H. Brill
Director, Dreyfus Fund Group

François V. Bujon de L'Estang
President and Chief Executive Officer, COGEMA, Inc.

Lewis I. Cohen
Economic Officer, European Bureau, Department of State

William T. Coleman, Jr.
Senior Partner, O'Melveny & Myers (Trustee, Brookings Institution)

Coleman Conroy
Administrative Assistant, Office of Congressman William J.Coyne

Brian Dean Curran
Officer in Charge of French Affairs, Bureau of Europe/West Europe,
Department of State

Lester A. Davis
International Economist, Office of Trade and Investment Analysis,
Department of Commerce

Régis de Laroullière
Financial Attache, Embassy of France

Gérard de Margerie
Financial Counselor, Embassy of France

Hélie de Noailles
Counselor, Economic Affairs, Embassy of France

Charles G. Derecskey
Program Director of Public Affairs, IBM Corporation

Jean-Claude Derian
Scientific Counselor, Embassy of France

Rimmer de Vries
Senior Vice-President, Morgan Guaranty Trust Company

Robert M. Dunn, Jr.
Professor of Economics, George Washington University

Alfred E. Eckes, Jr.
Commissioner, U.S. International Trade Commission

Michael E. C. Ely
Diplomat in Residence, University of St. Thomas

Robert D. Evans
International Economist, International Trade Administration,
Department of Commerce

Ruminska Ewa
Associate Professor, Central School of Planning and Statistics, Warsaw, Poland

Ava Feiner
Manager, International Policy Department, U.S. Chamber of Commerce

Geza Feketekuty
Senior Assistant U.S. Trade Representative

Tony Ferrarese
Press Assistant/Legislative Correspondent, Office of Congressman Berman

Lawrence A. Fox
Vice-President, International Economic Affairs,
National Association of Manufacturers

Paul Freedenberg
Economist, Committee on Banking, U.S. Senate

Julius W. Friend
Professorial Lecturer, History Department, George Washington University

Kiyohiko Fukushima
Manager of Washington Office / Senior Economist, Nomura Research Institute

Wallace Fullerton
International Economist, U.S. International Trade Commission

James K. Galbraith
Deputy Director, Joint Economic Committee, U.S. Congress

Jean-Louis Gergorin
Chef du Centre d'Analyse et de Prévision, Ministère des Relations Extérieures

Ruth S. Gold
Special Assistant, Economic and Business Bureau, Department of State

Otis L. Graham, Jr.
Distinguished University Professor, Department of History,
University of North Carolina

Joseph A. Greenwald
Counsel, Weil, Gotshal & Manges

Jean-Marie Guéhenno
Director of French Cultural Services in the United States, Embassy of France
Michael D. Hathaway
Staff Director, Committee on Energy and Natural Resources, U.S. Senate
Kathryn Hauser
Director, Telecommunications Services, Office of the U.S. Trade Representative
Stanley L. Heginbotham
Chief, Foreign Affairs and National Defense Division,
Congressional Research Division, Library of Congress
Robert Herzstein
Senior Partner, Arnold & Porter
John C. Hilke
Staff Economist, Federal Trade Commission
Roderick M. Hills
Of Counsel, Latham, Watkins & Hills
John W. Holmes
Director, European Regional Political and Economic Affairs, Department of State
Alain Hoyois
Head of the Economic Division, Commercial Office, Embassy of France
John Ikenberry
Assistant Professor, Politics Department, Princeton University
Ralph Johnson
Deputy Assistant U.S. Trade Representative, Executive Office of the President
Sidney L. Jones
Under-Secretary for Economic Affairs, Department of Commerce
Samuel I. Katz
Professor of International Economics, Georgetown University
Shinzo Kobori
Senior Vice-President, C. Itoh & Co.
Roman Kosinski
Specialist, Planning Commission, Department of Long Range Planning,
Polish Government
George D. Krumbhaar, Jr.
Staff Economist, Joint Economic Committee, U.S. Congress
Denis Lamb
Deputy Assistant Secretary for Trade and Commercial Affairs,
Department of State

Francine Lamoriello
International Economist, Office of European Community Affairs,
Department of Commerce

Andre Laude
School of Advanced International Studies, Johns Hopkins University

Denis F. Legras
Envoyé Spécial Permanent, Le Figaro

Lehmann K. Li
Senior Staff Member, Office of Policy Development, The White House

Seeley G. Lodwick
Commissioner, U.S. International Trade Commission

James G. Lowenstein
Former Ambassador; Managing Director, International Relations,
Consultants, Inc.

Richard T. McCormack
Assistant Secretary for Economic and Business Affairs, Department of State

Janice McCormick
Assistant Professor, Harvard Business School

Marci McDonald
Bureau Chief, Maclean's

James W. McKee, Jr.
Chairman, CPC International Inc.

D. Bruce Merrifield
Assistant Secretary for Productivity, Technology and Innovation,
Department of Commerce

Carl H. Middleton
Vice-President, Business International Corp.

G. William Miller
Chairman, G. William Miller & Co., Inc.

Ira M. Millstein
Senior Partner, Weil, Gotshal & Manges

Claude Moisy
U.S. Bureau Chief, Agence France Presse

R. K. Morris
Director, International Trade, National Association of Manufacturers

Philip B. Nelson
Staff Economist, Bureau of Economics, Federal Trade Commission

Ken Nichols
France Desk Officer, Department of Commerce

Thomas M. T. Niles
Deputy Assistant Secretary for European Affairs, Department of State

Jonathan Ogur
Deputy Assistant Director for Regulatory Analysis, Federal Trade Commission

Sue Okubo
Analyst, Central Intelligence Agency

B. Robert Okun
Executive Director, House Republican Research Committee,
U.S. House of Representatives

Allan Olson
Economic and Policy Advisor to the Assistant Secretary for Economic
Development, Department of Commerce

Van Doorn Ooms
Chief Economist, Committee on the Budget, U.S. House of Representatives

Rudy Oswald
Director, Department of Economic Research, AFL-CIO

Henry Owen
Chairman, The Consultants International Group

Thomas E. Petri
Member of Congress, U.S. House of Representatives

Clyde V. Prestowitz
Counselor to the Secretary, Department of Commerce

Alfred Reifman
Senior Specialist in International Economics, Congressional Research Service

Jacques J. Reinstein
Director, Rapporteur of Trade Committee, Atlantic Council of the United States

H. Chapman Rose
Of Counsel, Jones, Day, Reavis & Pogue (Trustee, Brookings Institution)

William V. Roth, Jr.
United States Senator, U.S. Senate

Catherine Rudder
Associate Director, American Political Science Association

James Sasser
United States Senator, U.S. Senate

J. Robert Schaetzel
Former Ambassador; Consultant, Honeywell, Inc.

Marjory E. Searing
Director, Office of Industry Assessment, Department of Commerce

Wendy Silberman
International Economist, International Trade Administration,
Department of Commerce

Kenneth S. Smith
World Business Editor, U.S. News & World Report

Philippe Souviron
Executive Vice-President and Manager, Crédit Lyonnais

Donald F. Terry
Staff Director, Subcommittee on Economic Stabilization, Committee on Banking,
Finance and Urban Affairs, U.S. House of Representatives

Regina K. Vargo
International Economist, International Trade Administration

Henry C. Wallich
Member, Board of Governors of the Federal Reserve System

Whittier Warthin
International Economist, Office of International Trade,
Department of the Treasury

John H. Watts
Chairman, Fisher, Francis, Trees & Watts Inc.

Leonard Weiss
International Economic Consultant; Member, Trade Advisory Panel,
Atlantic Council of the United States

Peter R. Weitz
Director of Programs, The German Marshall Fund of the United States

Sherrill B. Wells
Historian, Office of the Historian, Department of State

Jennifer J. White
Minority Staff Consultant, Subcommittee on International Economic Policy and
Trade, Committee on Foreign Affairs, U.S. House of Representatives

Mary A. Wileden
French Desk Officer, Department of the Treasury

Thomas M. Williams
Analyst, Office of European Analysis, Central Intelligence Agency

Chalmers P. Wylie
Member of Congress, U.S. House of Representatives

INDEX

Accor hotel group, 107
ADI. *See* Agence de l'Informatique
Aerospace sector, 90; civil applications, 51, 54, 55; companies, 50–51, 52–53; exporting policy, 51, 54; joint policy ventures in, 19; ministry control, 51, 52, 53; national independence and, 51, 55; structure, 52–53; successes, 7, 44, 54–55
Agence de l'Informatique (ADI), 204
Agence Française pour la Maitrise de l'Energie (AFME), 205
Agence Nationale de Valorisation de la Recherche (ANVAR), 25, 204
Aglietta, Michel, 91n
Airbus, 54
Alsthom-Atlantique, 41, 47, 49
American Telephone and Telegraph, 110
Andrews, William G., 99n
Antitrust laws, 27–28, 165
ANVAR. *See* Agence Nationale de Valorisation de la Recherche
Ariane, 55, 139
Armand-Rueff Commission, 149
Arms sales, 51, 54
Association Technique d'Importation Charbonnière (ATIC), 147
Auroux, Jean, 116
Automobile industry: debt, 78; emissions controls, 76n; employment, 76, 77–78; finance controls, 78; foreign competition, 75; investment controls, 78; price controls, 76

Balassa, Bela, 99n
Baldrige, Malcolm, 178
Bank of France, 27
Banks. *See* Financial sector; *and under individual banks*
Banque de l'Indochine, 16
Banque de Suez, 16
Banque Française du Commerce Extérieur (BFCE), 83–84

Barnett, Donald F., 110
Barou, Yves, 89, 95
Barre, Raymond, 91, 100, 200
Belgium 76–77n
Bérégovoy, Pierre, 207
Berliet, 23
Besse, Georges, 206
BFCE. *See* Banque Française du Commerce Extérieur
Biotechnology research, 139
Boussac, 204
Boyer, Robert, 91n
Bull. *See* CII–Honeywell Bull

Cap-Sogeti, 59
Carré, Jean-Jacques, 9
Carter, Jimmy, 175
CDF–Chimie, 29, 203
CEA. *See* Commissariat à l'Energie Atomique
Centre Mondial pour l'Informatique, 204
Centre National d'Etudes des Télécommunications (CNET), 43, 56
Centre National d'Etudes Spatiales (CNES), 43, 52, 55
Cette, Gilbert, 91n
CFDT. *See* Confédération Française Démocratique du Travail
CFP. *See* Compagnie Française des Pétroles
CGCT. *See* Compagnie Générale de Constructions Téléphoniques
CGE. *See* Compagnie Générale d'Electricité
CGP. *See* Commissariat Général du Plan
CGT. *See* Confédération Générale du Travail
Chambre Syndicale de la Sidérurgie Française, 64
Charbonnages de France, 45, 49, 206
Chevènement, Jean-Pierre, 101, 204, 205
Chirac, Jacques, 90
Chrysler rescue: bankruptcy option, 177; collapse, possible consequences, 176–177; government/business suspicions and, 178–79; information needs, 178; legislation re,

179; lessons of, 180; regulation as cause of crisis, 177–78
CIASI. *See* Comité Interministériel pour l'Aménagement des Structures Industrielles
CIDISE. *See* Comité Interministériel pour le Développement des Investissements et le Soutien de l'Emploi
CII–Honeywell Bull, 33, 41, 56, 57, 59, 135, 203
CISI, 57
CIT–Alcatel, 42, 56, 57, 58, 59
Citroën, 23, 135
CNES. *See* Centre National d'Etudes Spatiales
CNET. *See* Centre National d'Etudes des Télécommunications
Coal industry, 100, 147
CODEFI. *See* Comités départementaux d'examen des problèmes de financement des entreprises
Codevelopment policy, 205
CODEVI. *See* Compte de développement industriel
CODIS. *See* Comité Interministériel d'Orientation pour le Développement des Industries Stratégiques
COFACE. *See* Compagnie Française d'Assurances du Commerce Extérieur
COFAZ. *See* Compagnie Française de l'Azote
COGEMA. *See* Compagnie Générale des Matières Nucléaires
Cohen, Stephen S., 9
Colbertisme, 39
Comité Interministériel d'Orientation pour le Développement des Industries Stratégiques (CODIS), 24
Comité Interministériel pour le Développement des Investissements et le Soutien de l'Emploi (CIDISE), 24
Comité Interministériel pour l'Aménagement des Structures Industrielles (CIASI), 23–24, 203
Comité Interministériel pour les Restructurations Industrielles (CIRI). *See* Comité Interministériel pour l'Aménagement des Structures Industrielles
Comités départementaux d'examen des problèmes de financement des entreprises (CODEFI), 25
Commissariat à l'Energie Atomique (CEA), 43, 46–47
Commissariat Général du Plan (CGP), 14, 119, 120, 121, 123, 125, 126n
Commission de le Concurrence, 28, 149
Commission Nationale de Planification, 120
Common Market, 65, 66
Compagnie Française de l'Azote (COFAZ), 29

Compagnie Française des Pétroles (CFP), 48
Compagnie Française d'Assurances du Commerce Extérieur (COFACE), 83
Compagnie Générale de Constructions Téléphoniques (CGCT), 28, 58
Compagnie Générale d'Electricité (CGE), 16, 28, 33, 135, 203
Compagnie Générale des Matières Nucléaires (COGEMA), 48
Competition policy, 27–28, 41–42, 146–49. *See also* Deregulation
Compte de développement industriel (CODEVI), 129
Computer industry, 57, 99, 137
Concorde, 54
Conditionality, 169–70
Confédération Française Démocratique du Travail (CFDT), 204
Confédération Générale du Travail (CGT), 204–05, 206
Conseil National de Patronat Français, 98
Contrat de développement, 24
Contrats de plan. See Planning contracts
Control of French industrial policy: by ministries, 5, 17, 40–41, 43; by Parliament, 159–60; regional *v* national concerns, 19–20
Crandall, Robert, 111
Credit controls, 164
Crédit Lyonnais, 31
Crédits commerciaux classiques, 83–84
Crédits de politique industrielle, 23, 24
Crédits mixtes, 84
Cresson, Edith, 205
Creusot-Loire, 49

Dassault-Bréguet, 33, 41, 51, 53
DATAR. *See* Délégation à l'Aménagement du Territoire et de l'Action Régionale
de Calan, Pierre, 97n
Decentralization, 7, 19–20, 125, 194
de Gaulle, Charles, 14–15, 47, 97
Délégation à l'Aménagement du Territoire et de l'Action Régionale (DATAR), 15, 16
Délégation Générale à la Recherche Scientifique et Technique, 26
Deregulation: energy sector, 147–48; financial sector, 148–49; government promotion of, 149; macroeconomic policy and, 145–46; right wing, appeal for, 143; telecommunications industry, 148; transportation sector, 148; in the United States, 3–4
de Wendel, 16
Dreyfus, Pierre, 205
Dubois, Paul, 9

EC. *See* European Communities
Ecole Nationale d'Administration, 41
Ecole Polytechnique, 41
Economic policies. *See* Selective economic policies, General economic policies
Economic Plans, promulgation of, 97–98
EDF. *See* Electricité de France
Educational system, 39, 41, 162–63
EEC. *See* European Economic Community
Electricité de France (EDF), 45, 47, 147
Electronics sector: consumer electronics, 60; export policy, 56; *filière électronique* policy, 55, 56–57; integrated circuit production, 60; ministry control, 56, 58, 59, 60, 61; national independence and, 56; *plan productique*, 61; structure, 58–59; successes, 44, 58. *See also* Computer industry; Telecommunications industry
Electronic switching technology, 56–57
Elf-Aquitaine. *See* Société Nationale Elf-Aquitaine
Empain Schneider, 33
Employment programs, 104, 116
Employment reductions, 69, 72, 77–78, 109–10, 165
Energy sector: deregulation, 147–48; ministry control, 45, 48, 49, 50; modernization, 117–18; structure, 48–49; successes, 44, 45, 50. *See also* Nuclear industry; Oil industry
Equity finance, 78, 122
ESD, 58
ESPRIT. *See* European Strategic Program of Research and Development in Information Technology
Eurodif, 47
EUROFER, 70
European Coal and Steel Community (ECSC), 64, 134
European Communities (EC), 18–19; Commission of the European Communities, 69–70, 76–77n, 138, 139
European Economic Community (EEC), 76, 98, 134, 136, 137, 138
European industrial planning: cooperation, 137–38; high-technology efforts, 138–39; need for, 136–37; private sector initiatives, 140; research and development efforts, 137; shortcomings, 140; successes, 139
European Strategic Program of Research and Development in Information Technology (ESPRIT), 138–39
Evaluation of French industrial policy: complexity, 6–7, 32–33, 90; criteria, 109–11; Socialists' efforts, 208–10
Expansionary policy, 90

Export promotion: capital goods, 84–85; commercial missions network, 82–83; domestic budgetary constraints, 86; energy-related equipment, 118; foreign investment and, 86–87; risk insurance, 83; subsidies, 27, 28, 83, 84, 85–86, 87; successes, 84–85; trade barriers, 85; unfair competition, 82
Externalities, governmental role re, 173–74

Fabius, Laurent, 116–117, 133, 156, 158, 205
FDES. *See* Fonds de Développement Economique et Social
Fiat, 135
Finance Commission of the Seventh Plan, 21
Financial sector: credit controls, 164; deregulation, 148–49; export promotion, 83–84; industrial policy role, 207–08; public enterprises in, 29, 31
Fonds de Développement Economique et Social (FDES), 23, 65
Fonds Spécial d'Adaptation Industrielle (FSAI), 24, 69, 207
Foreign investment: increase in, 140–41; regulation of, 78, 86–87, 164
Foreign-owned companies, 141
Framatome, 41, 47, 48
French government, structure of, 156–57
FSAI. *See* Fonds Spécial d'Adaptation Industrielle

Gallois, Louis, 17
Gas industry, 45, 147
Gaz de France (GDF), 45, 48, 147
Gazocéan, 48
General economic policies: industrial growth and, 90, 99–100; mergers, 99; modernization, 99; successes, 102
Giraud, André, 43
Giscard d'Estaing, Valéry, 16–17
Government/business/labor cooperation, 120–21; in U.S. industrial policy, 167, 169–170, 182, 191–92
Grandes écoles, 39, 41, 43
Grands projets, 40, 99
Groupe de stratégie industrielle (GSI), 120–21
Groupement de l'Industrie Sidérurgique, 64
Grundig, 135
Guibert, Bernard, 99n
Guillaumat, Pierre, 43

Haberon, Jean-Yves, 159
Hannoun, Hervé, 32
Hanon, Bernard, 206

High-technology industries: European lag in, 136–37; European cooperative efforts, 138–39; investment strategies, 202–03; national independence and, 40, 44, 44–45; public procurement and, 44, 45; research and development, 42–43, 101; subsidies, 14–15, 24, 40. See also Aerospace sector; Electronics sector; Energy sector
Hispano-Suiza, 52
Hoechst, 135
Hoffmann, Stanley, 99n
Horizontal economic policies. See General economic policies

Iacocca, Lee, 176
IDI. See Institut de Développement Industriel
Indicative planning: decentralization, 20; forecasting, 120; government/business/labor cooperation, 120–21; government policies, coordination, 121–22; implementation, 122–26; origins, 14, 119; nature, 43, 80, 106–07; for steel industry, 63–64. See also Modernization
Industrial growth: domestic demand, 91; factors affecting, 89–91; general economic policies, 90, 99–100; macroeconomic performance, 88–89; monitoring, 125–26; selective economic policies, 90
Industrial policy: definition, 4–5; history of French policy, 13–17, 38–40; macroeconomic model of, 92–96; pragmatic nature of, 38; rationale, 5–6
Institut de Développement Industriel (IDI), 24–25
Institut Français du Pétrole, 46
Institut National de la Statistique et des Etudes Economiques (INSEE), 145–46
Integrated circuit production, 60
Intertechnique, 52, 59
Investment: entrepreneurship, 173; macroeonomic policy, 146; market economies, 185; in public enterprises, 129–30; in steel industry, 63–64, 65, 202. See also Foreign investment

Jacquemin, Aléxis, 9
Japan: auto exports, 75; industrial policy, 5, 37, 105, 166
Jeumont-Schneider, 49
Joint policy ventures, 19, 138
Joly, Pierre, 91n
Jublin, Jacques, 15n

Keizer, Bernard, 89, 95
Keynesianism, 36

Kis, 107
Kuisel, Richard F., 9

Labor: corporate decisionmaking, involvement in, 130–32; government and business, cooperation with, 120–21, 167, 169–70, 182, 191–92; labor market, 146; in public enterprises, 128–29, 130–32; relations with management, 77–78, 122
La Chapelle Darblay, 204
Lazarus, Simon, 167n
Le Pors, Anicet, 33
Les Gobelins, 39
Litan, Robert E., 167n
Loan Guarantee Board (U.S.), 179
Loi d'Orientation de la Recherche et de la Technologie (1982), 204
Lorraine, 71–72

McArthur, John H., 9, 98n
Machines Françaises Lourdes, 204
Macroeconomic model of industrial policy, 92–96
Macroeconomic policies, 145–46, 172, 199
Malinvaud, Edmond, 9, 101
Manufacture de Sèvres, 39
Marine-Firminy, 16
Market economies: investment and, 185; selective economic policies and, 168–69, 183–84
Marshall, Alfred, 191
Mathieu, Gilbert, 32n
Matra, 51, 52, 53, 56, 58, 59, 60
Mauroy, Pierre, 90, 199
Mercantilism, 38–40
Mergers: asset swapping, 135; company sizes, 135; general economic policies and, 99; government attitude toward, 27–28; insular nature, 135; merger movement, 15–16, 135; public enterprises, 135, 203. See also National champions
Merlin-Gérin, 49
Messier-Hispano, 51, 52
Ministries, French: aerospace sector control, 51, 52, 53; electronics sector control, 56, 58, 59, 60, 61; energy sector control, 45, 48, 49, 50; industrial policy control, 5, 17, 40–41, 43; personnel, 41, 43; regional branch offices, 20n
Ministry of International Trade and Industry (MITI) (Japan), 5, 166
Mitterrand, François, 13, 123, 194, 198
Modernization: adaptation concerns, 116; commissions, 120; conversion policy, 116–17; decentralized bargaining and, 122; economic success, relation to, 107; employment reduc-

tions, 109–10; energy sector, 117–18; equity finance and, 122; general economic policies and, 99; international cooperation re, 133; Ninth Plan goals re, 121–22; public enterprises, 117; qualitative dimensions, 119, 122. *See also* Indicative planning
Mondale, Walter F., 169
Monetarism, 36
Monetary policy, 27
Monnet, Jean, 20, 97, 119

National champions, 15–16, 41–42; public enterprises as, 29. *See also* Mergers
National currencies, stability, 108
National independence, French: aerospace sector and, 51, 55; electronics sector and, 56; high-technology industries and, 40, 44–45; policy primacy, 6, 103
Nationalization. *See* Public enterprises
Nuclear industry: electricity generation, 47; export policy, 50; growth, 46–47; sales of equipment, 50; successes, 7, 47, 104, 117, 118, 121

Oil industry: deregulation, 147; growth, 46; service companies, 46; successes, 107
Organization for European Economic Cooperation (OEEC), 98
Orléan, André, 91n
Oudiz, Gilles, 91n

Padioleau, Jean G., 9
Parliament: absence from policy debates, 157–59; control of industrial policy, 159–60; industry, problems in dealing with, 157; investigative activities, 158–59; legislative limitations, 156–57; office of technology assessment, proposed, 159
Pechiney Ugine Kuhlmann, 16, 28, 29, 135, 203
Petit, Pascal, 91n
Petroleum industry. *See* Oil industry
Peugeot, 23, 77, 78, 79
Plan Calcul, 59
Planification contractuelle, 65–66
Planning contracts: decentralization through, 125; for public enterprises, 42, 123–24; regional governments and, 124–25
Planning Reform Act of *1982*, 125
Plans sectoriels, 15–16
Politique de filières strategy, 17–18
Politique des créneaux strategy, 16–17
Pompidou, Georges, 15, 100
Porter, Roger, 111

Price controls, 73, 76, 149
Programmes prioritaires d'exécution (PPE), 123
Protectionism (U.S.), 8, 191, 197
Public enterprises: cooperation, 129, 131–32; efficiency criteria (market-based), 128–30; efficiency criteria (social), 130–32; false assumptions re, 144–45; financial losses, 208; in financial sector, 29, 31; financing and restructuring, 202–03; history, 42; in industrial sector, 29; investment concerns, 129–30; labor in, 128–29, 130–32; management of, 7, 31–32, 42, 78–80, 123–24; mergers, 135, 203; modernization and, 117; as national champions, 29; planning contracts for, 42, 123–24; privatization, 149; rationales for, 29; regional development through, 131–32; scope, 201–02; shortcomings, 106, 127–28; Socialist goals re, 127–28, 132, 144–45, 200; in steel industry, 64; value added shares, 28–29, 30–31
Public procurement, 25, 44, 45

Quatrepoint, Jean-Michel, 15n

Rausch, Jean-Marie, 159
Reagan, Ronald, 175, 190
Reflation policies, 199
Regional agencies, 15, 16, 20n
Regional industrial policy: decentralization, 19–20, 194; planning contracts, 124–25; priority development areas, 207; public enterprises, 131–32
Reich, Robert B., 167n
Renault, 23, 59, 141, 206
Rescue operations, 36–37; Socialist efforts re, 203–04; U.S. *v* French, 163–64. *See also* Chrysler rescue
Research and development: in European industrial planning, 137; funding, 25–26; high-technology industries, 42–43, 101; private investment, 150; Socialist efforts, 204; U.S.-French joint efforts, 142
Rhône Poulenc, 28, 29 135
Rohatyn, Felix, 176, 190, 192, 193
Roussel-Uclaf, 135

Sacilor, 28, 69, 203
Saint-Gobain–Pont-à-Mousson, 16, 28, 39, 203
Saint-Simonian movement, 39
Schorsch, Louis, 110
Schultze, Charles L., 171–72
Scott, Bruce R., 9, 98n

SDR. *See* Sociétés de développement régional
Selective economic policies: government's abilities re, 169; *grands projets*, 40, 99; industrial growth and, 90; legitimacy, 37; market economies and, 168–69, 183–84; phaseout, 196; profitability, effect on, 101–02; record of, 143–45; of Socialists, 17–18, 100–02, 204; in U.S. industrial policy, 167, 168–69, 181
SEMS, 57
SFENA–Crouzet, 52
SFIM, 52
SG2, 59
Sheahan, John B., 9
Shepherd, William G., 9
SNEA. *See* Société Nationale Elf-Aquitaine
SNECMA. *See* Société Nationale d'Etude et de Construction de Moteurs d'Aviation
SNIAS. *See* Société Nationale Industrielle Aérospatiale
Socialists: austerity period (*1983–86*), 205–08; coal policies, 100; evaluation of industrial policy efforts, 208–10; honeymoon period (*1981–83*), 200–05; ideological shift by, 209; industrial policies, 17–20, 199–210; macroeconomic policies, 199; public enterprises, goals re, 127–28, 132, 144–45, 200; rescue operations, 203–04; research and development efforts, 204; selective economic policies, 17–18, 100–02, 204; steel policies, 100
Société Européenne de Propulsion, 52
Société Nationale d'Etude et de Construction de Moteurs d'Aviation (SNECMA), 51, 53, 54
Société Nationale Elf-Aquitaine (SNEA), 29, 41, 46, 48, 135, 141, 203
Société Nationale Industrielle Aérospatiale (SNIAS), 41, 51, 52, 53
Sociétés de développement régional (SDR), 25
Sproat, Audrey T., 9
Steel industry: Common Market and, 65, 66; crises, 66–67; debts, 66, 67; employment, 67, 68, 69, 71–72; European intervention, 64, 69–71; four-stage intervention program 67, 69–71; history since *1945*, 65; indicative planning for, 63–64; investment in, 63–64, 65, 202; in Lorraine, 71–72; *1982* plan for, 71; *1984* plan for, 71–72; *planification contractuelle* process for, 65–66; public enterprises in, 64; Socialist policies re, 100; structural reforms, 67–69; trade union, 64, 70
STERIA, 59
Stoffaës, Christian, 9
Stoleru, Lionel, 9

Subsidies: allocation, 23–25; amounts, 21, 23; business failures and, 24; exports, 27, 28, 83–84, 85–86, 87; high-technology industries, 14–15, 24, 40; horizontal, 21; large companies, 32–33, 34, 35, 104; small and medium-sized companies, 24–25; unemployment, 24; uses, 22, 23; vertical, 21
Supply-side policies, 199–200

Talbot UK, 77
Targeted assistance. *See* Selective economic policies
Tax policies, 27, 164–65
Technip, 46, 48
Technocracies, interpenetration, 43
Telecommunications industry, 105, 139, 148
Telefunken, 135
Television programming, 35
Textile industry, 18–19, 107
Théry, Gérard, 43
Thomson-Brandt, 28, 33, 59, 135, 203
Thomson–CSF, 42, 52, 57, 58, 59, 60
Thurow, Lester, 167n
Tocqueville, Aléxis de, 210
Total–Compagnie Française des Pétroles, 41, 46, 135
Trade: free trade, 185–87; import restraints, 188–89; international trade growth, 134, 135, 142; liberalization, 133; trading blocs, possible, 186. *See also* Export promotion
Trade deficit, 130
Trade unions, 64, 70, 204–05
Transac, 57
Transportation sector, 148
Treaty of Rome (*1957*), 15
Trucking industry, 148
Turboméca, 51, 52

Unemployment subsidies, 24
United Kingdom, 77
United States: antitrust laws, 110, 165; automobile industry, 111; commerce, focus on, 163; deregulation in, 3–4; educational system, 162–63; foreign industrial policies, views re, 4; French culture, comparison with, 162–63; indsutry, government knowledge of, 178; policy conflicts, 170–71, 177–78; steel industry, 110–11; trade deficit, 185
U.S. industrial policy: allocation of funds, 184–85; alternatives, 172–74; components, 1, 4, 162, 197; coordination of government policies, 170–71; debate re, 182, 189–90; defense spending and, 184–85, 187; entrepreneurship and, 172–73; expansion, 187–

222275141

88; financial institutions, 192–93; French industrial policy, comparison with, 7–8, 61–62, 108–09, 161–65, 187, 197; goals, 166; government/business/labor cooperation, 167, 169–70, 182, 191–92; government intervention, promotion of, 167; import restraints, 188–89; Japanese model for, 166; loan guarantees, 176; political aspects, 161, 181; presidential leadership, 175–76, 190; protectionism, 8, 191, 197; rescue operations, 163–64; research and development, 142; right-wing support, 111; selective economic policies, 167, 168–69, 181; service economy, adjustment to, 192; state and local activities, 193–95; trade policy, 182. *See also* Chrysler rescue
Usinor, 28, 69, 203

Vernon, Raymond, 9
Vertical economic policies. *See* Selective economic policies

Young, John, 176

Zysman, John, 9, 61, 99